CRIMINAL ATONEMENT

ISBN-13 (Paperback) 979-8370584602

Library of Congress 1-12090719701

Disclaimer

All of the events listed in this book are true. Many of the names have been changed to protect the innocent as well as the guilty.

TABLE OF CONTENTS

Prologue

"Look where you are," "Look where you are," those words kept ringing in my head. My heart was racing, and my breathing was fast. It was hard to believe where I was standing— Africa, of all places, at the top of Victoria Falls. With my arms outstretched to the sky, the mist from the enormous amount of water cascading down around me, drenched my clothes. This was a very intense moment that I didn't quite understand. There I was, standing in this amazing, beautiful, awe inspiring place, where I imagined myself being so many years ago. Now I'm here, overwhelmed with different emotions that feel like currents of energy running through my body. Feelings of freedom, joy, and gratitude rushed through me as I stood there in awe, pausing to take it all in, and recalling all that I had been through since first learning about Victoria Falls.

My memory took me back to the time and place when I had first set eyes on this beautiful sight where I was now standing. It was a picture I had many years ago that I tore out of a National Geographic magazine and stuck to the wall of my prison cell with toothpaste. It was one of those large foldout pictures that went about three feet across in length. It was awe-inspiring looking at such beautiful scenery. The hours spent admiring it was like a temporary reprieve that helped ease my mind from the reality I was in. The National Geographic, along with other American magazines were hand delivered to me by someone from the U.S. Embassy. I vividly remember the sound the stack of magazines made when he plopped them down on the floor in front of my cell.

He was carrying a large, heavy stack that he was apparently tired of holding. When he made it to the front of my cell, where I was standing, instead of setting them down, he just let go of the stack and let them drop to the floor. The loud "plop" sound it made, when hitting the floor, reverberated throughout the cell block. Looking back, that was 25 years ago.

This all happened while I was confined to a dungeon-like prison cell in Bogota, Colombia. The name of the prison was "La Picota," and the year was 1992. My cocaine smuggling career had just come to an end. It would be the first of many different prisons where I would be incarcerated for the next 18 years. On the wall, in that very first prison cell, I had placed a picture of Victoria Falls. I had never even heard of it until then. Now I'm standing here, remembering when I looked at that picture everyday for months, before eventually being extradited to the United States and sentenced to thirty years without parole for possession with intent to distribute cocaine.

As I stood there in awe, my mind not only drifted back to that first prison cell in "La Picota," but all the years of incarceration that followed. It seemed like everything that had happened to me from then until now came rushing back to my memory all at once. Raising my arms up to the sky, I breathed quick, deep breaths as the tears ran down my face. I was free, mind and body. The moment was very intense, and I was flooded with a rush of gratitude.

Usually, I try not to think about all the years I spent incarcerated. Thinking about it just seems to bring me back when I do—remembering the horrible feelings that stayed with me. Feelings of hate, hopelessness, uncertainty, despair, and shame to name a few, were eating away at my stomach and toying with my mind constantly. Now those old feelings are all gone, having been replaced with new ones. Standing there, I was overtaken with happiness and gratitude. Grateful for where I am now and grateful that those horrible feelings no longer torment me.

Being incarcerated inside of various prisons for a very long time is not something I'm proud of or like to talk about. It is with great reluctance that I tell this story. I have asked God for forgiveness for the harm my actions have caused others and I am sincerely remorseful, and apologetic.

When I finally got out, I was determined to leave all that happened behind me. Better to let what happened in the past stay in the past. Up until now that I'm writing it down for all to read I have been good at keeping this information hidden. Except for my immediate family, no one I interact with is aware of my criminal background or that I've ever been in prison. Walking around bragging about being a convict is not how I roll. The guys who get out and keep the prison life mentality don't last long on the streets. It took a long time for me to finally wake up and realize the ignorance in the whole tough guy/gangster criminal attitude. Getting in trouble and committing crimes was how I lived my entire life. Starting in elementary school, living in a low income neighborhood, I regularly fist fought to gain respect from kids who bullied me. Growing up, I believed it was cool to break the rules and be a thug. I associated this behavior with being accepted, respected and thought of favorably by my peers. Several events happened at the peak of my "Tough Guy" attitude while I was locked up in the most violent prison in the United States, USP Beaumont. It changed the way I thought about what was cool and what's not cool. I learned from first hand experience that the consequences of this foul attitude was incarceration and death. Neither of which are very cool.

Beginning at a very young age, I demonstrated a total disregard for rules. Smoking my first joint at age 9, stealing bikes at age 12, and cars at age 14. I was convicted of my first felony, which was arson, for setting my high school on fire, at age 17. My entire life revolved around crime and incarceration. The only exception was about two years from age 18-20 when I was going to church and studying the Bible. However, If you were to meet me today you would be surprised to find out that I've ever been incarcerated at all. I don't talk or act like your stereotypical convict even though I have been in custody in over 30 different jails and prisons throughout my lifetime. Including four different jails/prisons in Colombia, and even passed through Guantanamo bay Cuba. I was on the Federal Marshals 15 most wanted list for two years and mentioned on the television show "America's Most Wanted." My last bit lasted 18 years in United States Federal custody. All day and all night. In 1989 I was busted with five kilograms of cocaine by the DEA in Houston, Texas. It was just me and the cocaine. No co-defendants. The DEA knew I was heavily connected and wanted my cooperation in exchange for a lighter sentence. I told the DEA I would cooperate but instead fled to Colombia. I stayed on the run living mainly in Santa Marta, Colombia for 2 years. During this time I was placed on the Federal Marshals 15 most wanted list. Needless to say, the feds were very angry when I ran. Finally, I was captured in Santa Marta, Colombia in 1992. Eventually I was extradited back to the United States to serve out a 30 year sentence. While incarcerated, I was not what you would call a "Model Inmate." Far from it. I carried myself by the "Convict Code," always trying to get away with as much as I could in prison and never backing down from unavoidable altercations. I don't consider myself a tough guy, but I have had a few run-ins in prison where it didn't turn out well for the other guy. Thankfully no deaths resulted in these altercations, but on three separate occasions, three different guys were carried out of the prison in an ambulance. Two of those three times, I was acting in self-defense. I've smuggled countless packages of dope through multiple prison visiting rooms, always had a knife, ran poker tables, and made hundreds of gallons of wine in multiple prisons. Having been locked up with thousands of different criminals over the years who were incarcerated for every imaginable crime, I have run into some very interesting characters, to say the least. I've hung out with top guys from various Colombian cartels. Met Italian Mafia crime bosses, a Chinese Triad, Japanese Yakuza, Russian mafia, Irish mafia, Mexican cartel drug traffickers, bank robbers, kidnappers, scam artists, hijackers, serial killers, terrorists and gang members from too many different gangs to list. Living with the mentally insane, psychopaths and sociopaths. We were all bunched together in a small, confined area for a very long time. I've been in prison riots, battles, race wars, watched men killed in front of me multiple times and witnessed numerous, brutal, merciless beatings. I myself have been beaten, pepper sprayed, stripped naked, handcuffed and shackled, then placed In a room full of urine and feces with hardly any ventilation at the hands of prison guards. I've been subjected to some of the worst, inhumane circumstances you could place a human being in. It was terrible. It was not fun at all. But God, through his abundant love and mercy, rescued my life from destruction and crowned me with loving kindness and tender mercies. After 18 years of miserable confinement, I was finally set free. I am not proud of all the crimes that I've committed, all the craziness and bad decisions that I've made. It's very embarrassing for me to tell this story. Revealing the strange conditions of my childhood upbringing is not easy to share. It is with great reluctance that I tell you my story.

PART I

TROUBLED CHILDHOOD

A Broken Home

My mother and father were divorced when I was just a baby, so I have no memory of them ever being together. My mother was from a very small town nestled away in the mountains of West Virginia next to the Potomac river called Berkley Springs. The people who lived in this area at that time relied mainly on the coal mining industry for work. They lived hard but happy lives. Everyone knew everyone, and most were related somehow. This part of the country has historical significance, as many battles from the civil war were fought in this area. The Mason-Dixon line that separated the north from the south was near my mothers home.

My mother was an only child from a broken home, raised by her mother under very meager conditions. Her father was a wild seed who remarried soon after she was born. His name was Pete Moss, and he was well known for his guitar playing, women chasing and drinking. He died before I was born, so I only remember the stories that were told about him and there were many. My Grandmother was just the opposite. She was an extremely responsible, hard working woman. She worked long hours at a nearby hotel while raising my mother alone. Mother had decided at a very young age that Berkeley Springs would not be her plight. She was eager to see and experience the exciting big world outside of the small West Virginia town she was from. Mother was a wild child like her father. She was very bold and adventurous. She didn't fit into the mold with the other young ladies of Berkeley Springs and always felt as if she didn't belong there. It wasn't until later in life that I discovered my mother ran away and married when she was just 16 years old. She fell for a guy in the military who was assigned to be stationed in England. She left with him on a ship and crossed the Atlantic to London. Extremely bold and unheard of for someone of that age, especially from a town that small in 1952. Her mother did all she could to raise her right and the relationship between the two was a very strong bond. My mother loved her very much. She was just an adventurous, fearless young lady, who desperately wanted to see the world outside of the mountains of West Virginia. The marriage to her military beau didn't last long. The fact that she had been married before my father was always kept a secret from us growing up. Not sure if my father even knew. It was only after her death that I found out while researching my family tree online. Eventually, mother got a job as an airline stewardess with Texas International Airlines. This job seemed to coincide with the adventure she was seeking. I'm sure she loved it and thrived in it. One of her layover routes was Lafayette, La. That's how she met my father. He also worked for the airlines at the Lafayette airport.

My father was from Lafayette as was his father, grandfather, great-grandfather, great-great-grandfather all the way back to the 1770s. He was a proud Cajun man steeped in Cajun tradition. He spoke French as well as English as did most of the Cajuns who lived in that area. My father was a good looking young man, fun loving and jovial. He was constantly laughing, telling jokes and was always the center of attention at the airport where he worked. He was a very fun guy to be around and this is what attracted my mother to him.

My Mother and father were married in 1960, and soon after, on my mother's birthday, August 1st 1962, she gave birth to my older sister Carla. I came along in November of 64. My mother and father's marriage was already in trouble by the time she was pregnant with me, and her pregnancy just prolonged the inevitable. Mother's wild streak was not ready to be tamed. She wanted to go out and have fun like her and my father did when they were dating. She loved the excitement of going to the horse races, which was a big thing in Lafayette. In the beginning of their relationship they would often go out. Now that she was married, my father was content with just staying at home after work, and lying on the couch reading a book or watching TV. Mother was not wanting to spend the rest of her life stuck in a house, in a small Louisiana town, being the quiet subservient housewife. That was just not her cup of tea. I guess she felt trapped and wanted more out of life. She thrived in a fast paced, live on the edge environment. Wasn't long after I was born that she left my father and took my sister and me with her to Houston, Texas.

She remarried a Texas oil field guy that she met while going to the horse races in Louisiana. I vaguely remember him because the marriage didn't last long enough to leave any impression. I was told that he was a drinker and a gambler. He was the father of my younger brother Lance but never lived with us from the time Lance was born. Lance is five years and five days younger than me. Lance was named after a Dallas Cowboy football player, Lance Rentzel. His middle name "Belmont" comes from Belmont Park in NY where they race horses. Apparently, his father loved to bet on the races. His father also had another son from a previous marriage who was around ten when Lance was born. He was a talented guitar player who somehow ended up living with us when he was around fifteen. This was the early 70s when everyone was weird anyway, but the circle of people surrounding our family was exceptionally weird, consisting of outcasts and hippies. My mother smoked pot, and so did the guitar playing stepson. Marijuana was always present in our household in those days. Mother was working in apartment management so our apartment was part of her pay.

We kids were left alone the majority of the time. I was constantly looking for fun things to do out by myself. Many times getting hurt or in trouble in the process. When I say getting hurt, I mean seriously injured many times. Once my mother went to a Washateria to do laundry and took me with her. As we pulled into the parking lot, I remember seeing a big electrical sign in the middle that you had to drive around. The sign had a plastic covering, around ground level, that had been broken and had a loose wire jumping around inside, causing sparks. For some reason I was drawn to it. While my mother was doing laundry, I crawled into the sign. Not sure if I grabbed the wire on purpose or touched it by accident, but I was electrocuted pretty badly. My hair caught on fire, and the jolt of electricity blew out through my joints. Later, I woke up in the hospital dazed. Another time when I was very young, an older kid from our apartment complex had gotten his kite stuck on the roof. Wanting the kite so badly, I tried climbing up to the roof of our apartment complex to get it and fell from the second story. As I came down my arm hit the wooden picket fence below and ripped a big chunk out of it. After regaining consciousness, I found myself trapped on someone's patio. There was no getting out because the gate was locked. I tried banging on the patio door but no answer. No one home and no one to help me. My arm was broken, and about two inches below my wrist, on the inside of my arm was a gash two inches square where the picket fence had ripped it open. You could see the bone, and I was bleeding badly. The only way out was to climb the fence. Out of breath from screaming for help and crying, I remember catching my breath and through much effort, climbed out. Somehow I made it to the apartment office where my mother was working, and once in the door I just collapsed unconscious. My mother held me in her arms while the stepson drove us to the hospital, speeding through traffic blowing the horn. That was the first time I broke my left arm. Eventually I broke my right arm and my left arm again on separate occasions. Each time I was climbing up on stuff and fell off. The grown ups would often tell me that I was "accident prone."

There was a phase I went through where I was fascinated with starting fires. Several times I would go into a dry field near the apartment complex and set it on fire just to watch it burn. It was fascinating and entertaining for me to strike a match and watch it burn. What else was there to do? Once again, we kids were left alone to entertain ourselves, and I ended up playing with matches underneath my mother's bed with my baby brother and burning our apartment down. We lost everything. Clothes, furniture, pictures, everything. After that, we were homeless, and our mother was jobless. We moved around alot. We lived with other people for brief periods of time. Me and my brother's room was someone's closet for a time. Whatever we had as far as food or clothing was a hand out.

Stepson/Stepfather

We ended up living in an upstairs apartment over a storefront business. It was called an "antique shop," but it was just a bunch of old junk. It was a run down, roach-infested crappy place. Pretty sure it had been condemned by the city to live in, and that's how we were able to afford it. Our vehicle at the time was a Volkswagen van. Your typical low-rent hippie mobile that barely ran.

It was here that I noticed my mother and the stepson started sleeping together in the same bed. I was too young to understand but instinctively knew the situation was not right. Their relationship was not that of a mother/son relationship but now that of two lovers. My mother pretended that it was ok but we were told to keep the part about him being her stepson and how old he was a secret. During this time the stepson had also taken on the role of disciplinary enforcer and started disciplining my brother and me, never my sister. This was done with the full endorsement and encouragement of my mother. By enforcer, I mean whipping us. He would use belts, tree branches, shoes, wire hangers, whatever. There was a wood shop there used to refurbish the junk that was being sold as antiques. Once, he spent a couple of days making a wooden paddle to spank us with. The whole time he was making it, he was telling us how we were going to get it if we messed up. He really got into the making of that paddle. First, he cut out the pattern on some hardwood. Then he sanded it out and stained it. He made a special handle to grip it with, and it had a leather wrist strap. Then he drilled holes in it and sanded it again. Looking back now, I see how sadistic he was. Grinning and taking pleasure in forming this weapon that he eagerly waited to use on us. If we did not answer with "sir" or "ma'am," we were getting it. He instilled a fear in my brother and me that I began to resent and hate him for. Consumed with an intense, burning hate, I fantasized about one day beating him to a pulp. He stood 6 ft 4 in and was very mean and intimidating. I was nine or ten years old at the time. Even though I was terrified of him, I still misbehaved. Seemed like everything fun to do would get you in trouble. He was 16 at the time and the half-brother of my younger brother Lance. Lance grew up calling him "pop," believing he was his father. We were told to keep it a secret about the stepson's true identity, so Lance never knew until years later.

Tough Neighborhood

From there, we moved to the Heights in Houston on Bayland ave. The Heights is one of Houston's oldest neighborhoods. All of the houses there were very old and run down in the early to mid-70s when we lived there. The houses were very nice at one time, and if you go there today, they've remodeled all the houses to be very nice once again. Just not when we lived there. It was a rundown low-income area. We were renting the house we lived in. With the exception of my father's house in Louisiana, this was the only house I had ever lived in. We never lived in a house before or after. We always lived in an apartment complex, and we moved from one complex to another quite often. The Heights is centrally located right outside of downtown Houston. Easy access to the freeways and the 610 loop that circles around Houston. I went to the historical Travis Elementary School, my 4th and 5th grade. Back then, it was a rough neighborhood. Mostly Mexican kids from low income families like mine. There were two other white kids in my class. Being white in an all-Mexican school and neighborhood had its challenges. Being a "minority" I was always the outcast "white boy." Fighting was a big thing at my school. Who could beat up who was where you stood in the Travis elementary hierarchy. That was your status. I wanted to be accepted and liked and thought of as a tough guy, so I found myself getting into several fights. Not so much that I wanted to, but that I had to. There was always a fight after school. Almost always, the fights I got into were instigated and arranged by other kids. Most of the kids just wanted to see a fight. Whenever I fought, most of the kids watching the fight wanted me to get beat up. I was white, and they were all Mexican. Once I was winning a fight against a Mexican kid, one of his friends jumped in to help him. Another time I won a fight quickly and had to fight someone else. They would not stand for me to win. I really didn't want to fight at all, I just wanted to be accepted. My home life was a battle that was tough in itself so there was no relief in staying at home. I was forever being told to get out of the house and go find something to do. "Go find some friends to play with." "Just go!" One afternoon after school, a Mexican kid invited me to his house. He was one of the more popular kids in our class and was considered tough. The fact that he was inviting me to his house made me think we were friends. When we got to his house, there were many people there. All of them were speaking Spanish, seeming mad and irritated that he had brought me there. They were all looking at me, laughing and speaking in Spanish. He went inside while I waited outside near his front porch. I had my back turned to his front door just waiting for him to come out, thinking we were going to play. All of a sudden, I felt this warm liquid being poured on my back. When I turned around, the kid was standing on his porch, pissing on my back, laughing. Everyone there started laughing at me. His mother started yelling in Spanish but she was laughing too. I felt so humiliated. The kid told me *"we're not friends!" "get out of my yard, white boy."* I took my shirt off and walked home. I was too embarrassed to tell anybody what happened. I never told anyone that story.

Looking back now on those days when I was attending Travis elementary school, I can see how the desire to be thought of as a tough guy coincided with being accepted. I understand now that this was a crucial time in my psychological development. I wanted to fit in and be accepted like every other kid. It seemed like I was always fighting an uphill battle because I was white. The constant daily abuse for being white went unchecked. No one ever spoke up for me or stepped up to have my back during this time, no teachers or any other adults. If I were to bring a complaint

15

home that I was getting picked on in school for being white, the response was for me to kick whoever's ass it was picking on me. Whenever I got into fights, I would get in trouble. My mother would tell me after the fact that I shouldn't be fighting. Just because I fought back didn't mean I won every fight. I got beat up a lot. When someone bigger or tougher than me kicked my ass, my parental instructions were to get an "equalizer." An equalizer was a weapon like a big stick or anything I could find to even the odds. I just wanted somebody to have my back but there was no one. No one ever had my back during this time. There was no one I could call who would come and check the bullies that verbally abused me for being white and poorly dressed.

Bayland Ave. is where we lived when my mother became a born-again Christian. She was on the couch watching TV, high from smoking marijuana and flipping through the channels, when she stopped on the 700 club. She felt convicted listening to Pat Robertson and wanted to change her life. She called the number they provided and prayed with someone on the phone. After praying the prayer of salvation, they recommended a church in our area for her to attend. The Church was named Evangelistic Temple or ET. It was a non-denominational church that believed in speaking in tongues and miracle healing. This is where we all started going. Mother stopped smoking pot, and it was no longer present in our house. As far as sleeping with her teenage stepson, her solution was to marry him. She could no longer "live in sin" so they must get married. Forget that he is the son of my mother's previous husband or my younger brother's half-brother or that my mother was in her mid-30s and he was 17. They had to get married to prevent "living in sin." That was their logic. They were married at E.T. church in the small chapel that was used for children's church. As I waited outside the chapel while the ceremony was going on, I heard people talking, very upset that this was happening in their church. One lady was very mad, telling her husband, "I can't believe they are allowing this to happen, this is not right!" I was standing next to them listening, so embarrassed. My mother was marrying this young jerk who I hated, and people who didn't even know him knew it was wrong. My mother was not working at the time. The teenage stepson/stepfather was the only one working, and we were broke. Food and clothing came from donations from people from the church. The owner of the house we lived in was always in heated conversations with mother about the rent. Mother and her new "husband" often argued and yelled at each other. Home life sucked.

Run Away from home

The so-called toughest guy in our 5th-grade class was a kid named Ted Vargas. Ted didn't have a physical advantage or possess any superior fighting skills. Several other kids in our class could beat him in a fight, including myself, but he had the title because of his older cousins. Everybody knew if you messed with Ted he had about 15 older cousins that would come to Ted's aid and beat you up. His cousins varied in age from the next grade up to high school. They were all older and bigger than we were. They had the reputation of being the bad kids. Little gangsters from the neighborhood who emulated the older gangsters. They all had bandana's folded a certain way hanging out of their back pockets, and of course they all wore white Converse All-Star tennis shoes, more commonly known as "Chucks." When someone like Ted has a big family he could call on to get somebody beat up that was called having "slack." The more "slack" you had, the more feared you became. Even older kids didn't mess with Ted because they knew if you messed with him you were taking on all of his cousins as well. Ted had the most slack. I had none.

Ted approached me one day after school, said he wanted to run away from home, and asked me if I wanted to join him. To me, this sounded like a good idea at the time. Ted was the toughest guy in school, so I thought this would be my chance to gain status and notoriety by doing some gangster stuff with Ted. Home life was not all that great anyway. We decided we would take a bus to Galveston. Once we got off the bus in Galveston we started asking directions to the beach. A Concerned citizen called the cops, and we were taken to the police station, where they called our parents to come get us. We waited in a large room in the police station where the cops were very nice to us. They gave us something to eat and asked us a lot of questions. Why were we running away from home? Why did we come to Galveston? What was our plan when we got here? They were amazed and bewildered that we were there. Each one that spoke with us informed us of how lucky we were that nothing bad happened to us. While waiting for our moms to pick us up, Ted and I started horse-playing. As we were wrestling around on the floor, it was surprising to find out how easily I could completely dominate him and throw him around. It was obvious then that Ted was all talk and couldn't fight very well. Now I wished someone from our school was witnessing how easily I was throwing Ted around. The desire to be accepted and respected back at school was so strong that it affected most of my behavior. Eventually my mother and the stepson/want-to-be stepfather came and got me. The jerk of a "stepfather" was very angry and threatening but I did not get a whipping that time. He said he wanted to but promised my mother he would not. I felt bad that my mother worried about me not knowing where I was. She was very distraught and seemed confused as to why I ran away. She asked me questions, trying to find out the reason. With the jerk she had married glaring at me with that hateful look that I understood meant he would beat my ass the first chance he got. The desire to open up and try to get her to understand why I was so unhappy was there but I don't think I was capable of articulating such complex feelings at that age. The jerk continued to be a jerk, and I continued to always get in trouble. Back in school, I found out that Ted's mother told Ted he was not allowed to hang out with me. We couldn't be friends. Apparently she believed I was a bad influence on him. All the cool kids didn't want anything to do with me because they all followed Ted's lead. I was devastated. This was really the main reason I ran away. To be accepted at school and thought of favorably. Assuming that since Ted and I had run away and we were even in jail together, I would for sure now be popular and cool at school. It didn't work out that way at all. Nobody wanted to have anything to do with me, including Ted.

Ted was killed later that year, just a few blocks from our house. A drunk driver ran him over as he was walking down the sidewalk, huffing paint with friends at 4:30am. He was eleven.

Go find Something to do!

My parental instructions were always the same growing up. GO! Go play, go find something to do, go find some friends to play with. Just go. So off I went searching for something to do. Hours walking by myself exploring. I walked the trails of buffalo bayou, catching snakes, climbing trees and just checking stuff out. Sometimes I would walk way over to the motorcycle shop "House of Wheels" on the freeway to look at the motorcycles. There was a dirt bike my size, a Yamaha 80 that I would sit on and dream of having. It made it worth the walk just to go sit on that dirt bike and imagine having it. The city bus stopped right in front of our house so sometimes I would just get on the bus and go for a ride with the change that I got from collecting Coke bottles. Someone taught me how to get a bus transfer downtown and take another bus to the Astrodome. When I had enough change for the bus ride, I would spend a whole day exploring the Astrodome by myself. There were metal chains that were used to block the public from getting in, but I lifted the chains up and crawled underneath and got in. Acting like I owned the place, no one asked me any questions. Because I was there so often, the head security guard believed I was the son of someone in upper management. He was a very nice man who was super cool to me. He even introduced me to someone one time as young "so and so," the son of "I don't remember who." I'm not sure if he really believed I was the son of someone who worked there or if he knew I was just a poor kid from the Heights exploring the dome all along.

One day I walked to Stude park, about a mile from our house. When I got to the park I saw a group of kids my age with baseball gloves looking like they were about to start playing. Walking over to where they were I asked if I could play too. One of the kids asked me, "are you here to join the team?" He said It was their first day of practice. He showed me an army duffle bag full of gloves and said, "just pick one out." WOW! I was so excited. It was hard to believe my luck. The coach came over, asked me my name, and then wrote it on his roster. Just like that I had joined a little league baseball team called the "Pirates." Never played baseball before, but neither had most of the other kids there. That first day of practice was the best day of my life so far. Playing baseball with the other kids was so fun. All the kids were about my age and everyone was very nice to me. The park was about a 20 minute walk from my house and that was the best walk home ever. The coach gave me some papers for my mother to sign. Man, was I excited! While walking home, I started rehearsing how I was going to plead for permission.

About a year before I tried to join the cub scouts, actually the "Webelos." but it cost money for the uniform, so I couldn't join. No money from home for a uniform. Mother just told me straight out that there was no money for a uniform and that was the end of it. If I whined or persisted in my request it would be met with loud shouting threats of punishment in my face by the stepfather. The stepfather had a way of shouting demoralizing threats in my face that would discourage me from asking for anything again. This wasn't the first time that I had to ask for something and was told that there was no money for whatever it was I wanted. I was getting used to being told that we didn't have money for things. They did have a program where scout uniforms were donated to underprivileged kids but I did not make the cut because I was white. Why do I believe this? The other kids that got donated uniforms were supposedly less privileged than me. They were not white, but they wore real converse all-star tennis shoes and made fun of me because mine were the knock-offs from the big basket in the grocery store.

Almost ALL the boys in my school wore "Chucks." Their mom's would bleach them white, and they wore colored strings. I dreamed of wearing a pair to school like the other kids. Instead, I wore shoes that made me an easy target for the other kids to pick on. Always being made fun of by the other kids because of the clothes I wore and the fact that I was white. No matter how hard I tried to fit in, it was impossible because I was white, and the other kids reminded me of it every day. White boy this and white boy that. This baseball team I was joining was different. Even though there were not many other white kids, we were all on the same team and I felt accepted.

The coach was Mexican and had two sons on the team who helped me learn the game. Everyone was very nice. No one was calling me degrading racial slurs like the kids at school. We were all just having fun practicing baseball. Whatever it took to be able to join I would do. Collect bottles or mow yards or whatever. After much negotiation on my part, agreeing to pick my grades up, quit getting in trouble, and do extra chores around the house, I was able to join. The coach would come by my house in his truck and pick me up for practice. The coach had me playing first base and I was batting 4th in the lineup, a spot reserved for the best hitter on the team. At the end of the season we were the best team in our league and I was the best batter on our team. The coach would take us out for pizza after each win. My mother and step father started coming to my games and I could hear them cheering me on. That was a great feeling that I had never had before. They liked it so much that the stepfather volunteered to be a coach the next year and my little brother Lance joined T-ball. The team they gave him to coach was a rival in the same league that I played in. Everyone assumed that I would be on his team because he was my stepfather. My coach of the Pirates was willing to trade me but he wanted 2 of the stepfathers players in exchange. I was the best hitter on the best team the year before and now I am 13 in a 11-13 year old league. The stepfather did not feel I was worth the trade, so I remained on the Pirates playing the season against my stepfather's team. Everything was different and awkward the second season. The stepfather cherished his new team. The cheering and support I got the year before were gone as we were opponents. He wanted my team to lose. It was not fun like the year before. The whole thing shifted to being about him, his team, and his players. I lost interest and never played baseball again after that second season.

After graduating from Travis elementary school, I was headed for Hogg Jr. High. The summer before starting at Hogg I walked over to the school several times just to check it out. I was excited and scared at the same time. My sister and I had not yet left to go visit our father in Louisiana for the summer so on one rainy day, bored and looking for something to do, I walked over to the school. When I got there I saw about 30 or so black kids playing football in the rain on the muddy field. I stood by the fence watching for about a minute until the other kids started talking to me. They asked if I was going to Hogg. I said, "yes, this will be my first year." Then someone asked if I was going to join the football team. "Yes," I said. I definitely wanted to join the football team, but I hadn't signed up for it yet and wasn't sure how to go about it. *"Well, can you play?"* One of the kids asked. "Sure I can play!" I said. *"Come, let's see then."* I was not expecting them to ask me to play, but I was very happy when they did. They told me to take my shoes off and put them over on the sidelines where all of theirs were. Every pair of shoes there were white converse all stars. Everyone called them "Chucks" for Chuck Taylor. I placed my crappy pair of grocery store basket shoes next to theirs and ran out to play. It was a blast. I was the only white kid there. All the other kids were black. It was a light rain, and the field was slippery and muddy, making it a lot of fun. Of course we were playing tackle, but no one was trying to hurt anyone. Everyone was nice to me and I even caught an interception that impressed the older kids. They kept calling me "Chaaalee" after another white guy "Charlie" who had played with the school team the previous year. *"He's another Chaalee,"* they would say. After we finished playing and it was time to go everyone was grouped up where the shoes were, retrieving their shoes. One of the kids asked me what size my shoes were. When I told him, he handed me a pair of Chucks that he thought must be mine. I never owned a pair of Chucks, and the temptation to take these was too much. I said thanks, see you guys later, took the shoes, and started walking home. We were all still too dirty to put the shoes back on so most everyone just started walking carrying their shoes. I was waiting to hear someone call out to me about their shoes as I walked away, but no one did. The further away I got, the more excited I was. After walking a few blocks barefoot I assumed the coast was clear and sat down on the street curb to wipe my feet clean. The rain water was running down the side of the street near the curb to the street drain, making it a perfect spot to sit and clean my feet. Sitting on the curb I cleaned my feet the best I could before putting on my new shoes. Putting those shoes on my feet was literally a dream come true. It was my first pair of "Chucks" and I had stolen them. Walking home, I felt a little guilty for taking those shoes. It was not the way I wanted to come into possession of my own pair. I really had fun playing football in the rain with all those black kids. They invited me in to play and accepted me when they found out I was starting school there too and was joining the football team. Everyone was cool to me that day. When that kid handed me those shoes, I couldn't resist the temptation. Thank you. Thank you very much, kid who gave me some other kids shoes thinking they were mine. That was a good day. Someone handing me a pair of Chucks was like winning the lottery.

Visiting Father on the Holidays

M y Sister Carla and I would travel to Louisiana to visit our father on every school break. We spent every summer, Christmas and Thanksgiving in Lafayette, Louisiana with our father. My sister and I could not wait to go visit our father in Lafayette. It was a huge contrast from living in Houston. We were shown a lot of love and made to feel like we were part of a family. My father remarried a Cajun woman from Lafayette. She was very pretty, and her and my father seemed to me to be the perfect match. Not to say they had a perfect marriage, but it was obvious they were meant for each other. They laughed a lot, and from what I could tell they got along really well together. My father lived in a 2 bedroom house on one square acre of land. A huge oak tree in his backyard surrounded a good portion of the yard. Underneath the tree was a table with chairs that provided a cool hangout spot where he would drink beer, laugh, and socialize. I used to think he was rich because of the difference between his and our living conditions in Houston. His house was on a dead-end cul-de-sac where all the neighbors knew each other and were like family. Everyone spoke french. French was preferred over English and English was spoken with a heavy Cajun accent. My father was a beer drinker and cigar smoker. He would drink up to a case of beer a day. He would drink and smoke and laugh. I loved his laugh. He laughed a hard, loud, uncontainable laugh. He loved to read. He was always reading a book. He loved me and my sister but never really knew how to interact with us. When he got home from work he drank his beer, smoked his cigar and read his book. We would eat and watch TV together; sometimes, he would take me to work. There was never any mentoring from my father. Never any teaching or advice or words of wisdom on how to live, which I so desperately needed. He was a man of few words. He worked building houses as far back as I can remember. He was a building foreman and then started his own business building houses. One summer, when I was 12, I went to work for my father at his construction site. The first day they had me shoveling sand in the 100+degree heat and no one told me to wear gloves. The next day, my hands were blistered so bad I couldn't hold anything.

My father had a younger sister Pat. My Aunt Pat. I pronounced it Ain't Pat. She was married and had two kids Joey and Susan. Joey was the oldest, about 5 years older than me. Susan was my sister's age, about 2 years older than me. Aunt Pat always made me feel so loved. She was the best. She use to call out my name in her thick Cajun accent, "HAVRELL!" "Come over here boy!" My earliest memory of Lafayette is watching the Mardi-Gras Parade and catching beads. The parade was passing down the street right in front of my grandmother's house.They were passing me around between my Aunt and Grandmother, and everyone was asking me, "do you know who I am?" "I am your aunt Pat, and I am your grandmother, we love you." They were giving me so much attention and I loved it. Aunt Pat married a Cajun man who was a golden gloves boxing champion. His amateur record was 145W-5L. He won the Golden Gloves national championship 5 times in his weight class. No money in professional boxing back then so he found his way into the real estate business. His son, my cousin Joey, was boxing as soon as he could stand. Needless to say, Joey knew how to fight very well. Joey was my idol growing up. Him and "The Fonz" on the sitcom "Happy Days". He was the coolest, toughest guy I knew, and he was my cousin. I knew he would have my back if anyone messed with me. I wished he was around when those kids picked on me in the neighborhood back in the Heights. Things would have been different, that's for sure. My cousin never walked around like he was a tough guy, but everybody knew he was and knew who his father was. In Louisiana, you got your driver's license when you were 15 and your learners permit at 14. He was already driving at a very young age and would take me for rides. I was very young. Joey never picked on me or shunned me away. When he couldn't hang out with me he would patiently explain why. The first time I smoked pot was with Joey when I was 8 or 9 years old. All the other cool, older kids were doing it and I wanted to be cool too. I didn't get high the first time I smoked and wasn't quite sure what the fuss was all about, but I had done it and now I was cool. My cousin Joey was the man. He had a line on the best smoke there was. Joey's dad, uncle Sid, stayed very involved with golden gloves boxing and owned the Louisiana franchise. They coached and trained the Louisiana team and traveled all over to boxing tournaments. One of the coaches was a pot smoker who had an outstanding weed connection and would supply Joey. Joey was the connection with the best smoke you could get. This was the 70s and everybody smoked. All the weed was imported from somewhere else, mainly Mexico. Joey would have Panama Red, Acapulco Gold, Thai stick, Colombian Gold, Maui Wowi, you name it. Every batch had a name. He sold out before he got the stuff. People would give him money in advance to make sure they would get some next time he scored. Joey was the coolest to me, and I wanted to be just like him.

During those holiday visits, much of my time in Louisiana was spent walking around by myself and looking for stuff to do, just like in Houston. My sister, Carla, was 2 1/2 years older and didn't really want to hang out with me. Her and our cousin Susan would hang out together, and I cramped their style. We were out of school but the grown-ups had to work so we stayed at our grandmother's house during the day, which was next to Aunt Pat's. We called her Gram, and she adored all of us. Her house was spotless at all times so whenever I showed up at her door, I was not allowed in until I passed a full inspection. She used to make a big commotion every time I wanted in the house because I was so dirty. I climbed trees and roofs, played with dogs, cats, frogs, lizards, snakes, ant piles, dug holes, played with the water hose and if there was a dirt pile around I was on it. I was always dirty as a kid. Just by myself being a little boy looking for stuff to do. One afternoon my Aunt Pat was across the street visiting her neighbor Mrs. Clemons having coffee while I happened to be exploring around Mrs. Clemons garden and found a grass snake. They saw me in her garden from the sliding glass patio door and waved at me to come over. Not wanting to lose the snake I put it in my pocket and went inside. My Aunt asked me, "What are you doing in Mrs. Clemons garden?" I said, "Just looking around for snakes." They both laughed. Then my Aunt continues to question me with her thick Cajun accent, "Why you looking in her garden for snakes? They not any snakes in there boy. Mrs Clemons is in that garden everyday." I said, "Yes there is, I found one." They laughed again thinking I was making up a story. "Where did you find one?" She asked. So I told them, "Underneath a piece of wood that was laying out there." Again they laughed and asked "What did you do with it?" I said. "I put it in my pocket." They thought I was making this whole story up and are laughing at what they think is some little boy's imagination. Then Aunt Pat said, "Let me see," so I pulled the grass snake out of my pocket and there it was, coiling itself around my hand sticking its tongue out. It was like a bomb went off. I've never seen my Aunt move so fast. You would have thought the house was on fire the way they both shot up from that table and started screaming. "Get that thing out of here boy!" They both ran behind the table yelling at me pointing at the door for me to get out. "OUT!" "OUT!" I ran outside thinking dang, it's just a little grass snake. Hope I'm not in any serious trouble over this. Afterward, Aunt Pat was laughing really hard about what had happened so I knew I wasn't in any trouble. Aunt Pat was the best. She used to love telling that story. Sometimes I wished my mother was more like Aunt Pat.

Always Moving and Changing Schools

Mother finally got a job managing an apartment complex again, and we moved from Bayland Ave. in the Heights to Webster, TX. We lived on Nasa road 1, just a few miles down the street from Johnson space center. Our apartment complex was right next to the school. Now I'm in 6th grade in a mostly all-white school, and still did not fit in. Most of these kids came from upper middle class families. I had never been around kids like this, and they were way different. Things I thought were cool in the Heights were not cool to these kids here. The clothes I wore were not cool here. My t-shirts were the ones with pressed decals on them that said Led Zeppelin or a picture of a muscle car. Now I had real Converse All Star tennis shoes (The ones I stole) that were white with colored laces. The other kids wore polo, Izod, and oxford shirts with topsiders or penny loafer shoes. Everything that was cool in the Heights was not cool here. To my great disappointment, once again I was not fitting in with most of the kids at school. The clothes I wore and the fact that I was an outsider made it difficult to fit in. There was still no money in our household. Mine was not a home where you could easily get a quarter to stick in the pinball machine. Just asking for such a thing would get me yelled at. If I wanted to play pinball or anything else that cost money, it would have to come from somewhere else. It sure wasn't coming from home. I got my first job at Mario's flying pizza, washing dishes. It was right across the street from our apartment complex. That job did not last very long. The movie "Jaws" was playing at the theater and a group of kids from the apartment complex were all going. I was scheduled to work that night but went to see the movie Jaws instead. Mario told me if I didn't come in to work that night, I would lose the job. I really liked having a job and especially getting paid but there was no way I would miss seeing Jaws with everyone else. Everyone was talking about this movie, and I just had to go.

The apartment complex across the street from ours was managed by the same company as my mothers. She was friends with the manager there whose youngest daughter I married while in prison years later.

Bad Friends-Stealing Bikes-Stealing Cars

From there, we moved again to Spring Branch where mother found another apartment job. Always the outsider, always the new kid, I was in 7th grade now starting Jr. High. I made friends with a couple of kids in our apartment complex right away. Our mother's both worked for the apartment complex. These were the bad kids who smoked cigarettes, marijuana, fought, skipped school and stole. My two new friends were brothers and were as crazy as they came. Describing them as wild and crazy boys would be putting it mildly. These boys were extremely wild and rebellious. At this point, I started doing crazy things and committing crimes. Looking back now I believe the way I behaved as a child was motivated by a desire for thrill and action in order to fill the loneliness, lack of action and direction that was missing in my life. Making friends with a couple of brothers who misbehaved more than I did probably contributed to my terrible behavior.

First, we started stealing bikes. We would completely disassemble the bicycles we stole and build our own custom bikes. All of our bikes were a mixture of parts from several stolen bikes. Frames from one kind of bicycle would be mixed with the tires, seat, handlebars and front forks from other bikes. One of my friends made a chopper using the forks from 3 or 4 bikes to extend the front wheel. We chunked many bikes in the dumpster after only taking the parts or a part we needed. The bicycle theft ring lasted only a few months until we got bored. Then we started stealing cars. The first time we stole a car was just a spontaneous act of boredom. We were walking through a parking lot and saw that someone had left the keys in their car. Bobby challenged his older brotherTerry to take the car.Terry was the oldest at age 15 and the ringleader of us 3. I was 14 and Bobby was 13. There wasn't muchTerry wouldn't do if you dared him. He jumped in with no hesitation, started it up and took off. We met him a block down the street and jumped in the car with him. We just went joyriding around abusing the car doing donuts and burnouts as much as we could until the engine couldn't take any more. We left the car where it quit running with smoke coming out underneath the hood. It was such a huge adrenaline rush that it wasn't long after that we were looking to do it again.

We would skip school and walk through parking lots looking for cars with the keys left in them. In those days, you didn't have to look long before finding keys left in a car. We sometimes stole two or three cars a day just to joyride around. The first car I ever drove by myself with no one else in the car was one I stole. I was 14. The other two had stolen multiple cars before I had stolen my first one. Even though I had never driven beforeTerry insisted that I steal the next one with the keys in it. It was my turn so even though I didn't know how to drive I did it anyway. Almost wrecked the car, not paying attention to the road and driving off into the grass. It was my first time driving and It was not as easy as I thought it would be. Several times I had to tell myself to calm down and concentrate on what I was doing before I wrecked. Finally, I was relieved to meet up with my other two friends and letTerry takeover driving. Typically we would joy ride around until wrecking the car somewhere or drive it to a nearby quarry where we would put a rock on the gas pedal and watch as it drove off the cliff into the water. Landrum Jr. High was my school at the time and missed more school than I attended. Suspended countless times until finally they expelled me, I was totally out of control and doing very crazy things that year. One morning I walked to the bus stop where the school bus picks up the kids in the apartment complex to go to school. It was my first day back to school after being suspended. Today I had to be on my best behavior because the young, evil stepfather threatened to beat me like never before if I got into any more trouble at school. Nothing new. More importantly, I promised my mother that I would do my best to stay out of trouble. If I made it a whole day without getting into trouble I was doing good. As I approached the school bus stop I saw my two crazy friends Bobby andTerry. As soon as they saw me coming they started motioning me to hurry up and come over like it was really urgent. It was cold and rainy that morning and the most badass car in our apartment complex, a brand new, blue Camaro Z28 with T-tops, was running with no one in it. The owner of the car was a young, very attractive blonde who had started the car and left it idling to warm up while she went back inside. Bobby andTerry were motioning me to hurry up and come on before the lady came back out. "Let's go!" They said with big mischievous grins on their faces. They were super excited at the chance to steal this brand new badass Camaro. "No, I can't go." I told them. "I have to go to school today." "I promised my mother." This was my first day back from suspension; if I didn't go, I would surely get a beating. After calling me a scared little girl and other bad names, they jumped in the car and took off. All the other kids at the bus stop watched in amazement at what they were witnessing. I got on the bus with the rest of the kids and went to school. Later that day, during the school lunch hour I was hanging out in the usual hideout spot we used to smoke cigarettes during lunch break. It was right across the street from the school behind a little strip mall. All the smokers went there to smoke cigarettes during lunch break. Of course, word had already gotten around and every one was talking aboutTerry and Bobby stealing that Camaro. As we were there smoking cigarettes and talking here came the blue Camaro speeding by.Terry was driving really fast showing off. He came back around with the tires screaming and the engine roaring right in front of our smoking spot. The day had warmed up, and the sun was now shining at midday. I went over to the car to talk to my two crazy friends. The T-tops to the Camaro were off now.Terry was driving with "Big girl" in the front seat. "Big girl" had a reputation of being the toughest girl in the neighborhood. Bobby was in the back like an excited dog full of energy.terry was telling me this was my last chance if I wanted to go. They had stolen some guns from "big girl's," parents house. Bobby was holding a pistol in his hand pointing it around in the backseat laughing and obviously anxious to shoot it. Terry said they were going to Ohio to visit his Aunt. Again I declined to go. They were laughing and joking and said the highway trip was going to be like "smokey and the bandit" Bobby was 13 at the time andTerry was 15. Off they went smoking the tires as they left. I went back to school and when school was over took the school bus back to our apartment complex. The next day at school I was called to the principal's office right away.

Two police officers in plain clothes were there waiting to talk to me. They wanted to know whereTerry and Bobby were hiding with the stolen car. The principal knew us 3 boys very well because we were always getting into trouble. She told the investigators if anyone knew where to find them, it was me. I told them I didn't know where they were, they told me they were driving to Ohio. They didn't believe that for a moment. Even after I told them they still wanted me to go with them and show them all of our hangouts. My principal said I would be excused from school that day because I was helping the cops look for Bobby andTerry. I knew they were not around but I went driving around with the cops anyway just to get out of school. After being driven around and questioned by the cops all morning they finally brought me home. It was then that I finally told my mother what was going on. She was glad that I chose not to go with them. The highway patrol caughtTerry, Bobby and "big girl" a few days later in Kansas. I found out later that Bobby was hanging out of the car, pointing the guns at passing cars and shooting at the tires of 18 wheeler trucks. They were eventually sent back to Texas and, not long afterward, were all on the streets again with juvenile probation. I stayed away from them both when they got back because they were calling me a pussy for not going with them. The boyfriend of the lady whose car got stolen was a Houston police officer. He didn't likeTerry at all and started harassing and threatening him.Terry did not back down or cower from him but instead threatened him back. Within a couple of weeks fromTerry's return and his altercation with the Houston Police officer the officer was found beaten to death. At the time,Terry was just 15 or 16 and was being questioned for capital murder.Terry had some new older friends and I quit hanging around with them. We all still lived in the same apartment complex, so we talked from time to time. They told me about the cop harassing him and then getting killed. The cops brought him downtown for interrogation and had been by our apartment complex several times asking everyone questions.

Back at school, I wasn't doing good at all. When I attended, I was very disruptive and always causing trouble. For the most part, I skipped school. It got to the point where my teachers and Principle quit reporting my absences to home because they didn't want my craziness there. One report card I received had straight "Fs" all the way down. Staring at that report card made me feel ashamed. This was not something I was proud of at all, instead I was very upset that this was what I had to show for myself. Other kids were running around excited and happy, showing off their achievements as I stood stunned looking at mine, feeling like a total loser. No way could I show this report card to anyone. When my mother would ask about it, I would lie and say I lost it. I failed the 7th grade and would have to take it again. I was only 14 years old and already a complete failure, committing crimes.

High School-Selling Weed-Setting School on Fire

We moved again as mother got yet another apartment job. This time it was off Memorial drive in Houston, where some really rich kids lived. This was the best, richest school district we had been to yet. Mother tried to get us in the best neighborhood she could. She was working as an apartment manager, and the stepfather worked as maintenance. Money was still scarce in our household. Most of the kids I went to school with were from upper middle-class or high-income families. They wore nice clothes and had nice things, but we did not. Once I got a dollar for lunch money from the stepfather when lunches were 65 cents, and he wanted his change back. If I wanted any money, I needed to get a job. I worked at Baskin & Robbins and then Krogers while going to Spring Forrest Jr. High. During my freshman year in High School, I started smoking weed just about every day and always knew where to get it. The kids I hung out with all smoked pot as well. I kept a part-time job to have a little money. During my Junior year I was in the distributive education class where I only went to school for ½ a day and worked the rest. The class counted as 2/3rds of my credit to pass the 11th grade. I was working as a stocker in a clothing store and also selling weed. After school I would be at work so sometimes people looking for weed would come to my work looking for me to buy weed. (before cell phones) I devised a way for them to come in like they were shopping and give the cash to a salesperson friend of mine. She would come back and give me the money, typically $25 for a ¼ ounce of marijuana. The person buying the weed would then go outside around back where the trucks came with deliveries. The door was locked but had about ¾ inch crack underneath it to slide envelopes of weed out. At first I started selling weed because I smoked and all my friends smoked so I would get a ¼ lbs. to save money. It got to where too many people were coming to buy weed and too much going out the back door. My manager got wind of what was going on and fired me. Now I would fail the Distributive Education class and have to repeat my Jr. year. Before my teacher of the D.E. class even knew I was fired, she lectured and embarrassed me in front of my classmates. Informing the whole class that if I did not get a near perfect score on my final exam, I would fail the year. This teacher had talked down to me on several occasions before in front of the class, but it was really bad this time. What she was saying had me boiling over inside with anger but I kept it all inside, trying not to let it show that what she was saying was bothering me. As she spoke to me in that degrading tone my mind was imagining the revenge or payback that I would unleash on her. With that mindset, I was given inner satisfaction and strength to hold the anger in as she spoke to me the way she did.

Years later, I would talk about this moment with a psychiatrist in prison, who explained that this type of behavior I was demonstrating was called passive-aggressive behavior. After speaking with the psychiatrist and understanding exactly what passive-aggressive behavior was, I could see how it got me into a lot of trouble.

Most of the kids in that class were seniors whose parents were successful business executives and owners. They got jobs working for their parents, wore nice clothes and drove nice cars and of course got preferential treatment from the teacher. I felt very humiliated and belittled after the teacher embarrassed me in front of them. She was drawing pleasure from my discomfort as she spat her words at me like I was beneath her class. It made me so angry. She spent several minutes speaking to me in front of everyone in the class about the trajectory of my life after I failed the exam. If I did not get a near-perfect score on the final exam, it was over. 24 hours until the exam. The guy who sat next to me asked, "What are you going to do?" "Are you ready for the test tomorrow?" My response was "We are not taking the test tomorrow." He looked at me as if to say, "Don't be ridiculous, we are taking the test tomorrow" but what he said was, "Bet." Now I had clearly made an outlandish claim, and this guy wanted to capitalize on my bravado by making a suckers bet. The odds of us not taking that test had to be at least a thousand to one. He thinks I am a sucker so, of course, I said, "Bet". We bet $5 that we would not take the final exam the next day. I was angry and felt I had to do something. Now I was going to do something and there was no turning back. That night, me and 2 friends broke into the school and poured gas all over the classroom and set it on fire. We poured so much gas we were lucky to get out of there without setting ourselves on fire. The next day at school everyone was obviously talking about what happened. All the burnt furniture was outside in the parking lot and all the doors were open to let the smell out. The distributive education class met in a different classroom that day. When I got to that class we were told our teacher would not be coming back and the test would be taken at a later date. The guy I bet $5 came over and paid me with that look on his face that said he knew I did it. I never bragged afterwards or told anyone it was me. The arson investigators quickly determined the fire was set on purpose and suspected it was a student from the D.E. class. Reward posters for any information concerning the arson were posted all over the school. The investigators were at our school everyday doing interviews, and rumors were going around about who it might be that started the fire. The teacher had a big verbal altercation with another student days before the fire where he cussed her out. He was originally the prime suspect but was cleared after passing a polygraph test. Someone from the

41

neighborhood came forward and told the cops that they saw my car leaving my house around 3:30am the morning of the fire. That person was drinking with friends in my apartment complex that night. He decided to leave and make his way home at the precise moment I was leaving. As he left my apartment complex and started walking home, he saw my car leave. He lived in the apartment complex across the street from the school. He again saw my car parked across the street from the school as he continued walking home. His testimony is what eventually led to me getting busted. That was my first Felony conviction. Arson. I was 17.

Bible School-Going to Church-Acting Right

I was arrested and then released on bond to await trial. During this time, my mother had just found out that the stepfather was cheating with a woman in our apartment complex. Not only was her husband cheating with this woman in the same apartment complex that she managed, but he was leaving my mother to go live with her. She was very hurt and crying all the time. She was devastated. It was hard for her to focus on anything else. My mother never let things get to her; this was the first time I had witnessed her so upset. I felt lost and alone with no direction. My behavior got me fired, kicked out of school, and arrested. I was physically ill, throwing up thinking about my predicament. My mother's advice was to pray. Go to church, Pray and read your bible. Get involved with the church. So I did. I prayed a sincere prayer asking for forgiveness. I prayed that God would help direct my life. I started reading my bible and going to church regularly. I found myself smiling all the time and feeling clean on the inside. My circle of friends were all church going Christians. Lakewood Church is where I started attending when John Osteen was pastor. I could not wait for church and never missed a service. I read my bible for hours every day. Lakewood was starting a bible school so I signed up. I could not get enough of the bible. I was addicted to reading, hearing, and talking about God. feeling charged with goodness, my mind was clear. My heart was full of joy and happiness and I felt good about myself. I signed up for Bible school because I wanted to learn all about God. Everyone assumed I was going for vocational training to become a preacher. Not that I was opposed to being a preacher, but that was not my motivation at all. At the time I was only 18 years old and searching for truth, direction, knowledge, wisdom and a better way to live my life. I got a job working for a preacher in his mail room filling book and cassette tape orders. I moved out of the apartment with my mother and got an apartment with my friend Jerry from bible school.

One day in bible school, we watched a reel-to-reel black and white film from the 50's of a missionary preacher named T.L. Osborne. He was in Africa preaching to a sea of people about Jesus and how Jesus healed the sick. In the beginning of the film you see them setting up the stage as people from all over start migrating in from every direction. Many deformed and crippled people struggle to come out and hear him preach. They showed a crippled man with calloused knees from scooting around all his life being healed and walking. He was in the audience and the crowd went crazy when he started walking. Many people knew him and now watched him walk. It was amazing. God was healing many people, and it was right there for you to see. We all walked out of that class in wonder and amazement. I remember seeing Jerry, beaming like a teenager in love for the first time. His face was noticeably different; you could tell the film got to him. He said he felt a strong overwhelming sense that this was God's calling on his life. He knew that God had spoken to his heart, and he was to be a missionary to Africa.

Once we had finished bible school, we were now awaiting the big graduation ceremony. I was leaving the church in my sister's car when another car ran a red light and smashed into me, puncturing my lung and nearly killing me. I was rushed to Ben Taub Hospital, where a tube was placed in my chest to drain the blood from my collapsed lung. I was unable to attend the Bible School graduation ceremony. Pastor John and Dodie Osteen came to see me in the hospital while I was still recovering from the car accident. When I recovered enough to leave the hospital and go back to church, T.L. Osborne was the guest speaker. Dodie called me up on stage and told the congregation who I was and what had happened. Then she asked T.L. Osborne to pray for me. He laid his hand on my head and prayed as the whole church prayed with him. I felt very honored. I continued to work for a preacher who traveled around teaching bible prophecy. Now I was driving a truck for him with his books and tapes and would set up in churches where he had speaking engagements. While driving his truck to a speaking engagement I was pulled over for speeding. The police took me to jail for driving while license suspended. Apparently, it had been suspended for a no insurance ticket I got a year before and did not know. Things kinda unraveled for me after this incident. My job was on hold because I could not drive. I was feeling guilty for having sex and not being married and felt like a hypocrite, so I slowly started missing church and hanging with the wrong crowd.

Part II

In and Out of Prison

State Prison First trip

One Afternoon I was shooting my .22 rifle down at the bayou with a friend, who had an air rifle that shot pellets. His neighborhood was on the bayou and his backyard opened up to it. The neighborhood constable got a call that we were shooting squirrels so he came running down the hill toward us blowing his whistle. Quickly, I tossed my rifle in the high weeds when we saw him coming. He was very angry because he saw the .22 shell casings but we told him we were only shooting the pellet gun. He searched the both of us and found I had a cheap souvenir Stiletto pocket knife from Mexico In my pocket. The kind that automatically Springs open when you press the button. He arrested me and took me to jail for a misdemeanor weapon charge. I was on probation for the Arson and had recently been arrested for driving while my license was suspended. I was processed into the Harris County Jail without a bond and placed on the 10th floor. The 10th floor is where they housed all the youngsters under 25 years old. The tank I was in was built to house 24 inmates but due to overcrowding, we had at least 60 in our tank at all times. The majority of the guys in there were black from the worst neighborhoods in Houston. They constantly yelled and screamed at the top of their voices like crazed animals. It reminded me of the primate section of the zoo but the primates are much better behaved. There were never more than five or six white guys in that tank at one time. Most of the blacks and Mexicans blamed the white man for all of their problems. The white man put them in jail. Never mind the heinous crime many of these young individuals committed, it was the white man's fault they were in jail. Their hate for white people dominated every part of the conversation.

Everything was racial. Most were obsessed with race. Jail is a very hostile environment to begin with but even more so if you are white. The whites are referred to as white BOYS. The emphasis on the word "boy" is meant to be disrespectful by referring to you as a boy instead of a man. The term "white boy" was actually one of the kinder references. Often whites are referred to as "Ho's" or bitches or "bitch ass white boy." Being a minority and the recipient of racial hatred was an everyday occurrence for myself and other whites in jail. There was nowhere to go to escape it. I had experienced this racial hatred before when I was in elementary school living in a mostly all-Mexican neighborhood. That experience was nowhere near as intense as the hatred directed towards me by the blacks in Harris County Jail. Not a day went by without hearing white mfr this or white mfr that. It wasn't necessarily directed at me personally but those hate filled words constantly echoed throughout the jail. It was a traumatizing experience that no one should ever have to go through. I could never forget it. It was here that I developed an unfavorable opinion of blacks because of the racial hatred I received from them. I had not yet realized that it was the behavior that I despised, not the race. They were rude, disrespectful, loud, obnoxious, ignorant, and without empathy. These behavioral traits would be offensive to anyone no matter who you are. After about four months of going back and forth to court, my probation was violated, and I was sent to Texas State prison. The judge decided to give me "shock" probation. Shock probation is where they send you to prison to "shock" you and then put you back on probation. I spent 6 months in Texas State Prison. I was sent to Pack 2 in Navasota, Texas. It was known as a gladiator farm because most of the prisoners there were under 25. Just a bunch of young testosterone-filled criminals wanting to fight all the time. Just like the 10th floor of Harris County Jail. In prison, we were forced to work out in the fields like modern-day slaves. Picking cotton, planting potatoes, clearing out thick stickerbrush, or just hitting on the ground with a garden hoe. They worked us like slaves without any pay. Wake-up call is at 3:30 a.m. and breakfast is served at 4:30 a.m. If you don't get up, you don't eat. Work call is at 5:30 a.m. If you were not in line for work when they called your name, they would go find you, beat you up, and talk nasty to you. You are talked to and treated worse than someone would treat an animal. Every minute of every day, you were reminded that you were in there to be punished. Slavery was technically abolished in 1865. However, a loophole in the 13th Amendment has allowed slavery to continue as a punishment for crimes. The state of Texas used this loophole to exploit slave labor. When you go to prison in Texas, you are literally the state's property. You are owned by the state and forced into hard labor without pay as punishment for your crime. if you refused to work you would be beaten severely and placed in a inhumane torture cell. It was very hard work, but it felt good to get some sunshine and exercise outside. I was in a fight while working out in the fields that caused me to gain respect for the short time I was there. We were working clearing some heavy thorn brush when a Mexican started talking crazy and disrespecting me. Calling me white boy and a bitch because he thought I was soft and apparently wanted to fight. I guess he just wanted to make a name for himself. He made his way over to where I was and took his shirt off like he was ready to fight. When he came at me and swung I ducked and went with his weight and flipped him on his back. I landed on top of him with his arms pinned underneath him. My knees were on his shoulders keeping him pinned down as I reigned down hard punches to his face cracking open big gashes on his eyebrow and breaking his nose. Every time I hit him I could hear something crack in his face. This was in front of about 300 guys who were all working out in the fields so word spread fast to the rest of the prison what had happened. The entire work crew went in early because of the fight I had been in.

They took the guy out in an ambulance so it was the talk of the prison briefly. That was my last day working out in the fields. After the fight, the guards rewarded me with a job in the kitchen. Everyone treated me with respect for the remainder of my time at Pack 2. A few months later, I was bench warranted back to Harris county and put back on probation. When I got out I lived with my mother and younger brother in the same neighborhood that I went to High School. I was only 21 and already a convict. I started hanging out with some of my old pot smoking fiends from High School and I enjoyed the notoriety of having been to prison. I told the story of Harris County Jail, my trip to Pack 2 and the fight I got in out in the fields. I thought of myself as a badass and portrayed myself as such in front of my peers. I identified myself as a criminal and rode around on a Harley Davidson hustling money by committing crimes.

Married and on the Run

My girlfriend at the time became pregnant. Sadly, I was not in love with her and did not particularly want to marry her but I felt it was the right thing to do. She threatened to have an abortion if I did not marry her. I've always believed aborting a baby was nothing less than murder. To me, it was just a selfish and easy way out of an inconvenient situation. Believing the best and only decision must be to accept responsibility, marry this girl, and try my best to support her and raise my child. I will try my best to give my child the best life possible. It is my intention to spoil him rotten and give him everything he wants. The best clothes, the best shoes, all the things that I never had. It was a dream to do and share all the things with my child that were never shared with me growing up. I'm going to be the best dad ever. That was my intention anyway. Unfortunately it didn't work out that way. Soon after I was married my probation was revoked for Burglary of a habitation. I had only been out of prison less than a year.

My new wife was 8 months pregnant, and now there was a warrant out for my arrest. Not wanting to go back to prison again and leave a pregnant wife, I left Houston and went on the run to Las Vegas. I stayed with my aunt Pat who had moved to Las Vegas from Louisiana years prior. My wife sent me a copy of her brother's birth certificate and I got a Las Vegas driver's license under his name. I bought a used car for 400 bucks and got a job at rent-a-center. After about 5 weeks I got an apartment and was able to furnish it for practically nothing with good furniture given to me from the rental center. My wife and new baby boy came to Vegas to live with me just three months after my son was born. Most days, I worked 12 hours a day and was being groomed for my own store by the corporate bosses. Everybody called me Keith. That was my new name in Vegas. My wife was very young and now stuck at home all day with the baby. That arrangement did not last long. She left Vegas with my son and went back to her mother in Dallas. I went back to Houston a month after.

Back in Houston, soon I found my old crew of friends and started selling weed again. Moved into a nice Two bedroom townhouse with an old friend from High School. My Las Vegas drivers license was the ID I used for everything. During that time there was a dry spell in Houston, and you couldn't find weed anywhere. I knew a lot of people who smoked weed and sold weed. Nobody had any and nobody knew where to get any at the time. Everyone we asked said the same thing, "if you find some before I do please let me know because I want to buy some too".

Finally, after weeks of looking for weed without any luck, a guy I knew brought over 100 pounds and wanted me to help him get rid of it. Because it had been so dry and everyone was looking for some we were able to sell it all within 6 hours. It was sold in quantities ranging from a quarter ounce to 10 lb. During this melee of transactions of getting rid of the weed a friend of the guy who's weed it was brought some girls over to my townhouse to show off. He was there under the guise that he knew someone who had the cash for 10 pounds. It was clear to me he just wanted to show off what was going on to the two pretty girls he had with him. This guy was showing off and had me very angry because thats how people get busted. They left with 10 pounds in a garbage sack then came back an hour later carrying the same 10 pounds. It was raining outside when he came back and I let them stand out in the rain for a while before opening the door, taking back the bag with the 10 pounds, and shutting them out. I didn't like the guy at all. He just rubbed me the wrong way.

Busted with Flour and a .357 Magnum

After all the weed was d, and my friend got his 60k he thanked me. It was just him and I talking about the wild night and he kept telling me what a good guy his friend was. The one I didn't like. He said his friend was a straight up guy and had been involved with large transactions before. His friend was looking for 5 kilos of coke; if I knew where to get it, I could make some money off the guy. So I told him I would ask. There was a guy I knew from Trinidad I met through selling weed who portrayed himself as a big coke dealer. He wore the Miami Vice style suits and shoes with lots of gold jewelry. He had that Caribbean accent and everybody thought he was a big Jamaican coke dealer. I contacted him and explained the situation. "What I think of the guy is he's a rich preppy punk but supposedly able to produce the cash for 5 kilos." "85-90k dollars." Trinidad suggested we rip him off and devised a plan. We went to the grocery store, bought 5 kilos of flour, and wrapped it up in duct tape. We bought a 1/4 ounce of real coke from a friend to show as a sample if the guy wanted to test it. If I could convince him to bring that money near me, I would take it from him. The deal was arranged for us to meet at his friend's apartment. Trinidad stayed out in the car with the duffle bag containing the 5 kilos of flour circling the parking lot while I went inside.

I was carrying a loaded Smith & Wesson .357 Magnum in my waistband under my shirt. After speaking with the preppy guy and his friend I told them the coke was in the parking lot but I needed to see the money before anything. His buyer friend came into the apartment with another guy.

Once we were introduced I thought he was going to shake my hand but instead of shaking my hand the guy quickly patted my waist and felt the gun. He started freaking out saying "he's got a gun, he's got a gun!"

I knew he was a cop at that point and tried to defuse the situation. I took the gun out and unloaded it in front of him telling them I had it for my own protection in case they were going to rob me. After much discussion the two left saying they were going to talk with their friend with the money. As soon as they left I started loading my pistol. I was scolding and cursing the two guys, telling them they set me up. "The guy is a cop!" I yelled. They pleaded with me that the guy was not a cop, making me angrier. As I watched, one and then the other left the apartment and I did not hear any commotion like cops had arrested them. Alone in the apartment now, looking out the windows wondering how I could Escape.

Thinking the coast might be clear, I put the pistol back in my waistband and walked out. Cops were everywhere. D.E.A. agents on the roofs of the apartment complex and running around corners yelling and pointing guns at me. They took my pistol from my waistband, handcuffed me, and sat me on a curb behind several of their cars. Already handcuffed and on the curb were three other guys. Two of which I had never even seen before. The other was the guy who's apartment it was. Through the cop's radio, who was standing near us, we could hear they were arresting Trinidad on the other side of the apartment complex.

While sitting on the curb with the cops five feet from us, I told the guy who's apartment we were just in to get the ¼ of coke out of my pocket. He was reluctant at first until I literally threatened him to tears until he scooted over where he could get in my pocket while his hands were handcuffed behind his back and got the bag of coke out of my front pocket. He did it and was able to toss it in the bushes behind us. Now I felt relieved because I knew this was our only real coke. The rest was flour. The DEA took us to their headquarters in Houston and put us in separate cells. They interrogated each one of us separately for hours. I was still very angry that the preppy guy set me up. He was the only one not arrested. During my interrogation, I told them the guy driving the car with the flour had nothing to do with anything. He was just giving me a ride. They let all the other guys go and took me to Harris county jail.

State Prison Second Trip

After a few months in county jail my court-appointed lawyer said they were offering me a plea deal. I had three felony charges pending against me: Arson, burglary of a habitation (for a VCR) and manufacturing and delivering a simulated controlled substance. (The flour) No indictment on the pistol that the DEA had taken out of my waistband. At this time the Texas Department of Corrections (TDC) was so overcrowded you were only doing about one month for every year of your sentence. By this time, I had already been in county jail for about five months and would also get credit for that time.

Feeling very satisfied with the plea deal they were offering me, I plead guilty to all three felony counts. In exchange for pleading guilty, they gave me a 10-year sentence on each charge to be served concurrently. If I kept out of trouble I would be out in less than a year! While I was awaiting transfer to prison in Harris county jail, the tank I was in was full of guys who had drug charges. The war on drugs was in full swing and many guys were getting busted. Everybody had a story to tell about how big time they were on the streets.

One guy, in particular, talked a lot and bragged how his brother was looking to buy 100 pounds of weed but couldn't find any. He said if his brother couldn't find it then that meant Houston was dry and there wasn't any to be found. I couldn't resist calling him out and telling him I knew where to get it right now. I thought the guy was full of it and was just talking to sound like a big shot. We had phones in that tank so I called a friend who also knew my weed connection. I told him what was going on and I thought this guy was just bragging and his brother doubtfully had the cash. It was arranged for my friend to call the guy's brother thinking the brother would give some excuse why he couldn't do the deal.

As it turned out I was wrong and the deal went through. That was the first time I had sold that much weed in one transaction, and it was from jail. A few Days after the deal went through I was transferred to prison and could no longer get on the phone. Later I received letters from home telling me my friend had moved into the apartment complex my mother was managing and he was making a lot of money selling weed. A total of 14 months was all the time I did on those three 10 year sentences before being released on parole. I paroled to my mother's apartment complex in Houston.

Selling Weed

My first night out of prison, the Trinidad guy took me out to a couple of strip clubs and spent a lot of money on me. He bought me new clothes and gave me cash. He arranged for a couple of girls to entertain me privately in a hotel room. At the time I thought he was just doing the right thing because I didn't snitch on him. Come to find out later he was a DEA informant trying to set me up from my first day out. My friend that lived in my mother's apartment complex was doing very well selling weed. We talked the first day I was out. He explained to me that he had cultivated a very nice clientele of mostly out of state buyers. He had five main guys that bought weed from him on a monthly basis. Each would get anywhere from 40-100 pounds at a time and always brought the cash. He sold an average of about 300-500 pounds a month making at-least $100 profit on each pound. He had a girlfriend that was living with him he wanted to marry. She was about to start at Texas A&M and they were moving to College Station. My friend had already purchased a house there and was just waiting for afew things to be finished then they were moving. He told me he was done selling weed and I could take over the clients he had. This was his big surprise gift to me for getting out of prison. He told me all about each person who came for weed. How much they bought, how often and for what price. He would be involved with the next transaction with each person to introduce me and we would split the profit. I was anxious to do a deal and make some money.

My friend was driving nice cars and had many nice things; of course, I wanted those things too. All my life I had watched other people with nice clothes, nice cars, living in nice houses with nice furniture but never enjoyed having anything nice myself. This was my chance to finally make some real money and I was very eager and excited to get started.

My friend told me about a couple of guys who wanted him to front them 100 pounds to bring to Wichita KS. They explained they had a buyer with the cash but the weed would have to be delivered. He was not going to front the weed so if I wanted to make a quick score we could drive up to KS and deliver it. We loaded up a van and drove all night to Wichita. We ended up staying there 3 days before getting all the money but other than that, everything went well. We had all the cash in 1000 dollar rolls, placed them in zip lock bags, and shoved down loose-fitting pants for the flight back to Houston. It was 80,000 total cash. We owed our guy 60 and split the 20k profit. It felt great having that money. As soon as we got back to Houston I got my own apartment and decked it out with all brand-new furniture. Out of prison less than a week and was feeling like I was on top of the world.

The first month was fast-paced, with my friend introducing me to his connections. He would tell them I was the one to contact for now on because he was getting married and was finished selling weed. Each time he introduced me we were doing a deal so I was making a lot of cash. I never had money like this before and it felt amazing. I bought a corvette which was the car of my dreams at the time and decked it out with all the extras.

I met a girl from Guatemala who was visiting her friends in my apartment complex. She and her friends were all in the hot tub late one night when a friend and I decided to test drive a jet ski in the pool. After the security guard made us leave I invited the group over to my apartment. They were all old friends from Guatemala. The girl was living in Miami with her parents when she found out her friends were all in

Houston so she came to visit for the weekend. They all came from very rich families. Linda's mother was English and her father was Guatemalan. Her father worked for the government of Guatemala. One of the guys in the group was the son of the owners of the largest beer company in Guatemala. Another was the grandson of a previous president of Guatemala.

We all hung out drinking and doing coke that night. Linda and I hit it off, and she ended up being my girlfriend and moving in with me. Her friend Freddy lived in my apartment complex and was a car dealer in Guatemala. He had a mechanic shop in Houston and was able to change numbers on stolen cars and produce legal blue titles. He hired drivers to drive the cars to Guatemala where he sold them on his lots. He drove a red Porsche 928 with Guatemalan license plates. Before I met him, I always thought he must be a drug dealer. During this time a lot of people were asking me about cocaine. Could I get any kilos? I knew of 3 guys who were looking for a cocaine connection to buy a kilo of cocaine. I did not know anyone who could get that much.

Trip to Guatemala

During conversations with Freddy I brought up that I was looking for a connection for kilos of cocaine. He said he knew some people in Guatemala whom he would ask. Before long I was traveling to Guatemala to meet his friends. Freddy was a successful businessman in his 40s with a wife and young kids. He owned several large car lots in Guatemala City with very expensive cars. He had 4 brothers who all worked for him.

They picked us up from the airport in 2 black BMW's. All the guys were armed and carried their pistols openly. We sped through the city as they showed me around town then eventually to the hotel. Freddy told them who my girlfriend was back in Houston, and they all seemed to know her. They brought me to a big billboard advertisement of a girl in a bathing suit drinking a Shangri-La soft drink and it was her. I was so proud.

These guys were acting like kingpins and treating me like I was a boss. The once bullied, lonely poor kid from the Heights was at this moment feeling like Tony Montana in Scarface. The acceptance and respect I sought after my whole life was finally happening abundantly. It was a major adrenalin rush. This was the kind of lifestyle I wanted. This is what I always hungered for

The hotel I was staying at was the tallest building in the city and the guy who owned it was who I was meeting, Freddy's friend. He lived on the top floor of the hotel. He was a Lebanese guy who everyone called "The Maharishi." The elevators to the top floor are separate and we had to go outside to get to it. Next to the elevator was a little police shack. When the police came out of the shack they asked to see ID's and the guys I was with went off on them, yelling and cursing in Spanish.

There were six of us and four were armed. The cops started being very apologetic as the guys were yelling at them. I think they were being overly aggressive to show off in front of me. We six then got on the elevator and headed up. The elevator opened to a bar lounge type area where 10 or 15 people were hanging out. Without acknowledging anyone we walked through that area to a different living room type spot that had couches, tables and chairs.

Freddy was the only one who spoke English and not very well. Everybody was speaking Spanish introducing themselves. We then all sat down on a big conference table that was furnished with fruits and various snacks. They all spoke Spanish for about 15 minutes, with Freddy and the guy (a Lebanese guy) doing most of the talking. I gathered he was vouching for me telling them he knew where I lived, knew my mother, knew my girlfriend, and I was a big weed dealer in Houston.

I had not spoken at all when the guy suddenly told me in English "*I think we can do good business together.*" He said my price for each kilo would be 7k if I picked it up in McAllen, TX. He could fly it to wherever I wanted and drop it but that would be 9k a kilo at a minimum of 400 kilos. He talked about plane routes and GPS coordinates as I listened, not knowing what he was talking about.

Finally, when I spoke, I told them the truth about my capabilities. "I have never even seen a kilo of cocaine before." "I am a weed dealer, and many guys were asking me about a kilo of cocaine." "I may be able to sell about five kilos a month but what you guys are talking about is way over my head." "I appreciate the offer and want to do the deal but I wouldn't know who to sell that much cocaine to." They were all cool with what I said and everyone still treated me very respectfully. We hung out, ate and drank. I had made new friends. It was an amazing experience, and it made me feel like I was on an episode of Miami Vice.

I was excited to get back to Houston and brag about my billboard model girlfriend. I told my friends all about the trip as they listened wide eyed. We all wished we could do a deal like that and make a quick million-dollar cash profit. Cocaine was a lot different than selling weed. It was way more dangerous. You could get robbed or set up to get busted if you didn't know everything about the person you were doing business with. On the other hand, many people were becoming millionaires overnight. It was all very exciting, and I thought if I could ever make a million dollars on one deal, I would never do another.

My girlfriend and I were getting along great. We went out to the flea market one weekend to buy some plants for the apartment when I ran into a guy with whom I was locked up, in county jail. He was a Colombian who was in the bunk right next to mine for several months. We started talking about what's been going on since getting out. He said his wife and kid lived in Miami but he had an apartment in Houston for his Texas parole residence. He said he has not been able to do any business since getting out and times were tough for him. I told him I was doing good, making money selling lots of weed. His lease was up in the place he was living and was looking for another apartment. My mother was the manager of the apartment complex I lived in and he could get an apartment there no problem. I helped him out getting the apartment right next door to mine. His two Colombian roommates were also in the same tank in the county jail with us. These guys were all serious and well-connected cocaine dealers. They had all been involved before with very large transactions of cocaine. They were all part of a network of Colombian distributors. I told my Colombian friend about the recent trip I took to Guatemala and what they offered me. He assured me he could have all the cash for 400 kilos in a week's time. He said he could have cash for 100 immediately. The price for a kilo was $18,500 dollars at the time and I was offered 400 kilos at 9k apiece. All I had to do was be the middleman between my Guatemalan and Colombian friends.

I spoke with Freddy and arranged another meeting with "The Maharishi." Soon I was traveling back to Guatemala and speaking with the man again. Rudolpho, my Colombian friend, told me exactly what to say and if I had any questions I would call him. This time when I went, I knew much more about how deals like this were done. Rudolpho had taught me a lot. The plan was to drop the packages of cocaine from the plane into the gulf at the designated GPS coordinates. It was an abandoned oil rig three miles offshore that my Colombian friends used before. We would leave from Kemah, near Galveston, in a fishing boat, anchor near the rig, and fish. Once the fishing boat was in position, we would use a radio to communicate that we were ready. The plane would then leave Guatemala and be on its way. We would continue fishing and wait for the plane to toss the cocaine out in the water. Then we would gather the packages, secure them up in the oil rig, then leave and come back the next day to pick them up. The meeting went well, and we all left feeling very optimistic. The price had changed from 9k to 11k a kilo but I would still make close to 3 million dollars. I was so excited I could hardly contain myself. The guy in Guatemala would put his end together and let me know. He said it could be 2 weeks or 2 months but we would be in touch.

Soon afterwards, back in Houston, Rudolpho and his crew had scored. A shipment of cocaine had come in from Colombia that they were tasked with distributing. He had been waiting for months and now he was rolling. He was not excited like I was when I told him about the Guatemalan deal. His attitude was let's wait and see what happens.

Homicide Investigation

At this same time my High School friend who set me up with the weed deals had just killed a guy. The jet ski I mentioned that I was riding in the pool the night I met Linda was stolen and the guy who stole it had stolen two. My friend bought one for $400 dollars and told the guy, (Leon) he may be interested in buying the other. Leon got impatient about my friend not coming back to purchase the second jet ski. Apparently, Leon drove by my friend's apartment late one night and shot out his bedroom window and put a couple of bullet holes in his car. We actually thought it was someone else and nearly retaliated against the wrong person. Then Leon called my friend and left a message on his answering machine. The message was very bad. Calling my friend a punk ass bitch white boy blah blah *"you better come get this other jet ski MFR!"* *"I know what room you and your girlfriend sleep in"* blah blah. *"The first time I shot up your house was just a warning"* etc... So my friend called him back and told him to meet him and he would give him the money for the other jet ski. When Leon came out to meet my friend, my friend shot him 14 times.

My friend moved into his house in college station right afterward. I still had the jet ski in my apartment. It was heavy, and I lived downstairs while my friend had an upstairs apartment. That is why it was there in the first place. The homicide investigators came asking questions about my friend and the jet ski. My mother was the manager and let me know they were there asking questions. They found out I had the jet ski and they wanted it. Because I would not talk to them or allow them in my apartment, they handcuffed me and put me in the back of the car. They told me they would get a search warrant and then I would be charged with interfering and theft by receiving. My girlfriend was crying and my mother was telling me to just let them see the jet ski. Finally, I agreed to let them in and they took the handcuffs off. They came into my apartment and checked the numbers on the jet ski to confirm it was the one they were looking for. Now they needed to transport the jet ski downtown to the police station. They remained at my apartment complex for hours waiting for transportation to take the jet ski. I wanted to be done with the whole ordeal, so I actually borrowed a van from a friend and transported the jet ski downtown for them.

Afterward I called my friend and told him everything that just happened. Wish he would have taken that damn jet ski with him when he left. I didn't have anything to do with the murder or the jet ski but now I am being handcuffed and questioned by homicide. A couple of weeks later the homicide detectives busted in my door and arrested me for theft by receiving. They had just come from arresting my friend in College Station for murder. He was actually in the back of their car while they were breaking into my apartment. The jet ski that I had allowed them to get out of my apartment and transported to police headquarters was what they were now charging me with. This was a pressure move by the homicide detectives to try to get me to talk. I was released on Bond. My friend was charged with murder, and I was charged with theft by receiving. He got a $10,000 Bond, while I got a $20,000 Bond. Go figure.

Busted with 5 Kilos of Cocaine

Both mine and my girlfriend's birthdays were in November, just a couple of days apart. We decided to get a hotel room to celebrate our birthdays. I had a kilo of cocaine that belonged to me. It was payment from my Colombian friends for a deal we had done earlier that week. I was having trouble getting rid of it because the color was an off yellow color instead of the brilliant white everyone was looking for. Although the cocaine was high quality, uncut from Colombia my prospective buyers were not interested because the color was not right. I took the kilo with us to the hotel room and we started using it. We stayed there for three days partying. I came back to our apartment on the 20th of November.

When we arrived back at my apartment, my Colombian friends who lived right next door to me were outside. It was obvious by looking at me that I had been doing cocaine. I had not slept in 3 days and looked pretty bad. My Colombian friends were very concerned about me. I told them I was having trouble selling the kilo they had given me because the color was not white. One of the Colombians told me, "I can change the color and have it repackaged for you." "OK," "Sounds good" I said, and gladly gave it to him to fix. Later that day, he returned with it and told me it was two and a half ounces short of a kilo. He also said if I didn't want to deal with it he would sell it for me for $14,000 dollars. Relieved, I was happy to let him do it and be done with it. He told me "It might take a couple of days to get rid of it but as soon as I do, I will give you the money." "No problem" I said.

I was asleep in my bed still trying to recover from the

cocaine binge, when I got a call from the guy from Trinidad. He was calling to tell me he needed 4 kilos of cocaine. He said he had a guy who was looking and willing to pay $18,500 dollars per kilo. I called my Colombian friend and asked for four kilos. I asked him to bring the one I gave him back and three more. A few hours later he arrived with four of his and the one that I gave him earlier. He had just gotten a new car, and the cocaine was in the trunk. He parked the car near my apartment and gave me the key. He told me to let him know when I was finished, and we would square up. I called the guy from Trinidad back and told him I was ready. He told me he was coming over with the money.

When he got to my apartment, he didn't have the money. He told me the buyer would not let him leave with all that cash. The buyer wanted to see the cocaine before turning over the cash. I was very uncomfortable with this and told him "I don't want to do the deal." However, after much back-and-forth, I agreed to meet the guy with the money. I had not eaten much or slept in the last 3 days so my mind was not right. I gave the trunk key of the car to the guy from Trinidad. I told him once he sees me leave with the money he can go to the car and get the cocaine. While I was in the car talking to the guy with the money it was obvious to me that he was a cop. I again said "I don't want to do this deal" and started to walk away from his car.

At that moment DEA agents came out of everywhere and placed me under arrest. The head DEA agent in charge was the same guy that had arrested me before with the flour. His name was AJ McFadden. *"Remember me?"* he said, *"It's not flour this time is it?"* I was in shock. My girlfriend Linda was still inside the apartment, sleeping in bed, oblivious to anything that was going on. I asked the head DEA agent if it was okay if I just told my girlfriend goodbye. He agreed to let me go back in the apartment with about 10 other DEA agents who immediately started searching my apartment.

They found and confiscated $22,000 dollars in cash that I had hidden in a box in my closet. They were also very interested in both Linda and my passports. Linda had traveled all over the world because of her dad. I had recently been to Guatemala twice. All of the stamps of our travels were in the passports. This seemed to make the agents even more interested in me.

What really sucked was sitting at my dining room table handcuffed to a chair watching all the DEA agents rummage through my apartment while my dog came and sat next to me. He put his head on my lap and looked up at me sensing something was wrong. "I'm sorry buddy," I told him, "I was just trying to make some money." As we were leaving my apartment, there was a DEA agent inside my Corvette grinding the gears trying to get it in reverse. I called out hey! hey! you're grinding the gears! The DEA agent that was escorting me to his car told me you'll never see that car again.

They took me to the DEA headquarters in Houston for extensive interrogation. They wanted me to tell them where I got the cocaine. They told me if I wanted out of the situation, I would have to cooperate. It was obvious that I was heavily connected, and they wanted to know about that connection. I didn't want to give up the Colombians because they were my friends. They were always very good to me and I would not betray them to save myself. However, I did want out of the situation I was in. Playing to their eagerness to make a bigger bust, I told the DEA that my connection was in Guatemala and I could get them a whole plane load full of cocaine if they just let me out.

After the initial interrogation, I was taken to the Harris County Jail. I was able to call my girlfriend and let her know what was going on. She and I devised a plan in which she would contact a friend in Guatemala to play the role of my cocaine connection. The DEA needed to corroborate whether or not what I was telling them was true. So, the trick was to get someone on the phone to act like they were sending me a plane load of cocaine. The DEA came to interview me again a few days later. I told them "The guy I am dealing with in Guatemala does not speak English so I will use my girlfriend as a translator." They asked me, "Would she be willing to help set the guy up?" I told them, "I would need to talk to her about it." They let me call her while they were in the room and listened to what I said. We had already talked about it in advance, so she was ready. They asked if she would come down to the DEA offices to make a recorded call to the guy in Guatemala. She did, and it was convincing enough for the DEA to let me out of jail.

Never had I any intention of cooperating with the DEA. It was all a con job to get them to let me out of jail so I could leave the country and go into hiding. My Colombian friends brought my mother a bag full of cash, $10,000 dollars to hire a certain lawyer. He was the same lawyer that had previously represented them. The lawyer was fully aware of my intentions and knew I was not going to rat on the Colombians. Even if I wanted to, I couldn't because we had the same lawyer. Smart move on the part of the Colombians. Part of the deal of me getting out was I had to plead guilty to the Firearms charge. The pistol the DEA had taken from me over a year ago when I got busted with the flour.

Finally, I was released on two separate bonds. The first was for possession with intent to distribute cocaine and the second was felon in possession of a firearm. Now I was out on three separate felony bonds. (Including the $20,000 dollar bond for 'theft by receiving' with the state.) Now I was to report to the bonds people, the DEA and the Federal Probation Department every day, as well as my state parole officer. Everybody was watching me. None of my old friends on the streets wanted anything to do with me. While out on bond, I continued to see the DEA on a regular basis. We were making tapes of the conversations with the guy from

Guatemala. I had sold all my furniture and some jewelry I owned that the DEA hadn't confiscated and I only had about $6,000 dollars cash. It was time to run and I was very desperate to get out of the country. Since the DEA knew I might try leaving the country, they held my passport. A guy I knew who lived in the same apartment complex had a passport but would not let me use it. Out of desperation I went into his apartment anyway and stole it.

Originally, Linda and I were planning to go to Guatemala, but my Colombian friends convinced me that I should go to Colombia instead. They had just made a bunch of money and were all planning to move back to Colombia as well. They told me they would even bring my dog to Colombia when they came. That was it then. I was going to Colombia.

Living in Colombia on the Run

Linda and I flew from Houston to McAllen, Texas. From there, we took a taxi across the border to Reynosa, Mexico. We caught another flight in Reynosa to Mexico City. From there we flew to Colombia. The stolen passport I was using had a picture that didn't look anything like me. It was nerve racking each time some official asked to see my passport. They just stamped it and handed it back without any questions though. Once we made it to Barranquilla Colombia I called the number of Carlos who was supposed to come pick us up. Carlos was one of the three Colombian guys who lived in the apartment next door to me. He and I were also in the same tank at the Harris County jail.

Instead of coming to the airport to pick us up he gave us his address and told us to take a taxi. My girlfriend did all the talking because I did not speak or understand Spanish at that time. As we drove through the streets of Barranquilla on the way to Carlos's house you couldn't help but notice the trash everywhere. What struck me as strange was in the middle of what seemed to be a ghetto-type neighborhood would be a few very nice houses. The houses were all made out of cement. Every house large or small had burglar bars on the windows and doors. The walls that separated each house had broken glass cemented to the top of the walls. Security was obviously a big issue there. As we turned into the neighborhood where Carlos lived, all the houses looked pretty nice. When we pulled up to Carlos's house there were about 10 or 15 people sitting outside waiting for us to arrive.

Carlos lived in a very nice neighborhood in Barranquilla in a nice, brand new house. He had armed bodyguards who worked for him. I later realized this was very common. I assumed this was where we were going to stay temporarily but that was not the case. After exchanging pleasantries with Carlos and his crew, he took us to a hotel down the street. The hotel was nice with a kitchen and living quarters inside overlooking the city. This is where Linda and I would stay until our other friend from Houston who was bringing my dog was to show up.

His name was Dario, and he had just recently married a Colombian girl he met in Houston who was from Cali. They arrived about two weeks after we did. I was so happy to see my dog. Dario had a sister who lived in Santa Marta, Colombia. Santa Marta is a beautiful beach town on the Atlantic coast about an hour drive from Barranquilla. His sister lived there with a guy who was also a "Narcotraficante" who worked with the Medellin cartel. He was soon to be leaving Colombia to go to Guatemala in order to help facilitate the transportation of cocaine into the United States.

Dario had purchased a house in Barranquilla that was currently under construction. We would stay in Santa Marta and take over the rent of the house his sister's boyfriend was living in. It was a small two bedroom bungalow with a maid quarter in the back. The beach was less than a quarter of a mile away. This area was called Rodadero. It is a very beautiful place.

The little bit of money that I had brought with us soon ran out. I was not working so Linda and I had to depend on Dario for our livelihood. My dog was a Siberian Husky and Santa Marta is a very hot place. My poor dog was suffering in the heat. In the best interest of the dog, I had to give him away to someone who would take care of him in a cooler spot. I loved that dog and had it since it was a puppy. Linda was not handling the situation well at all and understandably so. After about three months in Colombia, she informed me that she had missed her period and thought she was pregnant.

Linda owned a Thoroughbred quarter horse back in Guatemala. She suggested she go there to sell the horse and then return to Colombia. Her parents no longer lived in Guatemala but were now living in London, England. Our plan was she would make the trip to Guatemala, sell her horse and then come back with the money that she had gotten from the sale of the horse.

She called me after arriving in Guatemala to update me on the situation. She told me that she was unable to sell the horse because there was an outstanding bill with the stables that had been taking care of the horse. She also informed me that she had lost the baby. She said she had a miscarriage from riding the horse. She quit calling me after that and I had no way of contacting her. I was devastated. I loved Linda, and now she was gone. First my dog, then my girlfriend. Everything I loved was gone. Feeling very depressed and lonely, I started taking long walks on the beach by myself. Somebody once told me the best way to get over a woman was to get another woman. Fortunately for me the beaches of Santa Marta, Colombia did not have a shortage of beautiful women. I found this antidotal advice to be spot-on. Soon I was seeing many other women and the hurt of losing Linda slowly faded away.

It was 1990 and the cocaine trade was in full swing in Colombia. It was like living in the wild, wild west. Every night on the news they talked about Pablo Escobar and different atrocities around Colombia. It seemed like everyone I ran into was either in the cocaine business themselves or had a family member who was. Being from the United States, everyone wanted to get to know me. I was constantly being approached by people wanting to do a cocaine deal. They wanted me to be their American connection. So many guys quickly became very rich because of the cocaine trade. Narco-traffickers traversed about driving the best vehicles, wore the best clothes and had armed bodyguards surrounding them. The number of bodyguards you had was like a status symbol. It was actually quite necessary. In the beginning, Pablo Escobar was viewed as a folk hero around Colombia. He was an uneducated street thug who came out of extreme poverty to become one of the richest men in the world. People looked up to him and wanted to be just like him. However public sentiment started to change while I was there. He had gone too far and killed too many innocent people. Thousands were murdered. It got to where everyone had a friend, relative, neighbor or someone they knew who had been murdered because of Pablo Escobar. He was no longer the folk hero he once was.

My friend Dario and his wife were leaving to go out to their farm and asked me if I wanted to join them. I had just met a girl who lived not far from where we were staying so I decided to stay and hang out with her instead. She didn't speak English, and I didn't speak Spanish at the time. Before long, I realized she was certifiably crazy. Beautiful but crazy! After about a week of staying at her house I decided it was time to leave and return to my friend's house.

My friend and his wife had been gone for about a week and were not scheduled to come back for another two weeks. I was there alone in the house with no money and no food. The only thing there to eat was rice. I was so hungry. All I could think about was food. I was lying in a hammock outside, underneath the shade of two palm trees. As I was lying there, I noticed two large iguanas sunbathing on the leaves of the palm tree. Immediately I thought about eating them. I was so hungry that all I could think about was what I could eat. I went in the back where the clothesline was, made a makeshift noose, and attached it to a stick. My plan was if I could get the noose around the iguana's neck I would catch it, kill it and eat it. As I was trying to get the noose around its neck, the iguana fell from the palm tree. As soon as it hit the ground, it took off running, and I took off running after it. It got away but there was still one left. I was laughing to myself as I walked back to the palm tree to try to catch the other one.

While walking back, my neighbor who lived right across from me, came out to see what I was doing. He was a French guy about my age and to my surprise he spoke English. "What are you doing?" he asked. We had crossed paths many times before but he never spoke to me until that day. "You speak English?" I responded. "Yes, I speak a little." he said. "All this time I thought you didn't speak English because you never spoke to me." This really had me puzzled. "I don't know, my English is not that good," he said. Then he asked me "Why were you chasing the iguana?" Laughing, I told him the situation I was in. My friends had left, I had no money, and I was hungry. All I've had to eat for the last week was rice. He invited me into his house and pulled some leftovers out of the refrigerator for me to eat. Too hungry to be embarrassed, I still had my 18 karat gold necklace with a diamond embezzled lightning bolt pendant hanging around my neck. The watch I wore was a white gold Cartier Panther. Both pieces were worth a substantial amount of money. I thought about trying to sell them many times before but finding someone who I could trust to pay what they were worth was the problem. He told me he knew where I could get cash for my watch and necklace right now if I wanted to pawn them. It never occurred to me that I could go to a pawn shop and get cash for my jewelry. Up until that point I didn't even know pawn shops existed in Colombia. Tired of being broke, it was time for me to part ways with my shiny valuables. Off we went into Santa Marta to a pawn shop. They gave me the equivalent of $5,000 dollars for my watch and necklace.

I hated to lose them but being broke in a third world country is no fun. Now that I had money and met someone who spoke English, I felt totally relieved. My French neighbor's name was Herbert. He lived with his older brother who had a wife and small child. His brother had lived in Rodadero for over 10 years. The older brother used to rent small sailboats on the beach. Now he's moved onto bigger and better things and was encouraging Herbert to rent those same sailboats. They also owned two wave runners, and two windsurf boards. Herbert invited me to go into business with him renting these on the beach. He needed a partner. The sailboats needed a few minor repairs so I would be required to invest in the restoration. I would also help load and unload the equipment as everything was very heavy. I was all for the idea. Most of the days were spent hanging out at the beach, flirting with all the girls. Many days would go by without us renting anything. It was a lot of fun though, and I met a lot of new people.

Hardly anyone there spoke English, and since I didn't speak any Spanish, I had to learn. As time passed, I started picking up more and more Spanish. I never went to school to learn Spanish or had any formal training. I learned by just listening. After about a year's time I became fairly proficient in Spanish and was able to understand just about everything being said but couldn't speak it quite as well. My Colombian friends from Houston were busy with their own lives doing their own thing. People were constantly approaching me wanting to do business but would require that I travel back to the United States and there was no way I was going back.

Colombian and Venezuelan women, in my opinion, are some of the most beautiful women in the world. The women there outnumber the men by a ratio of three or four to one. It was crazy the amount of attention I received from women while I was there. They loved me partly because I was from the United States. One of these beautiful young ladies, my girlfriend at the time, worked in an office building right next to the beach. She had a phone in her office and was allowed to make international calls. It had been about a year now on the run and I had not told anyone where I was. Not once had

I contacted home during this time. My girlfriend encouraged me to call my mother using her office phone. After all this time on the run, I finally called her. My mother was very excited to hear from me and to know I was okay. She told me that I was on the Most Wanted list. She said that the police were looking for me everywhere. The Federal Marshals had visited all of my family members. My picture had been on television informing the public that I had been added to the Most Wanted list. My grandmother in Louisiana was watching her soap operas when my picture came across her television. She nearly fainted. They had convinced my mother that if I didn't turn myself in my life was in danger. I had been labeled as "armed and dangerous" and because of this, the police told her it was very common for cops to shoot first and ask questions later. My mother spent most of the conversation trying to convince me to turn myself in. It was never even a consideration in my mind. I felt very safe where I was. I believed at the time my mother was exaggerating about my fugitive status. When she told me I was on the most wanted list, I assumed it was Houston's most wanted list. After speaking with my mother, I decided to call my lawyer to see what he had to say about my fugitive status. He informed me that I had been added to the Federal Marshals 15 most wanted list. He explained the seriousness of being on that list. He told me a team of Federal Marshals were assigned to apprehend me. They would not stop until they found me and had all the resources of the United States federal government to do so. It was very serious. I could not believe what I was hearing. During the course of the conversation, I asked my lawyer what involvement, if any, did AJ McFadden (the DEA agent that busted me) have in this. My lawyer told me that AJ McFadden got promoted and was now working in Istanbul, Turkey. I still felt safe from the Federal Marshals where I was. No way was I going back. I was living in Paradise on the beach. Beautiful girls in bikinis were approaching me every day. It was like living in a dream. I was living like a rockstar. The attention I received from so many beautiful women there was unbelievable. I was having the time of my life.

One of my girlfriends at the time introduced me to someone she thought could help put me to work making some serious money. The work involved carrying a specially-made suitcase with the cocaine built into the suitcase. These suitcases were very professionally done. They would totally disassemble the suitcase and then rebuild it with the cocaine inside. The cocaine itself would be pressed and shaped to replace the hard solid pieces inside of the suitcase such as the wheel wells. I was introduced to a couple of guys who had been involved with this business for a long time.

Ramon and Eduardo, who went by the name "Yayo", were very interested in recruiting me as a mule to carry a suitcase. My problem was I could not travel with the passport I had. It was too risky. They told me they could get a new passport made for me with my picture on it. They also told me that I would be taking a suitcase somewhere in Europe, not the United States. They would pay me $25,000 dollars in addition to my airfare, hotel and traveling expenses. To further convince me how safe it was to carry one of these suitcases, they introduced me to an American guy who had done it several times. It sounded like a good deal to me at the time. Especially the part about the $25,000 dollars. I agreed to do business with them and carry a suitcase. For the next couple of months, they worked on getting me a passport.

We were in constant contact during that time. I had traveled back and forth to Barranquilla with them several times. Introducing them to my Colombian friends from Houston who talked very highly of me to them. We became good friends. They were having problems getting my passport made. The first guy they hired took the money and disappeared. The next guy they found did a very bad job. He made a total of three different passports, none of which were good enough to travel. Weeks turned into months and everyone was getting frustrated that things weren't coming together.

They explained that recently one of their suitcases had arrived in Canada safely. They were still waiting for the money from the sale of the cocaine. The money was there in Canada, but they had problems getting someone to bring it to Colombia. They told me a lady was originally supposed to fly back to Colombia with the money but hadn't done so yet. It was one excuse after another. They were getting tired of waiting for the lady to come with their money. They were looking for someone they could trust to transport the money from Canada back to Colombia.

I told them my mother would do it. She would jump at the opportunity to be able to come see me. They were all for the idea. I called my mother and explained the situation to her. My friends would buy her a ticket to fly from Houston to Montreal. Once she arrived in Montreal she was to call the Colombian connection who had the money. My mother was happy to do it. This was an opportunity for her to have an all-expense-paid vacation and be able to see me. We would meet in Maracaibo, Venezuela. Everything went according to plan without any complications.

Mother in Venezuela

I was able to cross the Colombian/Venezuelan border using one of the fake passports that was made for me. At that time the border crossing was not difficult at all. When they saw an American with a blue passport they just stamped it and told you to go on through. Never questioned me or looked twice at the passport.

I met my mother at "Hotel del Lago" in Maracaibo, Venezuela. It was so nice to see her after all this time. I had lost a lot of weight and she just cried when she saw me. She had never seen me so thin. We hung out for a couple of days seeing the sights and going out to eat. I explained to my mother my plans to carry a suitcase to Europe. The money she was carrying from Canada was the proceeds from one of those suitcases. I explained how good these suitcases were made. Many people were doing it and making a lot of money. I would have already gone, but we were having problems getting a good passport made. My mother had brought my real passport that the DEA had confiscated from me but later returned to her. No way would I try to use it to travel but it was nice to get it back.

The Colombian guys were anxious to get their hands on the money, fearing that my mother and I would just disappear with it. We were in constant contact over the phone. They told me my passport was almost done, and it looked really good. They sent someone to the hotel to meet us to get the money. When the guy came to get the money, he also brought a suitcase with 4 kilos of cocaine built inside of it. I was to hold on to the suitcase until it was time for me to go. Both my mother and I were very impressed with the quality of the suitcase. Even after being told that the suitcase held 4 kilos of cocaine, there was no way of discerning where it was. We checked out of "Hotel Del Lago" and went to a different hotel that was much less expensive. We were running low on the cash that we had and both of us were getting impatient. Every day I spoke with Colombia on the phone. They were still waiting for my passport to be completed.

My mother argued with me to let her travel with the suitcase. The prospect of making a quick $25,000 dollars was very enticing. After days of debating what to do I agreed to let her take the suitcase. I called Ramon in Colombia and told them my mother was wanting to travel with the suitcase. They were all for the idea. The next day after that phone call, a man showed up at our hotel with a bag full of cash. The plan was for my mother to board the plane in Maracaibo then travel to Aruba then to Curacao. From Curacao she would travel to Amsterdam. Once she cleared customs in Amsterdam she was to check into a hotel and call me. We purchased the tickets, and I took her to the Maracaibo Airport to see her off. The suitcase was very good but needless to say we were still both very nervous. Once her bag was checked in, we both sighed in relief. She arrived in Aruba shortly after leaving. After a brief stay in Aruba, she made it to Curacao. Again, I was relieved and confident that she would make it without a problem.

I waited nervously by the phone to receive her call that she had made it to Amsterdam. I waited and waited but she never called. I called Ramon in Colombia and told them that my mother had not called. After three days without hearing from her, it was evident that she had been busted. I felt terrible. I could not eat or sleep. It was the worst feeling ever. Writing these words now, I am again overwhelmed with guilt. How could I allow my own mother to travel with that suitcase of cocaine? Now I would have to call my sister and brother back in the States to tell them what happened. My sister was extremely angry. My mother had already called her from Amsterdam so my sister knew that she was in custody. She told the police as well as my sister, that she did not know the cocaine was in the suitcase. My sister asked me, "What have you done to MY mother!" She was too angry to talk with me and understandably so. I had never heard my sister like that before or since. I felt like the lowest scum of the Earth. This was all my fault. I could have stopped my mother. I could have just said no, but I did not.

More Suitcases

I was on the phone daily with Ramon and Yayo in Colombia. I wanted them to bail my mother out of jail or at the very least, pay for her lawyer. They tried to calm me down and tell me they would do everything they could. The money I had was running out. I was staying in a hotel and eating all of my meals out. Each time I called Colombia it cost money as well.

Finally, someone came from Colombia to meet me and give me money. It was the brother of Yayo. His name was Leonardo but went by Nano. He explained they had four other suitcases at the Colombian/Venezuelan border that they were waiting to bring to Maracaibo. They had several other people waiting to transport the suitcases to Europe. He told me that once they get the money from the delivery of any of these suitcases, they would be able to get a lawyer for my mother. I went with him to meet these people who were also staying in a hotel in Maracaibo and I acted as a translator.

It was a couple from Denmark. They had been waiting for almost two weeks for the Colombians to bring them the suitcases. They were very impatient and ready to leave. They said if they didn't receive the suitcases in the next three days they were leaving without them. After we left the meeting with the couple from Denmark the Colombian guy explained the problem to me. The old man who had delivered the suitcase to me that my mother took was the person who was supposed to bring the suitcases across the border. He had not been paid and was unwilling to transport anything else until he was paid. He was owed $5,000 dollars.

They were trying to get the money together for him but it was taking time. I offered to do it myself. "They don't even check when I go across the border," I explained. "They see me as an American tourist with a blue passport and I just walk right through," Continuing to explain that I could do it easily. "They never even look at my bags," I said. That same day he and I traveled back to Colombia. We went to the house of the old man who they called Uncle. He lived in a remote area on a farm near the Colombian/Venezuelan border. He was not happy at all about the idea of my carrying the suitcases. He was pretty much holding the suitcases hostage until he got paid. There was a lot of arguing and yelling but when it was all said and done, we left with two of the four suitcases.

We drove during the night to Maicao, Colombia. The next day I got a seat in a carrito going to Maracaibo. A carrito is similar to a taxi. It's someone's private car used for the transporting of paying customers. They seat one passenger in the front and three in the back. The plan was for me to travel back alone with the two suitcases to Maracaibo. Once I arrived, I was to meet the couple, confirm and write down all their flight information. I would not give the couple the suitcases until right before we left to go to the airport. The suitcases were never to leave my sight until they got on the plane. I was to stay in the airport and watch them get on the plane and not leave until I saw the plane leave. Then I was to call back to Colombia and let them know what happened. We reached the Colombian /Venezuelan border about an hour after we left Maicao.

Everybody had to get out of the car and go through customs. I went to the toilet area first and stood around to see how everyone was acting. Next, I went through the line to get my passport stamped. No one even asked to look at my bags. I got back in the car and off we went. No problem whatsoever. I arrived in Maracaibo as the sun was setting. I checked back into the same hotel that I had left from earlier. I took a shower, changed clothes and left the suitcases in my hotel room. The couple from Denmark were staying in a hotel just a few blocks down the road so I walked over to speak with them. When I got there the lady at the desk told me that the couple had checked out earlier that day. It was hard to believe what I was hearing. They were not supposed to leave until the next day. Now I must use the phone and call the guys in Colombia. A taxi took me to the place where I could make an international call. It took about an hour before I finally got through to someone in Colombia. Finally reaching someone, I told him I had made it there, but when I went to speak with the couple, they had already checked out of the hotel. Apparently, they had already known this and told me *"oh, yeah, they changed Hotels. They're staying at hotel Astor because it was cheaper."* It was good to know all was well, but I was relieved and pissed off at the same time. All the running around, being stressed out and coming to find out the couple were staying in the same hotel as I was.

We met later that evening, and I copied all their flight information. They were flying from Maracaibo to Caracas and then from Caracas to Madrid, Spain. The next morning, I brought them the suitcases. They packed all their stuff and left me two very nice suitcases which they had traveled there with. We all took a taxi to the airport. Once inside, I hung back, watched them check in, get on the plane and the airplane left. When I left the airport, I took a taxi straight to the place to make an international call. The guys in Colombia were waiting for my call and answered right away. I gave them the flight information and told them I watched the couple get on the plane with the suitcases. They were very happy. They told me to call back tomorrow evening and they would have confirmation from Madrid. The next evening, I called many times and never got an answer. The following morning, I called again but didn't get an answer. I was back and forth from the hotel room to the place where you make international calls for three days straight without getting any answer. Finally on the fourth day my friend's wife answered the phone. She said Ramon was in Barranquilla and told her to tell me everything was fine and someone would be coming to the hotel to talk to me soon. I told her I needed to speak with Ramon and asked when he was going to be back from Barranquilla. She told me she was not sure. He was there on business and he should have already been back. I called back the next day and spoke with her again. This time I was very angry and could not hide it. I told her to tell Ramon that everything was NOT okay and I was about to return to Colombia. She told me no, no, don't come back. Leonardo is on his way to see you; he's already left Santa Marta.

Thankfully Leonardo arrived soon after the phone call. He told me that the couple had made it to Madrid with the suitcase. He gave me some cash as well. He told me Ramon and Yayo had been in Barranquilla celebrating. I asked about the money for the lawyer for my mother. He told me don't worry, they would take care of it. They had a lot of things going on but he was sure that Ramon was going to contact someone in Amsterdam about helping my mother. He stayed drunk most of the time we were together. He kept telling me don't worry, everything will be okay. They had two more European people in Maracaibo waiting to take the other two suitcases. They wanted me to stay in Maracaibo and deliver the suitcases just like I did last time. They would pay me $1,000 for each suitcase. His uncle would bring me the suitcases. All I had to do was hold on to them until it was time for the Europeans to go to the airport. I was to make sure that they got on the plane with the suitcases and call back with confirmation.

Call to Guatemala

L eonardo stayed in Maracaibo for less than a week. He seemed to stay drunk the whole time. The night before he was to go back to Colombia, we went out to eat at a nice restaurant. As we talked, drank and danced with the girls, I noticed it was November 17th— Linda's birthday. There was a phone in the back of the restaurant that you could use with a phone card and make international calls. I was pretty drunk and decided to give Linda a call. I had the number of one of her good friends named Luis. He was one of the guys who had been to Houston who was in the hot tub the same night I met Linda, the night I was riding the jet ski in the swimming pool. He answered the phone, and I greeted him "Hey Luis, how are you?" "This is Harold, do you remember me from Houston?" "Are you still in contact with Linda?" "Today is her birthday and I'm calling to wish her a happy birthday." "How is everything going over there?" Luis sounded very strange and apprehensive. He was telling me "*I don't want to get involved.*" He sounded very scared and not really wanting to talk to me. I was confused and a little drunk. I was asking him "what are you talking about?" He explained to me that Linda had been shot, and her husband was murdered. She had recently married the mayor of Guatemala City. The guy had just been assassinated a couple of days ago and it was all over the news. Linda, who had also been shot, was in the hospital under police investigation. The parents of the guy who was murdered are saying that Linda and I conspired to have him killed so she would inherit his money. It was all over the news and it had just happened. They were linking her connection with me to the murder of her new husband. Stunned, I could not believe what I was hearing. Completely surprised because

I had no idea she was even married. I asked him to repeat it several times to make sure I understood him correctly. He was very uncomfortable talking to me and wanted to get off the phone. He asked me to please not call him again because he didn't want to be involved. Walking back to the table, I was in a daze. Leonardo was drunk and acting like a fool trying to dance with somebody's girlfriend. Heated words were being exchanged as I came back from using the phone. Right away I had to get in between him and the guy to try and calm the situation. Afterwards we paid the tab and left. There was no use of trying to talk to Leonardo about what I had just learned on the telephone. We both went back to our hotel rooms, and he left for Colombia the next day. All this new information about Linda I just kept to myself.

Back to Colombia

After Leonardo left, I stayed in Maracaibo for around three more months. Ramon gave me one excuse after another about hiring a lawyer for my mother. My sister back in the United States kept me informed about the situation with mother. The Dutch government appointed her an attorney who was representing her case. Mother was eventually given a 3-year sentence.

I delivered one of the two remaining suitcases to a Norwegian guy who traveled to Canada with it. The uncle came and got the last suitcase from me. Ramon told me both of the two suitcases had not made it to their destination. They had lost a lot of money over the last few months and were struggling to send me more money. I met a very nice girl during this time who became my girlfriend. We spent every day together. She was a very special girl who I probably would have married had the circumstances been different. After several months staying in a hotel in Maracaibo, my money was running out. Ramon kept telling me "Two weeks." Two weeks would pass and he would tell me another two weeks. Finally, I had enough and decided it was time to return to Colombia.

When I arrived back in Santa Marta, I first went to my friend Dario's house by the beach. I told him all that had happened while I was in Venezuela. Dario was very upset to hear about my mother and how Ramon had not done anything to help her. He said whatever I wanted to do as far as retribution, he had my back. He told me I was welcome to stay with them there but they soon moving to Barranquilla. The house that he was building was finished.

My first day back In Santa Marta I ran into my friend Herbert, the French guy who lived next door to Dario's house. He told me that Linda had been calling his house trying to get ahold of me. He said she had called the last two Saturdays and was going to call back again this Saturday. He said she was calling from London, England. Very interesting, I thought. I was definitely curious to hear what she had to say, especially after finding out all that stuff when I called on her birthday. I was looking forward to talking to her and finding out what was happening.

Within a couple of days, Ramon found out that I was back in Santa Marta and came by Dario's house looking for me. He never got out of his truck. He just asked me if I wanted to take a ride so we could talk. I went back in the house to tell Dario that I was going with Ramon to talk. Dario had a .38 revolver that he handed me to take. He did not know Ramon and was not sure what his intentions were. I tucked the pistol in my waistband and got in the truck with Ramon. He was very nice and apologetic. He was telling me how sorry he was about what happened to my mother. He wanted to do something but just was unable because he didn't have the money. Two other suitcases had gotten busted. He lost a substantial amount of money. He promised he would make it up to me. He said he had a great business opportunity for me if I was interested. Would I like to come to his house for dinner to discuss this new opportunity? I was broke and had no idea how I was going to make any money. Of course I wanted to hear what he had to say. In the back of my mind, I wondered if he was just trying to set a trap to kill me. He had to know that I was very unhappy and possibly wanted to cause him harm.

We drove to his house in Santa Marta. Ramon lived in a nice house surrounded by high walls and an iron gate. He had two armed guards as well as a live-in maid. He introduced me to his wife and three young daughters. I was very apprehensive going there but everyone was very nice to me. After we ate dinner with his family, Ramon and I went out into his backyard to talk. Eduardo and Leonardo came over as we were sitting in the backyard. I started feeling extremely paranoid and thinking about the pistol in my waistband. Both of these guys carried pistols all the time. My first thought was they were about to kill me. I was very nervous at this point. After greeting Eduardo and Leonardo they sat and we all started talking. They were apologizing to me about what happened to my mother. They were telling me the same things that Ramon told me on the drive over. They were very sorry for what had happened and wanted to make it up to me. They told me that they wanted me to go to Australia. The price for 1 kilo of cocaine in Australia was $100,000 dollars. They were not going to risk me carrying a suitcase but wanted me to go and receive the cocaine they sent. They had a connection there who would buy the cocaine from me. My job would be to receive the suitcases and sell the cocaine to their Colombian connection. The Colombians there in Australia were from Medellin and could not be trusted to send back the money. I would pay the mule and keep $5,000 for each kilo for myself then send the rest back to Colombia. They had some big-time investors from Santa Marta and Barranquilla who were trying to establish a trustworthy connection in Sydney, Australia. It all sounded very enticing to me. I was relieved that they were not there to kill me. Ramon invited me to move into his guest house while they ironed out the details. I went back to Dario's that night and moved into Ramon's house the next day.

Phone call from Linda

Saturday came, and it was time for Linda to call. I went to Herbert's house to see if she would call at the designated time she said. Sure enough, she called right on time. What she told me blew my mind. She told me that she had not lost the baby after all. She had the baby, and it was a little girl named Kristina. When she arrived back in Guatemala, things didn't work out the way we had planned. Right when she arrived, the police detained and questioned her about my whereabouts. The police frequently followed her and questioned her concerning me. She was unable to sell her horse because of the outstanding bill at the stables where it was kept. She was scared and did not know what to do. She did not want to come back to Colombia with me only to be broke and trying to raise a baby. She ended up getting married to a guy whom she knew for a long time. The guy was from a very well-to-do family and was into politics. He was actually the mayor of Guatemala City. She told him that she was pregnant with my child but he wanted to marry her anyway. She felt that this guy could give her and the child she was carrying a much better life than I could. She felt like it was best to lie to me and say that she had lost the baby so I would not interfere with her new life. The guy's parents were totally against their son marrying her. Not only was she pregnant with someone else's child but that someone else was a drug dealer living in Colombia and wanted by the police. They were against this marriage from the beginning. They never liked Linda. They were only married for just a few months when the guy was killed. She told me he normally had bodyguards with him wherever he went, but that night it was just her and him together. They were exiting out of a restaurant where they had just eaten when two guys on a motorcycle pulled up next to them and opened fire with an automatic weapon. In a spray of bullets, he was killed and she was shot. She was over 8 months pregnant at the time. While she was in the hospital, they looked at her as a suspect in her husband's murder. It was all over the news. They were reporting that she had recently come from Colombia pregnant with the baby of a "Narcotraficante" who was on the Most Wanted list in the United States. He was on the run living as a fugitive in Colombia.

Police were investigating whether or not her marriage to him was all an elaborate scheme to have him killed so she would inherit his estate. It made for great news and kept people glued to their television, but it was all untrue. It was the parents of her husband who started pushing this conspiracy theory. Now that she was the widow she was also the heir to the guy's estate who apparently was very rich. The parents could not stand Linda and did not want her to have any of that money. While she was in the hospital, she was under police guard. Her mom and dad were living in London England at the time and flew down to Guatemala to be with Linda while she had the baby. After she had the baby they took her back to England with them. That's where she is now. Living in London, England with her parents. We talked for a very long time, and Herbert was getting uncomfortable and wanted me to get off the phone. I told Linda I had to get off, and she said she would call me back at the same number next Saturday at the same time. I agreed to be there. I wanted to talk to her more. It was difficult to process all this new information. It was both stunning and exciting to find out I had a baby girl! Her name was Kristina with a K, and she's living in London, England. Wow!

After I hung up with Linda, I went to talk to Dario. I told him everything that Linda had just told me. I also told him about the conversation I had when I called Guatemala from

Venezuela on November 17th. Dario told me he already knew some of the information I had just told him. His sister's brother, whose house he was staying in, was living in Guatemala. He was the guy working with the Medellin cartel that went to Guatemala. Linda and I met him before he left. He was in contact with Linda when she first arrived in Guatemala, at first they were friends, but they had some kind of falling out. I asked Dario why he didn't tell me any of this before. He said he thought it was best that I didn't know because there was nothing I could do about anything anyway. He thought it was best if I just forgot about Linda. Dario and his wife moved to Barranquilla that same weekend. That was the last time I saw or spoke with him.

Now I was staying in Ramon's guest house. We were driving back and forth to Barranquilla two or three times a week. He introduced me to several big players from the Atlantic Coast cartel. They were about to invest a lot of money sending me to Australia. My only stipulation was that there must be work for me when I got there. What I didn't want was to wait like I did in Venezuela for a suitcase to arrive. They had to assure me that there was cocaine already there before I went. No way would I risk being stuck on the other side of the world with no money. I met the guy who was going to take the suitcase to Australia. I also met the guy who was making the suitcase. They explained to me every step of the operation and how it would work. The suitcase the guy was going to carry only had two kilos. This was much easier to conceal and was virtually impossible to detect. They would even test the suitcase with drug-sniffing dogs before it left Colombia. The plan seemed to be coming together and everyone was very optimistic.

The next Saturday came, and I returned to Herbert's house to receive Linda's call, just like before she called right on time. Herbert was convinced that this call was costing him money even though Linda was calling direct. He insisted that

I only talk for a few minutes; this was the last time she should call using his phone line. Wanting to know all about the baby, there were so many questions I wanted to ask. We didn't talk long and I gave her the number of Ramon' neighbor so she could call me there. We set a time for her to call me back the next day on the neighbor's phone. I asked her what she was doing nowadays, and she told me not much, just taking care of the baby and working out. She said that she had joined a gym near her house and when she wasn't home, she was working out at the gym. She asked me what I was doing, and I told her I was planning on leaving Colombia. I didn't tell her where I was going. I just told her that I was leaving the country. I was tired of living in Colombia. The next week she called again. Linda told me her father didn't want the baby to grow up without its father. He wanted to help me get out of the situation I was in. He was all for the idea of me coming to London to help raise the baby. She said her parents owned a house in the city and another house in the country. She was staying with her parents in the house in the city. She told me her father offered to give her and me the house in the country to live in and raise the baby. It all sounded like a really good proposition to me at the time. My only concern was what would I do for work? What kind of job could I get to support her and a baby? She told me that she had become friends with the owners of the gym that she was attending. They suspected she was from a Latin American country because of her Spanish accent. During the conversation, they asked her if she knew anyone who could get cocaine? She told me that these two guys were very rich. She knew that they sold illegal steroids out of the gym. If I could supply cocaine to them, it might be the answer to my financial problems. I told Linda I might be able to do something, but I wasn't sure. I told her the next time you see these guys ask them how much cocaine they were looking to buy and how much were they willing to pay? She said she would talk to them and let me know.

After that phone conversation, I told Ramon all that had transpired. Linda's father wanted me to move there and help raise the baby. Also the part about the gym owners who were asking about buying some cocaine. Ramon told me if that's what I wanted to do he was all for the idea. We could do the same thing we were planning to do in Australia but in England instead. He said the price for a kilo of cocaine in England was around $40,000 dollars. Although it was a lot more money in Australia, he had too many partners in that deal. If I went to London, he and I could work directly together. I was hoping that Linda's friends were serious and not just talking big to impress Linda.

Several days went by and Linda called back to the neighbor's house. I was at Ramon's house when she called. The neighbor came over and told me I had a phone call. I rushed over excitedly to take the call. Linda told me she talked to her friends at the gym and they were very excited. They could buy two kilos of cocaine right away. They were willing to pay $40,000 dollars a kilo. She had quoted me the same price that Ramon told me. This convinced me that the guys knew about the business. I told her it shouldn't be a problem at all. I would let her know something soon. Linda tried to tell me everything in code and seemed to be very uncomfortable talking about it. We quickly changed the subject. I asked her how the baby was doing. She said fine. She was sleeping. Every time I asked her about the baby, she was very vague with her answers. The baby was always sleeping when I asked about her. I never heard her cry in the background. I even asked Linda to wake her up so I could hear her cooing or something. She did tell me the baby looked like me. She said she had my eyes, making me so anxious to see her. I asked Linda to send me a picture. She would always quickly change the subject. She never wanted to talk in-depth about the baby. I thought she was just being overly protective. Linda had been through a lot, so I didn't want to push the subject too hard.

After we got off the phone, I went and talked to Ramon. I told him what Linda had just told me. The guys said that they could afford two kilos right away. They said the price was $40,000 dollars a piece in London. This also made Ramon feel more comfortable and optimistic that the guys were for real. Again he told me if that's what I really wanted to do he was ok with it. We would start coordinating plans to make it happen right away.

Suitcase to London

A lot of time, money and effort went into coordinating this project. Many people were involved. **First** the guy whose cocaine it was. He was willing to front the cocaine and wait to get paid once it was sold in London. **Second**, the guy who made the suitcase. The suitcase had to be purchased brand new. He would spend days building the cocaine into the suitcase. He would wait to get paid when the suitcase arrived in London. **Third** was the guy who was carrying the suitcase. His airline ticket and travel expense had to be paid upfront. He would get paid for carrying the suitcase once he arrived safely in London. **Fourth** were the investors who would front the cash for the new suitcase, the airline ticket and travel expenses. **Fifth** was my travel expenses and airline ticket. Ramon would coordinate all of this together. It was not easy but Ramon is very good at putting deals like this together. The most difficult part was getting the investors to hand over the cash. Ramon had made a lot of money sending suitcases all over the world. In the past, it was much easier than it was now. Ramon still had a reputation for being very successful at transporting suitcases. Things were coming together, but it was taking a long time. Ramon was trying to talk me into letting the guy carrying the suitcase meet the buyers directly. I refused. I wasn't going to let them cut me out of my own deal. The suitcase was ready, and they had the money for the carrier's plane ticket and travel expenses.

Ramon decided to send the guy with the suitcase to London before obtaining the rest of the cash. He reasoned that once the guy was there with the cocaine, it would be much easier to convince the investor to invest more money. Even if he couldn't find more money to send me, he would use someone else's connection to sell the cocaine. The guy made it safely to London with the suitcase. Everyone was very excited when he called. Ramon was now actively trying to sell the cocaine to someone else in London. He told me as soon as we got the money, we would do it again. Linda would call me once a week. I never gave her any details but kept telling her that we were working on it. She kept asking me what's taking so long. She said the guys at the gym were asking her when I was coming. They were starting to act like she was making everything up. I told her the cocaine was already there. It cost a lot of money to get it there. Now it was going to cost even more money to send me there. It looks like they're going to sell it to someone else. They promised me once we got the money, we would do it again. If those guys were serious, they would send me the money for the plane ticket. She called me back and told me the guys were willing to buy my plane ticket to London.

This was great news. It was the last piece to the puzzle. I was so excited and so was everybody else. I gave Linda the name on the fake passport that I would be traveling with. The guys bought the ticket, and it was waiting for me. We called the travel agency to confirm the ticket had been sent. They told us they did indeed have the ticket. Everyone was so excited. We had a big party the night before they took me to the airport. The next day we drove to the airport in Barranquilla from where I would be departing. So many people came to see me off. Three Toyota Land Cruisers full of people taking me to the airport. We stopped at the travel agency by the airport to pick up my ticket. I went in by myself while everybody waited outside. I sat across the desk from a beautiful Colombian girl who was typing out my ticket. We talked and flirted with each other as she was getting my ticket ready. I was so happy. Right before handing me the ticket, she said, *"Oh, this ticket is coming from Istanbul, Turkey."* Meaning whoever sent the ticket sent it from Istanbul. I felt like I had just been shot. The only person in the world I knew in Istanbul Turkey was AJ McFadden. The DEA agent who had busted me twice before. She handed me the ticket and told me she wished she was going with me. I was in total shock. Linda was working with the DEA and had been setting me up all this time. I was so stupid. Now I had to go outside and tell the gangsters waiting to take me to the airport. They had invested so much time and money and effort into this project. They might just kill me when I tell them. I walked out with the ticket in my hand still in shock. When everybody saw me come out with the ticket in my hand, they were all smiles. I got in Ramon's Land Cruiser and told them the DEA had sent the ticket. The origin of the purchase was actually written on the ticket. Istanbul, Turkey.

Ramon asked me, "Everything went okay?" "You got the ticket okay?" I told him yes but I could not go because the DEA sent this ticket. "What do you mean the DEA sent this ticket?" I told him it was sent from Istanbul, Turkey. The DEA agent that busted me in Houston was in Istanbul Turkey. At first, they didn't want to believe it. They kind of laughed and thought I was being overly paranoid. Just because the ticket was sent from Istanbul Turkey does not mean the DEA sent it. Maybe the guy's partner lived in Istanbul. Linda did tell me that these guys were Lebanese. I explained to them the phone call I had with my lawyer a year earlier. He told me that I was on the Federal Marshals 15 most wanted list. He also told me the DEA agent who had busted me was now working in Istanbul Turkey. I'm 100% certain that I'm being set up. If you guys still really want me to go, I'll go. Just know that they'll be waiting for me. I'm going to be arrested. The police are probably waiting for me at the Barranquilla Airport. Needless to say, everyone was very disappointed. There was a lot of cussing and yelling as everyone else in the group discovered what had happened. It was a very intense situation.

Part III

18 years of Incarceration

Arrested in Colombia

As we drove back to Santa Marta, we talked about what to do next. The guy with the suitcase was staying in a hotel in London and was out of cash. They were worried about losing the suitcase. Ramon had a connection in Amsterdam who would front the cash for the guy to take a train from London to Amsterdam with the suitcase. Once the guy delivered the suitcase to Amsterdam, Ramon would have cash again. I would have to lay low at Ramon's house until they could put the deal together in order to send me to Australia. I told them If I went back to Ramon's house, I would get busted. "They know where I am. As soon as I don't show up in London they're going to come and get me." They told me to call Linda tomorrow to let her know that I missed the plane. "Tell her we had car problems and were unable to make it on time not to worry and that the ticket is still good." The plane leaves once a week for London and I will be on the next one. As long as they think I'm still coming, they won't come and arrest me here. I was very paranoid about going back to Ramon's house. They kept telling me not to worry because this was Santa Marta. "You are safe here. It's only temporary." Ramon had a farm where I could stay, but some relatives of his were there at the time. I could stay at the farm the next week when they left.

The next day I called Linda. It was hard talking to her, knowing that she was setting me up, and the DEA was probably listening on the other line. I told her we had car problems and didn't make it to the airport on time. I did get the ticket, and it was good till next week. I gave her the flight number and told her not to worry, I would be there next week.

She sounded a little upset and impatient. She told me that she would tell the "buyers" what happened. I cut the phone call short and told we would talk again before I left. Two days later she called me back. The neighbor came over to inform me I had a call. We started talking and Linda was acting like she was very upset that I didn't make it. She kept going on and on about the inconvenience I had put her through. All the while I knew she was lying, and the DEA was listening to the call. The more she talked the angrier I became. Then she started talking about the baby. She said she got the baby all dressed up to meet me at the airport. She also told the baby she was going to meet her father. It was more than I could take. I could no longer contain my anger. I told her I knew she was lying. She was setting me up this whole time, using the baby to pull at my heartstrings. She started to deny everything, telling me I was wrong, and I didn't know what I was talking about. "Why do you think I'm setting you up?" She asked. She said I'd been smoking too much pot, and I was just being paranoid. I told her I knew the ticket was sent from Istanbul, Turkey. She tried to tell me that was because the gym owners were from there. I asked her "Do you know who else is there?" "AJ McFadden." "He's probably listening in on this call right now." She hung up, and that was the last time I ever spoke with her.

I went back next door to Ramons' house in a hurry. I told him, "I gotta go man. I got mad at Linda because she was talking about the baby and I told her that I knew she was setting me up. I got to go man, they're going to come get me." I was looking out the windows, sure the cops would be there any moment. Ramon was laughing and telling me to calm down. "This is Santa Marta," he said, "The cops will not come get you here." Again I tried to explain to him how serious it was being on the Federal Marshals 15 most wanted list. "Don't worry," he said. "I'll take you out to the farm next week. Just stay around the house and don't go anywhere by yourself. Moses and Benjamin won't let anything happen to you." Moses and Benjamin were Ramons' bodyguards. I couldn't stand still. I knew I had to get as far away from that telephone as possible. At least it was the neighbor's phone and not Ramon's. There was nowhere for me to go. My friends from Houston were now living in Barranquilla. I hardly slept that night. I was up early the next morning and paced around the house all day.

Everyone was telling me to chill out and calm down. "They're not coming to get you here, this is Santa Marta. You're not Pablo Escobar." They thought I was being ridiculous. Nothing happened that next day and I started to feel better. I was up early again the following morning. Moses and I were out in front of the house smoking a joint. The cleaning lady was using the water hose spraying the driveway. We moved closer to the road to get out of her way. As we sat underneath a palm tree in front of Ramons' house smoking a joint, a van came to a screeching stop right in front of us. The side door slid open and out jumped several police officers carrying automatic weapons. Moses instinctively pulled out his pistol. At that same moment several other undercover cop cars pulled up quickly with police jumping out. Military soldiers dressed in fatigues were running at us from every direction. Everyone was screaming. I tried to get inside the gate, focusing mostly on Moses and his pistol. There was no escape. They kept yelling at me to get in the van. Moses was yelling back at them saying they were not taking me. What was my charge and why were they taking me? "*We have an order, we have an order,*" they screamed. Moses argued with the pistol still in his hand. They told him to put his gun away, but he told them to put theirs away. "Where are you taking him? Why are you taking him? What law has he broken?" Moses asked. "*We have an order, we have an order,*" they kept saying. "An order for what?" Moses asked, "How do you even know you have the right man?"

One of the police officers in plain clothes had a paper that said "WANTED" at the top. It was a picture of me obviously sent from the Federal Marshals in the United States. It did not look anything like me. However, it showed my tattoos. I had a cloud with a lightning bolt tattoo on my right arm. The officer lifted up my shirt and saw the tattoo. There was no arguing that I was the right person. They had orders to bring me in, and that's exactly what they intended to do. I got into an unmarked car with the police officer who seemed to be in charge, but they never handcuffed me. They took me down to the Santa Marta jail where I spoke briefly with the captain before he jailed me. Eduardo (Yayo) was the first to visit me. Visitors could walk right up to the cell and talk through the bars. He was all smiles and very jovial telling me not to worry that they would get me out. He said they had a good lawyer who was talking to the captain trying to reach an agreement to free me.

As the day went by several other people stopped by. Everyone had smiles on their faces telling me not to worry that they were getting me out. Just like Yayo and each time I thought they would let me out. The day turned into nighttime and I was still in the cell. The plain clothes police officer who had driven me to the jail came to visit me at night. He told me the next morning they were going to take me back to my house to get all of my belongings. He kept asking me if I understood what he was saying. I took this to mean that someone had paid him off and they were going to let me go the next morning. Maybe they wanted to make it look like I escaped or something.

The next morning, the guy came back to my cell and asked if I was ready to go. Again, he explained that he was taking me back to the house to get all of my belongings. Did I understand? I thought to myself cool, they must have paid this guy off, and he's about to let me go. Before we left, they wanted to fingerprint me and take my picture. After that was done, we walked out to where the police vehicles were. I was not handcuffed and we were still inside the police station walls. I could see several large military transport trucks being loaded up with soldiers. Each one of these vehicles probably held 30 to 40 guys. I thought to myself they must be going on some military exercise or something. I got into the car with the officer who had brought me to jail the day before. I sat in the front seat with him while two other cops were in the backseat. Since they never handcuffed me, I took that as a good sign.

The military trucks full of soldiers left about 15 minutes before we did. When we finally got to Ramons' house, I realized they were not letting me go. The trucks were there blocking off the entire block. No traffic in or out of that area. All the neighbors were outside wondering what was going on when we pulled up to Ramons'. The cleaning lady was standing in the front with Ramons' wife. I went inside by myself to collect my belongings. All the police were waiting outside for me. I packed all of my stuff in my suitcases. Once I came outside, there was a small crowd of people, mostly neighbors who had come to say goodbye. Everyone was so nice to me, crying and hugging me. The cops helped me load my suitcases in the car and off we went, straight to the Santa Marta airport. Two of the cops flew with me on the plane to Bogota.

Prison in Bogota

When we arrived in Bogota a group of the Colombian special forces police were there waiting for us at the airport. It was obvious from how these guys moved around that they were a highly trained team. All of them were heavily armed and casually well dressed. They looked and acted like a group of badasses who were ready for whatever, whoever and whenever. If you didn't know they were cops, you could easily mistake them for bad guys. They escorted me from the airport to the jail in a three car caravan. Myself in the backseat of the middle car with the two guys who escorted me from Santa Marta sitting on either side of me. The driver and his partner sat up front. The lead vehicle was a Toyota Land Rover with a driver and 4 guys armed with automatic weapons. The chase vehicle behind us had the same. We raced through Bogota to the jail. At one point we were forced to stop very briefly because of traffic. As we were coming to a stop the doors to the lead and chase vehicles swung open and out jumped two guys from each vehicle holding automatic weapons. They menacingly stared at the occupants of the cars around us in traffic. The people all around us were sitting in their cars, scared shitless. They remained looking forward with both hands on the steering wheel, not daring to make eye contact with the armed men who had just stepped out on the street. The traffic started moving again, and they quickly got back in the land cruisers and off we went. The ride was exhilarating, and it was an impressive show of force that flattered my gangster ego. It also made me realize I was looking at some serious charges.

We arrived at the jail in Bogota and I was booked straight in and placed in a cell within 30 minutes of my arrival. I was allowed to have all of my belongings, including my 3 suitcases in the cell with me. The cells were like caged cubicles. A 4 ft cement wall separated the cells. On top of the cement block walls were bars that went straight up to the ceiling. Standing up in your cell, you could see through the bars others standing up in their cells. The frames of two bunk beds were in each cell but everyone had a cell to themselves. No toilet or sink, just a cell with two beds. If you needed to use the toilet, you had to ask permission and they would let you out to use the toilet. The mattress was a yoga mat. No sheets, no blanket, no pillow, nothing. if you wanted sheets or a blanket you had to have someone from outside bring it. They asked if I knew anyone in Bogota who would bring me a blanket. *"It gets very cold at night and you're going to need a blanket."* I didn't know anyone. I'd never even been to Bogota. They allowed me to use the phone to call someone I knew in Santa Marta to see if they knew someone in Bogota that would bring me a blanket. I called Eduardo. Thankfully, he had a friend who owned a restaurant there and told me he would call. Eduardo's friend showed up just a few hours later with a pillow, sheets, a blanket and a plate of food from his restaurant. I was too sick to eat and gave the food away.

Early every morning, they let us out one by one to take a shower. It was very cold there in the mornings. No one wanted to get out of bed and get naked first thing in the morning in the freezing cold. What made it worse, there was no hot water. The water was ice cold. It would take your breath away. I remember stripping out of the many layers of clothes I slept in to keep warm. Trembling in the cold, my body was full of goosebumps before getting under the shower of ice cold water. Everyone watched to see who would get up to shower and who would stay in bed. It was like a test of your manhood. Were you tough enough to handle a little cold water? If anyone did not take a shower, they were made fun of the rest of the day by every inmate including the guards. They would be called weak or soft. Too delicate to handle cold water. No way was I going to be labeled soft. I was a high profile inmate whose every move was monitored and talked about by everyone there. I wasn't going to miss a shower. I was the first one in that cold ass water every morning. Guys would ask me where I was from, assuming I must be from somewhere cold and used to bathing in the cold water. No, I'm from South Texas. Close to the Gulf of Mexico where it is warm most of the time.

This jail was a police station jail. The police faction that ran this station was called the f2. It was a special arm of the Colombian police. People arrested off the streets went there as they awaited to see a judge and most everyone would go to prison after seeing the judge. The whole process was very quick. It was very common for someone who got arrested off the street to be sentenced and in prison in less than a month's time. While there, they brought in five guys who had been busted for making cocaine out in the mountains. It was late at night and I was sleeping when they brought them in. Their clothes smelled of a very strong chemical like base cocaine. The whole place reeked of the smell of cocaine for days after they came in. One of the guys who had been busted was placed in the cell right next to mine. After he was there a couple of days, we started talking. He had been to prison before and knew he was going back. He told me all about the prison system. There were two main prisons that most everyone would go to from that jail. La picota or La Modelo. There was an ongoing debate over which one was worse. Neither one sounded like a very good place. Within a week of being arrested, he had already seen a judge and had been sentenced. He was now waiting to go to prison. His wife came and brought him several boxes of things he would take with him to prison. Clothes, hygiene items, books, and cash. He had a shoebox full of precious stones. They were all wrapped in wax paper inside the shoebox like a filing cabinet. Even

111

though we were in different cells, the bars were the only thing that separated us.

He would hand me one wax paper at a time to check out the different precious stones he had. I couldn't believe he was taking all of this with him to prison. He explained to me the more money you have in prison, the better off you are. He had been trying to talk me out of one of my suitcases. He gave me two very large Esmeralda's and a handful of uncut emeralds for one of my suitcases. The next week he was on a bus to prison. All the other guys arrested with him were gone shortly after. I thought for sure the Federal Marshals would be there to pick me up any time. I had no idea they were going to send me to a Colombian prison. When they told me to pack my stuff because I was going to prison, I thought they were joking. I had never seen a judge nor was I sentenced. I wasn't even charged with any crime in Colombia. The buses that took you to prison ran once a week on the same day but this was not one of those days. The lieutenant who ran the jail told me I was going to La Picota. I grabbed my suitcases and followed him outside. They never handcuffed me. Outside was a caravan of police officers waiting to transport me. I rode in the middle car with three other police officers. In front of us was a Land Cruiser full of police and in back of us another Land Cruiser full of police. They all wore bulletproof vests and carried automatic weapons. They were a different group of special forces Commandos but acted the same as the group who brought me there.

When we pulled up to the prison, I was apprehensive to say the least. I had no idea what to expect. I carried my bags as they escorted me into the prison. Once inside the main gate of the prison I was met by a large group of high-ranking government and prison officials. The warden, the director of all prisons for Colombia, the captain, some people from the American embassy and several other ranking prison guards. The Commandos who dropped me off spoke briefly with the group they handed me over to and then left. The warden was extremely nice as he welcomed me to his prison. He told me not to worry and they would put me in a safe spot. I was the only American prisoner there. We walked down the main hall to where I assumed my new cell block would be. It seemed like the entire prison population was up on the bars watching us as we walked down the main hall. Everyone was yelling at me, trying to get my attention. They weren't being mean or disrespectful, they were just trying to get my attention. I was being escorted down the hall by quite a large entourage. Everyone wanted to see what was going on. Word got around that they were bringing in an American Narcotraficante. It was like I was a celebrity or something.

We walked all the way to the end of the hall to what seemed like a remote part of the prison. We went up the stairs to a second floor cell block. I waited outside with the rest of the entourage while the warden went inside. The door remained open so I could see him inside. It did not look like a prison cell block at all, instead It was very nice. I could see a large polished cherry wood conference table with very nice leather back chairs. A matching china cabinet sat near the conference table full of very expensive looking coffee cups and dishes. Everyone inside was dressed very nicely. I could see the warden talking to one man who was dressed in jeans, an oxford dress shirt and wearing ostrich-skin cowboy boots. His body language showed that he was very upset with the warden. From my point of view, it looked like he was the one in charge, not the warden. It looked like he was scolding the warden. Whatever he was saying, the warden was listening with a bowed head. I had no idea what was going on. The whole scene did not make sense to me at all.

The warden came out and spoke to the group who was waiting with me. I could only pick up a few words. He said we have a problem; they don't want him in there. The warden spoke with the group for a few minutes then turned to me and said "don't worry." Then they opened the door to the cell block directly across from the one he had just gone into. It was completely empty. They told me this is where I will be staying temporarily and to pick any cell I wanted. The warden said someone would come by to explain everything. Then they shut the door and locked it behind me and all of them left.

The cell block was a long straight hallway with 66 cells on one side. The doors were metal with a small, barred opening around eye level. The cells were just a concrete box. No bed, light, sink or anything. literally a concrete box. I walked around, and checked out every cell looking for the best one. They were all the same. The different colored paint was peeling off the walls. Drawings and scribbled words were on all the walls that had paint. It was like being in a dungeon, a very old, filthy dungeon. The toilets consisted of four holes in the cement floor located at the front where I had just entered. An old rusty pipe stuck out the side of the wall near the toilet area for water. I later found out that the water only comes on twice a day. After a couple of hours, the guards returned and opened the unit door. They told me they were letting someone in to explain things to me and answer any questions I had.

The guy they let in had blond hair, blue eyes and looked more American than I did. I assumed he spoke English so I addressed him in English. I was surprised to find out that he did not speak English. He was a prisoner from another unit in the prison. He was a member of FARC. The Revolutionary Armed Forces of Colombia. They were a paramilitary guerrilla group that had carried out most of the large terrorist attacks in Colombia. They were all housed in the same unit in the prison. He explained to me the unit next door that they were trying to put me in was for the "extraditables" or "duros". All of the guys in that unit were big-time narcotraficantes who were awaiting extradition to different countries, mostly to the United States.

When Pablo Escobar recently turned himself in, they changed the law in the Colombian Constitution. Part of the deal was Colombia could no longer extradite a Colombian national. Now all of those guys were in limbo. They could no longer be extradited but Colombia didn't want to just let them out either. They did not want to let me in there until I signed a waiver stating that I had never met or done business with any of those guys before. Apparently, you could seek a sentence reduction by lying and saying you heard or discussed doing cocaine transactions with these guys. He explained that all the guys over there were millionaires totaling around 25. They used their own money to remodel their entire cell block. All the empty cells were being used as storage. He told me not to worry they would clean out a cell for me. It might take a couple of weeks because they had to meet with the lawyer first and instruct him to draw up the paper for me to sign.

After we talked a while, he left and said he would find me a cot to sleep on. He returned a little while later with a fold-up military cot. He also gave me some sleeping pills. He told me before I went to sleep to make sure that I put newspaper in all the cracks of the door because the mosquitoes got really bad. The guards came by at 9:00 p.m. to shut my cell door. They didn't use a key to lock, they used nuts and bolts. I took the sleeping pills and was out like a light. I forgot to put the newspaper like he told me and woke up during the night with mosquito bites all over. The next day I got a visit from someone from the United States Embassy. He brought me a stack of magazines and a little bag with basic hygiene items. The visit was very formal, and the guy was not friendly at all. I was happy to see him at first but after a few minutes, it became evident that he viewed me with complete contempt. When he got to the front of my cell where I was standing, he very rudely just dropped the magazines on the floor. It made a very loud "Plop" sound that echoed throughout the cell block. He asked to see my passport and when I handed it to him, he just grabbed it and stuck it in his pocket. He said "I'm confiscating this."

After he left, I started thumbing through the magazines. National Geographic, People, Rolling Stone and Men's Health magazines. National Geographic was my favorite by far. One of them had a fold-out poster of a waterfall. It was very beautiful and I had never seen it before. It was Victoria Falls in Africa. I took the picture out and hung it on my cell wall. Looking at that picture gave me a brief escape from the dungeon I was living in. I would lie on the Army cot and imagine what it must be like to be standing in a place so beautiful. Vicariously I would go there daily in my mind. After a couple of weeks they were ready to move me to the other side. Someone brought me the paper to sign and the next day I moved over with the bigshots.

I was given a cell about halfway down the run. No running water or toilet or sink inside. It did have an electrical socket, a light bulb in the ceiling and a light switch by the door. I set up the cot and unpacked a few of my things. I brought the waterfall picture with me and hung it on the wall. While unpacking and settling in, a few guys came by to introduce themselves. Everyone was very nice. After I got settled in, one of the guys gave me a tour of the place and let me know the do's and don'ts. The big cherry wood conference table with the leather back chairs near the front was off-limits. It belonged to Jairo Correa. He was the guy wearing the ostrich skin boots I saw talking with the warden. He was the highest ranking member of the Medellin cartel in the unit and probably the richest guy there. He was also the one mainly responsible for remodeling the cell block. Everyone pitched in but Jairo Correa contributed the most.

All the cells that weren't being used to live in were being used as storage pantries for food. There were huge burlap sacks full of every kind of vegetable of which you could think of. There were meat freezers and refrigerators inside them as well. There was a kitchen area used for cooking with a six-burner stove and oven. Next to that was a sink and dish area. This was the only unit in the prison allowed to have knives. They had Plates, pots and pans, blenders, food processors, juicers, you name it. All the cutlery you could possibly need to cook. There were tables and chairs in this area that everyone used to sit and eat. The guy showing me around told me I could help myself anytime I wanted. He showed me a pantry full of food that I could help myself whenever I was hungry. The toilet and shower area was all the way in the back. They had three toilets situated in private stalls behind closed doors. Three showers that were also private and a sink area with a row of 4 sinks with a large mirror. They even had a steam room with eucalyptus leaves. Everything was very clean and looked brand-new. Everyone's cell was made as luxurious as possible. They all had nice beds, mattresses, custom-made shelves, TVs, sound systems, and some had video game systems. All the cells were the same size 9x11, but you were allowed to make it as nice as you could afford to. These guys were millionaires so their cells were very nice. I was the only one there who was not a millionaire. My cell consisted of an Army cot, two suitcases, and a National Geographic picture on the wall.

Everyone kept an empty milk jug in their cell in case you had to pee during the night. The guards came into our cell block only to lock the doors at night and then to unlock them in the morning. 9pm was lockdown. They reopened at 5 in the morning. Visitation was Saturday and Sundays 9am until 3pm Saturday and was male-only. Sunday was female and children. All visitors were allowed in the cell block and the guards were not present in the cell block during visitation. They only came back at 3 p.m. to escort the visitors out when visitation was over. On Saturdays, Jairo would sit at his big conference table visiting with his lawyers and other cartel

117

members discussing business. On Sundays when their wives would come, everyone would be in their cells with their wives. They would come out and eat together then go back inside their cells. Needless to say, everyone looked forward to Sundays. I remained in that cell block for about 4 months. I got to know everyone there and hear their stories. Jairo was friends with a guy from Santa Marta named Rafael "El Mono" Abello. Everyone in Santa Marta knew who "El Mono" was. He was arrested and extradited to the United States before I came to Santa Marta. I heard all about him and met his brother but not him. His brother actually lived a few houses down from where I was staying in Rodadero and was the one to whom I gave my dog. Everyone talked about "El Mono" in Santa Marta. He was like a folk hero. He owned several apartment complexes that were the nicest ones in Santa Marta. Jairo told me he was best friends with "El Mono." They were together in Bogota doing business when Mono was arrested and extradited to the United States. Jairo talked very highly of him, and I guess because I was living in Santa Marta, he loved to talk to me about "El Mono." Jairo turned out to be a very likable guy. He was full of himself at times but was cool. He helped me out a lot. He got me a bed for my cell. He introduced me to his friends and lawyers who came to visit him on Saturdays. He asked his lawyer to advise me on my situation with extradition. He even arranged for a female to come visit me on Sundays. Everyone referred to her as my "wife" even though they knew she was hired to visit me. Jairo was educated and cultured. Not your stereotypical narcotraficante. His wife was a young pretty girl named Claudia. They had two kids together while Jairo was locked up.

While I was there, they brought in a guy named Ivan Urdinola. He was a big-time billionaire narcotraficante. It was all over the news when he had been arrested. They put him in the empty unit on the other side where I originally was. Jairo seemed very excited and anxious to talk with him. They

118

would let him in our unit once a day to shower, but then he had to go right back. Jairo bent over backward to take care of him while he was next door. The warden would allow Jairo to go next door to talk with the guy a few times while he was there. He was only there for about a week then they transferred him to La Modelo. The guy was on the news every night for about a week or two straight. They were calling him the biggest narcotraficante to be arrested since Pablo Escobar. He was not part of the Medellin cartel. Most of those guys were either dead or already in the prison Pablo built. He was part of a cartel called Norte del Valle Cartel. They called him "El Rey de la Amapola, " meaning the king of heroin. Jairo treated him with a lot of respect.

Several months passed, and I heard nothing from anyone concerning my extradition back to the United States. Jairo's attorney informed me that the extradition process could take years. He recommended that I waive extradition. He told me once I get back to the United States, it was up to the judge to give me credit for the time I was doing here in Colombia. He said because I ran, the judge would probably not give me credit for the time I was doing there. He agreed to contact the Colombian prosecutor on my behalf to let them know that I was interested in waiving extradition. The prosecutor came to see me days after being contacted by Jairo's lawyer. He told me I could waive extradition and the Colombian government would expel me. They were expelling mc for entering the country illegally. He brought papers for me to sign stating that I was waving extradition. I was ready to get back to the United States and start my sentence whatever it might be. The sooner my time started in the States the sooner I got out. I signed the papers and the prosecutor left. He told me the United States was anxious to get me back in their custody so the process should not take long. Within two weeks of signing that paper, they told me to pack my things I was leaving.

Custody of the United States

I packed up my suitcases and said my goodbyes. The warden and a cadre of prison guards escorted me to the front gate. The Commandos were there to transport me. Again, I was never handcuffed. First, they drove me to the offices of Interpol, where I was fingerprinted and had my picture taken. From there, I was transported to El Dorado International Airport. I was escorted through the middle of a very busy airport with a dozen armed Commandos surrounding me. It was quite a scene. They took me to a police headquarters that was located inside the airport. As soon as we got in there, I asked to use the toilet. The Commandos were assembled again, and they all escorted me to a public restroom inside the main airport. They entered the restroom ahead of me and cleared it out of all people before I went in. The way they treated me you would have thought I was some big time narcotraficante. Everyone in the airport was looking at us and I could only imagine what they thought. In a weird way, I relished all the attention I was getting. All this for five kilos of cocaine. They took me back to the police headquarters in the airport, where I sat and waited. A couple of hours passed and I was getting hungry. I had not eaten all day. I asked the police officer in charge if I could get something to eat. The Commandos who had escorted me earlier had already left. The guy in charge agreed to let me eat something.

He and I walked through the busy Airport to a Burger King that was located inside. I hadn't had Burger King in two years and no telling how long it would be before I was able to have it again. We waited in line, like any other person in the airport. I was not handcuffed, and I was carrying both of my suitcases. While we were waiting for my order the call came over his radio that my plane was waiting for me. Two other officers came to meet us at the Burger King and told us to hurry. Forget the hamburger they are waiting for you. The guy in charge was nice enough to let me wait for the hamburger and as soon as they handed me the bag and a drink, off we went. No time to eat the hamburger. They told me I could eat it on the plane. All this time I thought I was getting on a commercial airline. We walked towards the boarding gates and through a door leading to the runway.

We kept walking and walking further out on the runway until I could see a small plane off by itself. I then realized it was waiting for me. A group of people stood outside the plane. It was a mixture of people from the United States Embassy, U.S. Marshals, Colombian military, and Colombian dignitaries. I was approached by one of the marshals who asked for my name, date of birth, place of birth, mother and father's name, social security number and then I asked to see my tattoos. Once he was certain I was the guy they came to get, he told me to turn around so he could handcuff me. I refused to be handcuffed and started arguing with him. Somewhere I had heard that it was illegal to be handcuffed on an airplane, especially if flying over water. I had never been handcuffed the whole time I was in custody in Colombia.

The Marshal got very serious with me and showed the pistol he was carrying on his side. He told me they were going to handcuff me, but he would allow me to be handcuffed in the front so I could eat my hamburger. He told me he would shoot me if I gave them any trouble on the plane. He was very serious, and I believed him. I boarded the plane handcuffed and escorted by two Federal Marshals. Once we leveled off in the air, they allowed me to eat my hamburger, still handcuffed, of course. We flew from Bogota to Guantanamo

Bay Cuba. While the plane was being refueled, one of the Marshals escorted me inside to use the toilet and wait for the refueling. We were only there a little over an hour. However after 9/11, and Guantanamo became famous for housing terrorists, I would bring up the fact in conversation with guys in prison that I also was in custody at GITMO. From there we flew to Homestead Air Force Base in Florida. The plane taxied very close to where the Marshals' car was parked. We got off the plane and went straight into the car. We drove directly to the Miami Dade Courthouse where I was placed in a Courtroom holding cell. From there they took me to a Federal Detention Center in Miami. The same place where they were holding Manuel Noriega. I was secluded from the general population and placed in a special housing unit. I was there about a month then was sent to Montgomery County Jail in Texas, where I would await sentencing. I had already pleaded guilty to the felon in possession of a firearm and possession with intent to distribute cocaine. While I was on the run the state of Texas decided to charge me with several bogus armed robberies. I was actually in Maracaibo, Venezuela when these robberies occurred. They knew it wasn't me but charged me anyway. The lawyer my mother paid with the money brought to her by the Colombians still represented me in my federal case. I wanted to withdraw my plea of guilty, but they would not allow it.

The only thing in question was how much time they were going to give me. The new federal sentencing guidelines that just came out in 1987 would determine under which guideline I would fall under and thus what sentence I got. I was interviewed by the federal probation officer, who determined my guidelines based on my prior criminal history and I answered all of her questions truthfully. I found it a little strange at the time that she asked me so many questions about the first time the DEA busted me with flour. I explained truthfully that I never intended, nor did I have the capability to produce 5 kilos of cocaine at that time. I had never even seen a kilo of cocaine back then. My sole intention was to rip off the prospective buyer. The feds never even charged me with that incident. It was turned over to the state, and they charged me with manufacturing and delivery of a simulated controlled substance. (Flour) I was never charged with the pistol I was carrying either until after I was released from State Prison and busted again by the DEA with real cocaine. At the end of the interview, I asked her what sentencing guidelines I was looking at? She informed me with a big smile on her face, "360 months to life, and that's no parole." She seemed pleased to tell me that! I could not believe it. How could this be happening? Was this how the law worked with the feds? How could it go from if I cooperated that I would only get a couple of years in a minimum security prison to 30 years with no parole? My crime never changed. What changed was the Federal government's attitude toward me because I ran. They had let me out of jail to cooperate but instead I fled the country. Granted I obstructed Justice by not showing up for sentencing but 30 years? I know I broke the law and expected to be punished but the punishment did not fit the crime.

Child molesters, rapists, murderers and all sorts of evil doers were not punished so severely. I was sure that this would not stand. Somehow these guidelines were not right. They couldn't be right. I engaged in an illegal transaction involving less than 5 kg of cocaine. I didn't understand how she arrived at those guidelines but I was confident that my lawyer would argue effectively on my behalf. I was totally ignorant of the law. I tried reading my pre-sentence investigation report and making sense of it but it was like reading another language. I lazily put all my trust in my lawyer to argue my case effectively, but his argument did not prove to be effective at all. When it came time for my sentencing in front of a packed courtroom, the judge sentenced me to 360 months. That's 30 years without parole. I was shocked and in total denial. I could not accept the fact that this was a real sentence. It made no sense at all. My lawyer told me later not to worry, that I had a good chance of getting it reduced on appeal. I was confident that this sentence would not stand. My mind would not accept that I would have to do the next 30 years in prison. I knew intuitively that somehow this sentence was not legal. If you murdered someone in the state of Texas and got a life sentence, you came up for parole in seven years. I watched a guy kill another guy on the streets and only got probation. It was ruled self-defense, but he still killed a guy. I didn't kill anyone. There was no victim in my crime. After sentencing, I was transported back to the Montgomery County Jail where I would wait to go to prison. When the guys in my tank in the county jail asked me how much time I got, I told them 30 years but I'm going to beat it on appeals. I talked with my sister on the phone from the county jail who was crying and very upset. She was in the courtroom when I was sentenced. She seemed more devastated than I was. I consoled her telling her that I would beat it on appeals.

A couple of months after I was sentenced, the Federal Marshals transported me to the El Reno Oklahoma transfer unit. Before getting on the bus, we were stripped naked, searched thoroughly then issued different clothes to wear. I was handcuffed in the front with a belly chain around my waist and a black box that fit over the handcuffs. The black box was used to restrict hand movement even further and to prevent from picking the lock of the handcuffs. The belly chain went through the black box and was secured with a padlock. I had leg irons around my ankles. The bus took us to the airport in Houston where the Federal Marshals had their Air transport or "Con Air" as it was called. The bus pulled right up on the runway next to the airplanes. I was the first one they called off the bus.

One of the Federal Marshals had me stand separately from the rest of the group. A media crew with cameras recorded the entire event. I was the first placed on the plane before any of the others were even allowed off the bus, then the rest followed. The media crew also got on the plane and recorded us throughout the flight to Oklahoma City. I later found out the media crew was there to document my capture. I remained at the El Reno transfer unit for about 3 weeks. This is where I was issued my federal inmate number 51134-079. This would be the number by which I would be identified throughout my federal incarceration. I was designated to the United States Penitentiary in Leavenworth, Kansas. When it was time to leave El Reno to be transported to Leavenworth, again, I was taken by bus to the airport. Just like before I was the first one called off the bus. This time, the Federal Marshals separated me from the group, took a Sharpie, and marked a big "S" on my t-shirt. Most of the guys getting off the bus were being transported on the large Federal Marshals 727. Some of the guys had buses waiting for them while others had vans. Oklahoma City, being situated in the center of the United States, was the Federal Marshals' main hub for transporting federal inmates. I was being transported on a small Learjet which only held eight people with four being Federal Marshals. Only one other prisoner was on the plane when I boarded. He was a big-tattooed Japanese Yakuza guy, who was being taken to Marion, Illinois. From Oklahoma City, we flew to Marion to drop him off and then pick up another guy who would be dropped off in Terre Haute, Indiana before finally only flying me to Leavenworth, Kansas. I was transported from the airport in a van with three Marshalls and myself. There was a chase car with two additional Marshals escorting the van. When we pulled up to the prison I was escorted in through the front door by two of the Marshals.

Leavenworth

Pulling up to any prison for the first time is very intimidating. Leavenworth was no exception. Looking at its massive walls and the huge 5-tier cell blocks from outside going in, I had a fresh 30 year sentence and felt doomed. Once inside the prison, the Federal Marshals removed the handcuffs, belly chain and leg irons. They told me good luck, and then left. From there, I followed the lieutenant down to R&D to get processed. I was fingerprinted, had my picture taken, and then asked a series of questions. Did I have any problems with anybody that was in the prison? Have I ever testified on anyone? Had I ever cooperated with the police? Was I affiliated with any gangs? I answered no to all the above. They issued me my prison uniform and gave me sheets, a pillowcase, and a blanket. From there I was escorted to my new housing unit. B upper. The guard escorting me just opened up the door to the unit and told me to see the unit officer, in the office around the corner. Then he locked the door and left. The unit consisted of three tiers of cells that ran about 150 yards down the unit on two sides. The solid steel doors to each cell were not locked at this time so everyone was free to roam about the unit. There was a Coke machine, snack machine and microwave oven in front next to the unit office. Nothing like Texas state prison at all. As I was standing there waiting to speak with the unit officer holding my blanket and sheets, it was evident that I was new to the prison. Some guys came over to ask me where I was from, where I was coming from, how much time I had and what my charge was. Everyone asked the same four questions when meeting some unknown new guy in federal prison. Even though I had been in custody for almost a year, I was still

126

looked at as just coming off the street because this was my first prison in the federal system.

After seeing the unit officer, I was assigned to a cell on the second tier. I walked over to my new assigned cell and looked in. Nobody was in the cell then, but all of their personal belongings were. I felt like an intruder. I just placed my sheets and blanket on the top bunk, walked out of the cell, and left the door open. Some other guys came by and asked me the same four questions. They told me the guy whose cell I was moving into was at work and would be back in a few hours. They said to go ahead and make my bed and settle in. After a while the unit started filling up with guys getting off work. Most of them worked out in Unicor. Unicor is the name of the federal prison industries. Each federal prison has a Unicor that manufacturers different products for the government. Unlike Texas state prison, the feds paid you for your work. Unicor was the highest paying job you could get in the federal system. Everybody had to work but there was a waiting list to get into Unicor and you had to have clear conduct to work there. My new cell partner was a bank robber from California who went by the name of "mule." This was his second trip back to the feds for robbing a bank. He had a 12-year sentence and had been down for 6 years. He told me all about Leavenworth and all about the federal system. He was an old convict who had seen it all. While we were still talking the guards started yelling count time so everyone went to their cells and got locked in.

Mule informed me everyday at 4pm in every federal prison in the United States, it's count time. Prisoners must be standing for this count. While we were locked in the cell waiting to be counted, "Mule" started advising me on the best way to do my time. #1 Don't get yourself in debt. This means don't gamble, don't get any drugs on credit and don't borrow anything from anyone. #2 Don't join any gangs and don't associate or hang out with any gang members. #3 Do not mess with any homosexuals. #4 Do not disrespect anyone. This includes talking bad about somebody behind their back. It's almost guaranteed that they will find out and then be obligated to do something to you. #5 Get a job or find a Hustle. Being in prison is bad enough but being broke in prison is the worst. The guards soon interrupted our conversation by yelling, "Two row, stand-up count!" Mule told me to stand while the guards walked by and counted. You had to stand. if not, they'd write you up, probably take you to the hole, and most definitely lose all your privileges. After the guards walked by and we were counted, mule turned to me and said, with a smile on his face, "That was your first stand-up count!" He continued, "You've got many more to look forward to." Still smiling he said, "Just think, the guard who is going to tell you to stand up for count before you get out has not even been born yet!" Then he laughed loudly. I told him I didn't expect to have this 30-year sentence permanently. I planned on beating it on appeal. He laughed again. He said he didn't mean any disrespect, but the reality is everyone thinks they're going to beat their sentence on appeal and hardly anyone does. But good luck, he said sarcastically.

We continued talking while locked in the cell, awaiting the count to clear. Mule was telling me all about Leavenworth. The prison was built in the late 1890s and was one of the 3 original federal penitentiaries. Throughout the years it housed some of the most notorious criminals in United States history. Many "high-profile" inmates were currently occupying the cells around us. Italian mafia crime bosses, Colombian drug lords, Mexican cartels, Chinese Triads, Irish mafia, kidnappers, Airplane hijackers, you name it. High-profile guys whose crimes had made worldwide headlines. Books were written and movies were made about some of these guys. The fact that I was on America's Most Wanted, the Federal Marshals 15 most wanted list, captured in and extradited from Colombia wasn't going to impress anyone here. At that time, Leavenworth was full of "High-profile" guys. Big shots on the streets but not anyone special in Leavenworth. They were just another number like everyone else. No one treated them with any awe or extra respect because of what they did or who they were on the streets. Nobody in Leavenworth was just your average guy who broke the law. Everyone here did something extreme or they wouldn't be here.

Mule explained to me the seating arrangements in the chow hall. The blacks occupied one side of the chow hall and the whites the other side. The Mexicans and other races sat in the middle. The tables against the white section wall were reserved for the Aryan Brotherhood. Typically in the white section, guys from Texas sat together in their area of tables. California white guys had their tables, as did New York and Boston guys. Whatever state you were from is who you were expected to hang out with. These were your "homeboys." When mule found out I was from Texas he said, "you have a lot of homeboys here," and he would introduce me. Groups of guys who hung out together were referred to as "cars." If you were, for instance, an Asian guy from Montana and hung out with the white guys from Texas you would be considered "Riding in the Texas car." Almost never would you see a black guy riding in a white car or vice versa. The blacks had their cars, and the Mexicans had theirs. Everything was very racially divided. Within each racial group there were subgroups. The blacks from the West Coast did not get along with the blacks from the East Coast. The Washington DC blacks didn't get along with anybody. Texas Mexicans did not get along with California Mexicans. Southern California Mexicans did not get along with Northern California Mexicans. Native Americans had their subgroups according to their tribes. Biker gangs who were at war with each other on the streets had a truce in prison. Hell's Angels, Outlaws, Bandidos, Mongols, and El Forastero's all ate at the same table. The prison gangs had their own cars. The most notorious and dangerous gang in Leavenworth and in the entire federal system is the Aryan Brotherhood. Each and every member of the "AB" are extremely dangerous killers. Out of all the violent killers in prison, and there were many, these guys were typically the baddest of the bad. There were several other gangs in Leavenworth and it was wise to know who belonged to which gang so you could stay out of their way.

I was introduced to a few guys from Texas in our unit. It was customary for your "homeboys" to hook you up with hygiene items when you first arrived at a prison. Shower shoes, soap, toothpaste and shampoo. The hygiene packet the feds gave you when you first came in was not so good. When our unit was opened for chow I went with the guys from Texas to go eat. The seating in the chow hall was just how mule explained it. Everything was racially-divided. I remember being amazed at how good the food was while the guys at my table were complaining how bad it was. You would never see food like this in a Texas prison. They had a self-serve salad bar as well as an ice cream machine that you could serve yourself. After we ate, they showed me around the prison. The movements are every hour on the hour for 10 minutes. While the units were open for the evening meal it was open movement until the evening meal was finished. During open movement, you were allowed to walk to the outside yard, the recreation center or if It was your day to go to the commissary, you could go there to buy things you needed out of the prison store. You could never go to a housing unit that you were not assigned to. Once the move is over you are locked in the area that you are in for an hour until the next move.

I was shown around the prison and introduced to a few other guys. Because I had just come from Colombia, I was introduced to a Colombian who worked in the prison factory with one of the guys from Texas. The Colombian guy was from Medellin and was the nephew of Griselda Blanco. (Black Widow) We spoke briefly and when he found out I was living in Santa Marta, Colombia he told me there was another Colombian guy here from Santa Marta. He will introduce me tomorrow in the chow hall. The next day when I came into the chow hall the guy from Medellin called me over to the table where all the Colombians were sitting together. The guy he introduced me to from Santa Marta was Jose Rafael Abello, "El Mono." This was the guy I heard so much about while living in Colombia. "El Mono" was one of the biggest Colombian drug dealers ever to be extradited to the United States. Second only to Carlos Lehder. I felt like I was being introduced to a celebrity. I told him I had just come from "La Picota" in Bogota, where his friend Jairo was. I was locked up in the same unit with the "extraditables." He was amazed to hear that I was extradited from Colombia and sentenced to 30 years for only 5 kilos of cocaine. He invited me to sit down at their table so we could talk more. This may sound like no big deal to most people unfamiliar with "prison politics." However, in prison, especially in Leavenworth at that time, sitting at someone's table in the chow hall indicated to the rest of the prison population it was the "car" you were riding in. Who you sat and ate with was of great significance.

I had not yet gone through the line to get my food so I sat down and spoke with him briefly. The other Colombians at the table were urging me to go get my food, then come back and sit with them. I thanked them for the invitation and said I was honored that they had invited me to eat with them but I was supposed to meet some guys from Texas. Some of their faces instantly changed as did the mood of the table. Obviously, they felt disrespected because I did not accept their invitation to eat with them. After a couple of minutes talking with "El Mono," one of the Colombians at the table said, "Hey, aren't your friends waiting for you?" Mono Immediately fired back at the guy for interrupting our conversation and being disrespectful. The guy replied in

Spanish that other Colombians were waiting to sit down and I was taking up a seat. Heated words were exchanged between the guy and Mono. Other Colombians at the table were joining in the debate, some taking Mono's side and others taking the side of the guy who wanted me to leave. As I stood up to leave, I smiled and told them all it was very nice to meet them. I told Mono I would see him around and we would talk later.

Tensions were very high at the table as I left. I got in line to get my food and then went over and sat in the white section at a table with some guys from Texas. My conversation with Mono at the Colombian table did not go unnoticed. One of the guys at the table I was now sitting casually asked who I was talking to at the Colombian table. He was curious whether or not it was a co-defendant of mine or someone I may have known in another prison or on the streets. I told them I had been living in Colombia for two years on the run and was arrested there and placed in a Colombian prison. The guy I was talking to was from the same town I was living in Colombia. Everyone on the Atlantic coast of Colombia knew who he was. Practically everyone in Colombia knew who he was. He was probably the biggest cocaine dealer to be extradited out of Colombia. Definitely the biggest cocaine dealer in this prison. Nobody knew or cared who "El Mono" was. He was very low-key in prison. That was a good thing for Mono. If the wrong guys knew who he was, they would extort him for money. He would be forced to pay "protection" to stay on the yard.

The advice I got from the guys at the table was I better be careful. Some of the guys who sat in the white section may try and cause you problems if they see you sitting with the Colombians. They said I could sit with whoever I wanted but trying to switch back and forth would be a problem. The guys at my table weren't the only ones who said something to me about this. For several days after I met with Mono in the chow hall various white guys whom I just met would come up to me and say "I heard you were sitting with the Colombians in the chow hall, be careful." It was a little unsettling to me, to say the least. I was just starting a 30-year sentence and didn't want to get off on the wrong foot. Word gets around quickly in prison. Everyone is watching you especially if you are new. Nothing you do or say goes unnoticed. Everyone talks about everyone else. I explained to mule, my celly, what had happened. He told me not to worry about it. Those guys who were talking were just idiots. They like to talk like a bunch of old women. They weren't anyone to worry about. They're just "wannabes." Mule told me I didn't do anything wrong. Some of the white guys were always looking for drama and always looking to cause someone else trouble. He said I should be careful about my own "homeboys." Be careful about everyone for that matter. Be respectful but don't get too close to anyone. Choose wisely who you hang out with.

Mule's advice was always solid. Leavenworth was full of idiots. Not everyone there was an idiot though. There were some very intelligent people there too. That was one of the things that amazed me about Leavenworth. Some of the guys I met there were the smartest guys I've ever encountered. Really, really smart guys. Some super-intelligent guys who had whacked-out beliefs, and some were emotionally unstable. All of them had done some dastardly deed to end up in Leavenworth. Before I knew who was who, I would find myself talking to various guys who initiated conversations with me, not wanting to be rude or disrespectful I would listen to what they had to say. Some guys wanted to tell me their whole life story. Most just wanted to brag about how notorious they were on the streets. Talk talk talk talk talk about some really crazy stuff. After the conversation, someone would come up to me and say they saw me talking to that guy, be careful, that guy's crazy. Then someone else would tell me to be careful talking to the guy who just told me to be careful talking to the other guy. After a while I found out who the guys were to avoid.

It took a while, but I started to settle into a "routine" in Leavenworth. I found a workout partner and started lifting weights every day. I got a job out in the wood shop doing nothing. Everybody had to have a job, and that's where they assigned me. Too many people were working out there, so most of us just hung out, played cards, and drank coffee all day for $26 bucks a month. My name was on the waiting list to work in the prison factory. The wait was about one year. I had been in Leavenworth about four months, just settling into a routine, when I was called to my case manager's office. He informed me that I was going back to Texas to face charges for three armed robberies. I couldn't believe it. I knew I had been charged for these robberies, but everyone knew I did not do them. I assumed they would drop the charges after it was stipulated in federal court that I was in South America during those robberies. These were completely bogus charges. This was how the feds were able to justify putting me on the Most Wanted list. They were mad because I ran. These were completely false charges placed on me by dishonest, vindictive public servants. The feds had just given me a 30-year, non-parolable sentence for possession of cocaine. These types of sentences were supposed to be reserved for the most heinous crimes. Apparently my sentence was not enough to satisfy their thirst for revenge. The state of Texas wanted a piece of me too. About a week later, I was transported back to Texas. I was placed in the overcrowded Harris County Jail In downtown Houston to face serious charges in which I was completely innocent.

I had been in Harris County Jail four times before. The first time I was just 17, and still in high school. Now, I was 27 and back for the 5th time. I knew what to expect, getting processed into the jail can take anywhere from 24 to 72 hours before you are assigned to a "tank." Most tanks consisted of 24 bunks, some had 12. Almost all of them had more people than bunks. If no bunks were available, you had to find a spot on the floor. The four previous times I've been to this jail, it was so overcrowded that they were putting more than 60 people in a 24-man tank. You could be in there for months sleeping on the floor. This time was different. Three new jails had recently been built in Harris County as well as multiple prisons all over Texas to help relieve overcrowding. I was assigned to a 24-man tank and given the only empty bunk. It was a bottom bunk, at that. The tank I went into was considered a "convict" tank. Everyone assigned to this tank had been to prison before. Some of the guys had new charges and others were there for parole violations. Just about everybody was going back to prison. Nobody in there was getting out on bond. My first court date was soon after I arrived at the jail.

The court appointed me an attorney as I could not afford my own. He came and introduced himself to me as I was waiting in the court hold over cell. I briefly explained to him the facts surrounding my case. I had nothing to do with the robberies, and I was out of the country at the time they happened. He seemed very confident and very eager to help. He gave me the impression that he was ready to fight and take it to trial if necessary. A couple of weeks later, he came to visit me in the jail where we spoke more in-depth about my case. He was very interested in my federal cocaine case. He talked a good talk so I let him do my federal appeals as a court-appointed attorney. Each time I went to court, which was about once a month, my lawyer would tell me some BS excuse as to why they were not dismissing my case. I would sign a reset paper waiving my right to a speedy trial. After going back and forth to court for 9 months and nothing had changed, I was angry and tired of living in the Harris County Jail. I refused to sign the reset paper and told the attorney we would take it to trial. Finally he went and spoke with the prosecutor who noticed my case for the first time. After realizing that I was already doing a 30-year, non-parole sentence with the feds, the prosecutor dismissed all the robbery charges against me. Nine long months in that stinking Harris County Jail for nothing. Shortly after the charges were dismissed, I was transported back to Leavenworth by two Harris County deputies wearing plain clothes. They used a regular comercial airline to transport me. They also had me wearing plain clothes and had me handcuffed in the front with a jacket covering the handcuffs so as not to draw too much attention to the fact that I was a prisoner being transported. The deputies brought me all the way in the front door of Leavenworth. They took off the handcuffs and handed the lieutenant my paperwork in the middle of the center hall. I was processed back to my cell block in B upper in less than an hour from arriving at the prison.

Back "home" in Leavenworth now, I was given the update on what had happened on the yard while I was gone. The guy who lived two cells from me before I left was killed. His name was Renee. He was a gang member from the Texas Syndicate or TS as they are called. I spoke with him a few times because he was from Texas and lived right next door. He was the guy to see if you needed your radio fixed. That was his hustle. I know this because he fixed my radio. Now I am discovering that he was murdered. He was murdered by a former Texas Syndicate gang member who had recently joined the California Mexican Mafia. Sounds pretty crazy, I know, but that's what happened. The former Texas Syndicate member turned California Mexican Mafia was in the hole when he changed gangs. Then he was let out of the hole onto the yard. Members from both gangs met out on the yard. I heard the story from multiple people who were out on the yard when it happened. Everyone who saw it said Renee went out like a warrior. The other Texas Syndicate guys out there with Renee ran away after initially, briefly engaging the California guys in combat. Renee was the only one who did not run away. The California guys swarmed on him like a pack of hyenas and stabbed him to death. The prison was on lockdown for several weeks after the murder. I was glad to have missed all the drama. This incident started a war between the California Mexican Mafia and the Texas Syndicate that eventually spilled over into all federal prisons and onto the streets. It became California Mexicans against Texas Mexicans. Every prison yard throughout the federal system that tried to put California and Texas Mexicans together ended up in a riot. Many guys were transferred during the lockdown. Mostly Mexicans from Texas and California.

Because a bunch of guys got transferred out of Leavenworth, it worked in my favor. It moved my name up on the slow-moving waiting lists I was on. Once you've been in Leavenworth for one year, with clear conduct, you are eligible for a single cell. Even though I had been out to court most of that time, it still counted. Shortly after returning to Leavenworth, I was given a single cell. I also got a job working out in the factory, making a little more money. I stayed mostly to myself while at Leavenworth. I worked out in the factory, lifted weights out on the yard and tried to stay away from any drama. Six or eight months after I returned to Leavenworth and got my single cell, the case manager called me in his office to tell me I was being transferred. My security level had dropped as a result of the Texas robbery charges being dismissed. I was no longer classified as "maximum security" but now at "high security" level. I was being transferred to the FCI in El Reno, Oklahoma.

El Reno

I arrived at FCI El Reno with the hope of escaping. My direct appeals had just been denied and my out date was still 25 years away, which was if I behaved and didn't lose any good time. Most of the older convicts I talked to told me the same thing: escape was a more realistic option to get out of here than winning your appeal for freedom. There were a few guys who I talked to that had been to El Reno and they all said the same thing: yes you could escape from that place. The guys who had been there gave me advice to get a job with the landscaping crew working out on the yard. This would give me access to parts of the yard that no one else had, allowing me to see where the most vulnerable spots were.

El Reno has a really big yard. By "yard," I mean the space outdoors in which you are allowed to traverse. The housing units were very spread out with many blind spots. The recreation yard was huge. The prison factory, where most people work, is a long walk from the housing units. Prisoners are given a lot of space to move around within the razor wire perimeters of FCI El Reno. The prison yard was beautifully landscaped and well-maintained. There was green grass everywhere, including in front of the units that you are not allowed to walk on. Some of the units also had bushes and small trees with mulch and flowers in front. Along the sidewalks were raised flower gardens enclosed in brick. You'll never see beautiful landscaping on the Yard in a higher security USP like Leavenworth where I just came from. It is a very noticeable contrast between the two security levels. You won't see a tree or a flower bush in a USP.

El Reno was opened in 1933 and was designed to house younger prisoners aged 18 to 26. It later opened to all age groups in the late 70s. When I got assigned to that yard in 1994, one of the housing units was still being used as a transfer unit for the Bureau of Prisons. El Reno is located more or less in the center of the United States, so that's why the feds use it as a central transportation hub for federal prisoners. Guys from all over came through there. Some guys were being transferred from one prison to another. Some guys had been bench warranted to court after already being in prison and were either going to or coming from court. Other guys were just coming into the system and hadn't been to their assigned prison yet. That was the case with me the last time I came through here. It was a mixture of many different guys with different security levels.

There was always some kind of drama going on in that transfer unit. The wrong guys would inevitably be put in together, or someone would disrespect another, and somebody's head would get busted or someone would get stabbed. When I came through the transfer unit the first time, I was on my way to Leavenworth with a fresh 30-year sentence. I remember a loudmouth guy claiming to be a "made" Italian mobster who got beat up. He claimed to know Gene Gotti. At that time, Gene Gotti, the brother of John Gotti, was doing a 55-year sentence there in El Reno. For those who do not know, John Gotti was a famous Italian mobster. He was the boss of bosses/shot caller for all the Italian Mafia crime families in the U.S. His name was all over the news back in the 80s and 90s. Everybody knew who John Gotti was. Everyone coming through El Reno knew that Gene Gotti, the brother of John Gotti, was doing time there. Guys like this guy would come through trying to act like a big shot and throw Gene's name around. Where he screwed up was, he sent a message through one of the guys working on the yard to tell Gene he was there. He said Gene knows him from the neighborhood. If Gene really knew the guy, he would send over a big care package with whatever the guy needed. Things like coffee, cigarettes or any items from the main yard commissary, whatever the guy needed. When you are in the transfer unit, you don't have access to those things that guys who are assigned to the main yard have access to. The guys who were assigned to the yard were able to make commissary. If you were in transit, you were just passing through and did not get to make commissary. The transfer unit was on the yard just like all the other housing units but it stayed locked down and segregated from the rest of the inmate population who were assigned to El Reno. If you knew someone who was on the yard, you could send word to them, and if they wanted to they could send you a care package. Just because you know someone doesn't necessarily mean they are going to send you something. Guys in prison don't just give away their commissary because they know somebody who's passing through. All that stuff costs money, and everybody is trying to survive. You must be well-liked and respected to get a care package sent in from someone on the yard. So everyone was nice to this guy, thinking he was friends with Gene Gotti and was about to get a big care package. I'm sure not everyone has heard the phrase "having your covers pulled," but this guy had his covers pulled. That's when someone claims to be someone or something they are not and hides underneath the covers of that lie. The guy that got beat up looked and sounded like he could be the guy he claimed to be but he wasn't. He turned out to be just another loudmouth looking for attention. Word came back from the yard that Gene said for the guy to go fuck himself. He didn't know him and had never heard of him. What happened next was some really funny shit. Almost everyone in the unit started verbally abusing the guy really hard. Those of us who were not hurling insults were laughing our asses off. Finally, the guy had all he could take and got in his feelings. He became butt hurt because his covers had been pulled and some of the things being said were too much for him to take.

He started lashing back verbally until someone beat the shit out of him. The whole thing was very comical. It would not be the last time I witnessed a loud mouth having his covers pulled and subsequently getting his ass beat. It actually happened very often.

Now, as I arrive in El Reno for the second time, it was under much different circumstances. I won't be going to the transfer unit, instead, I'm assigned to the main yard. When guys on the main yard found out that I came from USP Leavenworth with a 30-year sentence, I was treated with a higher level of respect than a regular guy coming in. The prisoner population in a federal FCI is much different than the prisoner population in a federal USP. USP stands for United States Penitentiary. FCI is a federal correctional institution. Most guys coming from a USP to an FCI automatically receive respect. Many white guys approached me right away and hooked me up with whatever I needed. Guys were offering me a job in the prison industry factory. There was a waiting list about a year long to get out there as these were the best jobs. Factory jobs paid the most. These guys had been working in the factory for a long time and had some pull with the "C.O's" (Correctional Officer) that ran the factory. I told them thanks for the offer, but I wanted to move around outside as much as possible and asked about working on the yard crew instead. I couldn't tell anyone, but my focus was on escaping. If I could just get a job on the landscaping crew, I would have access to see the most vulnerable spots in the yard.

I was soon introduced to a guy in my unit who worked on the landscaping crew. He was a tattooed up, "Nazi Lowrider," youngster from California they called "Opie." He got his nickname from the Opie Taylor character played by Ron Howard on The Andy Griffith show. Red-haired and freckled faced, he had 5150 tattooed on his neck. 5150 is the California state code indicating a person is being held against his will due to mental disorders. Yes, he voluntarily tattooed this on his neck. He was a big kid around 6'1 220 and full of tattoos. Nazi Low Riders are an all-white California prison gang. They strongly support the Aryan Brotherhood and are often used as "Torpedoes" to carry out dirty work in order to impress members of the A.B. A "Torpedo" is someone who is told to "go get that guy." A "Torpedo" will stand by waiting to be called because he wants to advance his prison resume and good standing by "carrying out work." Inevitably guys show up in prison who are marked to be assaulted. Some guys may have owed money or told on someone in a different prison. Other guys may have committed a crime against a child or a sex crime. Word gets around fast who someone is. If there is dirt on someone, they will not last long in a USP. Someone will assault or kill them. FCI's, like El Reno, were definitely not as serious as a USP. This Opie character had not been to a USP but tried hard to carry himself like a hard core convict. He had the talk and the look of a prison convict, but I soon found out it was all an act. He was just a scared kid trying to bluff people into believing he was a badass. He is another one which I witnessed having his covers pulled. Someone introduced me to him because he worked on the landscaping crew and could get me on with them. Opie was eager to get me on with the landscaping crew. Just so happens, the guy who had the riding lawnmower job was about to go home in six months. He had been working landscaping and riding the lawnmower for nine years. They want to replace him with someone who has more than 15 years left on their sentence. Opie talked to the boss and got me to work out there. If I proved to be dependable and on time, I would get the riding lawnmower job when the dude went home. This was one of the most coveted jobs in the prison for obvious reasons. You get to ride around on a lawn mower, all over the yard, while everybody else is locked in somewhere. Very cool job, and just what I needed. I couldn't have asked for a better job to scope out the place and plan my escape. Each morning, the landscaping boss would lay out the work plan for the day. He would say something like, "You guys are going to mulch the flower beds in front of the Utah unit today, and you guys are going to be working in front of the chow hall." We all got along well together, and everyone worked.

Before the feds decided to take all the free weights out of the prison system, El Reno had one of the largest weight piles in the Federal system. The outside wreck yard was full of weights, as was inside the gym. If you wanted to work out with weights in the feds, El Reno was one of the best places to be. I took full advantage and continued to work out, lifting weights almost daily as I did in Leavenworth. I had been working out consistently for about three years at this point and was in really good shape. Most everyone there lifted weights, and most everyone there was in really good shape during that time. They also had punching, speed, and timing bags to do boxing training, if you chose to do so. I took full advantage of all the workout equipment. Working out not only kept me in great shape but it also made me feel really good. I hardly ever went more than two days without working out. There was weed on the yard, and you could buy a "dime" for two books of stamps. A book of stamps was worth $5 dollars at that time so ten bucks would get you high. Whenever there was weed around, I was always on the hunt to get some. Smoking weed was my thing. I loved to smoke weed. It was a good day if I could get high while riding around on the lawn mower cutting grass.

My main focus was on escaping. Every day that I went out to work on the yard, I was constantly looking for a vulnerable spot to escape. I had the riding lawnmower job that enabled me to see parts of the yard that no one else was allowed to get close to. Surrounding the prison were two 10-foot tall fences with razor wire stacked up high between the two and on the very top of each. That razor wire was no joke.

It's razor-sharp with needle-like barbs every few inches. It is laid out loosely in large circular coils that are designed to entangle and severely cut whatever touches it. Not an easy obstacle to overcome. The fence itself has motion detectors that immediately alert the cops if someone is on it. Around the entire outside perimeter of the two fences was a road that armed prison guards in trucks patrolled. Multiple trucks are constantly circling the outside perimeter. They are spaced out between each other in roughly 3 to 5 minute intervals so that a truck passes by any given part of the fence about every three minutes. After months of looking at the perimeter of the fence and studying the timing patterns of the trucks I found the perfect spot to make my escape. It took me several months before I had an opportunity to even go look at this spot. That area was considered "out of bounds" to everyone.

It was in the factory area of the prison near an old building that was no longer in use. Nobody had any business being over there, and if you were seen in that area, you were going straight to the hole. I could get away with it once, I suppose. I thought being on the riding lawn mower gave me an excuse and I would probably just get a warning if a cop saw me there. I was only told to go out to the factory area to cut grass about once a month. Each time I went, I would try to check out a spot I had never seen before. This area looked really good from a distance, but I was never able to get close enough to see it well. I had been thinking about checking it out for awhile before finally getting up the nerve to go. One day the time came to go out to the factory to cut grass, and I boldly made my way over to the "out of bounds" area on the lawn mower to check it out. My adrenaline was rushing through me as I checked it out. Right on the other side of the fence was a big water tank. The road that the trucks drove on was on the far side of the water tank. This made it so when the truck passed, it was further away from the fence than normal. There was hardly any razor wire in-between the 2 fences here and only 1 row of it coiled at the top. This was the best spot. I was tempted to just go for it all at once without a plan because it looked so appealing, but then I thought better of it. Even if I did make it over both fences without being seen, then what? Just run and hope for the best? I didn't have any idea what to do after I went over the fences. No money, no outside help, no ID, and I'm wearing prison clothes. I was sure to fail if I tried it now. Still the adrenaline rush was intense, and it alone almost compelled me over the fence. Not today I told myself but I'll come back again and next time I'll be prepared.

After I had been in El Reno for well over a year, my mother came to visit me. It was the first time I had seen my mother since Maracaibo, Venezuela. She had served 3 ½ years in prison in Holland for five kilos of cocaine. Now she was out living and working in Houston. She drove up to see me with a long-time friend of the family, and they stayed for the weekend. The first day of visiting, my mother came by herself to visit me. We had much to talk about since we last saw each other. She told me the whole story of the failed trip to Amsterdam. I felt terrible as I sat there listening to the details. How could I have allowed her to carry that suitcase? So stupid. I have repented about it so many times and asked God to forgive me.

Something good that came out of it all was that mother had lost over 50 pounds while away. She was in much better health than I ever remember seeing her. Now she was full of energy and optimism. We talked and talked and talked through the day on that first day of visitation. It was the first time we could speak openly. We had spoken before on the phone but knowing that we were being listened to we never opened up about what happened. We always spoke in code on the phone. Mother loved to speak in code and she was very good at it.

There was so much catching up to do. It seemed like the time passed in a flash and visiting was over. It was so good to see my mother. She would return the next day to visit me with our friend John. John was a few years older than me. We have been friends with him and his sister since I was 11 or 12 years old. Because of the age difference, we never really hung out together, but we knew each other for so long we were like family. It was nice to see John, and I was very grateful that he had accompanied my mother on the drive up from Texas to see me. He was a true friend. When we were approaching the end of visitation on the second day my mother got up from the table and said, "Why don't you and John visit for a while?" "I'm going to the restroom." John and I sat across the table from each other, talking for a while, when suddenly he asked, "Do you still smoke weed?" As I answered "yes," he continued saying, "Because I brought you some." He had a mischievous grin on his face and I noticed he was clutching a bag of chips from the vending machine in one of his hands. He said, "I made some balloons full of weed and put them in this chip bag for you." I couldn't believe it! John totally surprised me. I had no idea this was coming. You hear about guys bringing in weed this way but I had never done it. There were cameras all over the visiting room and a cop sitting at a desk just a few feet away from where we were. I didn't feel like they were paying too much attention to me, but my heart was racing and my adrenaline level went up in an instant. John was trying to act cool but the more he tried the more you could tell he was up to something. I told John to give me the bag, so he pushed the bag across the table to me, and when he did, the bag was open and several of the balloons came rolling out across the table. It was right there for anyone to clearly see. Colored balloons full of weed just spread out on the table in front of us. I quickly grabbed the few that had rolled out on the table and threw them in my mouth. John and I look at each other in shock, and he says, "Do you think they saw that?" I laughed, with my mouth still full of balloons, trying desperately to swallow them down while drinking coca cola. Once I could speak, I said, "I hope not, but we are about to find out." If they saw what had just happened they would be at our table right away, terminating the visit and escorting me to a dry cell. A dry cell is a cell with no sink or toilet. The cop sits right outside the cell door watching you. When you need to poop you must poop in a pan while the cop watches and then he will pick through your shit looking for contraband. If someone is suspected of swallowing balloons they are taken straight to a dry cell.

Luckily they never came, and I continued to swallow the rest of the balloons that were in the bag. It's not that easy to swallow because some of them are a little too big. Eventually I swallowed them all. John had wrapped up 23 balloons of weed. About an ounce. The non-biodegradable balloons would protect the weed inside of it as it passes through my system and I would come out in my poop. Soon after, the visitation was over and we said our goodbyes. I returned back to my housing unit with a big smile on my face. It was great to see my mother and John and I had swallowed 23 balloons of weed! I'm carrying an ounce of weed in my belly! This was the best feeling I've had in a long time and I couldn't wait until they came out. When I got back to my unit, I didn't tell anyone that I swallowed balloons. The process of retrieving the balloons from the poop was very nasty. First I put paper in the toilet bowl, so the poop doesn't sink into the water. I must dig through my own poop to get the balloons out then wash them thoroughly. Once everything was cleaned, I opened the balloons to try out the weed. I rolled a little weed up in a rolling paper and made a nice size joint. The weed was strong, and it got me very high. The only downside was it didn't taste all that great. Matter of fact, it tasted like shit. That's what happens when you bring weed in by swallowing balloons. Even after you triple wrap it you still get a little seepage as the balloons travel through the entire digestive system.

Nevertheless, it was awesome having the weed sack in prison. Just a little pinch of weed, about enough to go across a rolling paper, was $10 dollars. I had a whole ounce. Now I was smoking weed and my locker was full of commissary. I went from not having anything in my locker and trying hard just to get credit for a little pinch of weed to having more commissary than my locker would hold and smoking big joints. What a huge difference that made on a guy's quality of life in prison. It was like winning the lottery. I'm still locked up, but it made doing time much easier. The weed didn't last long, but it was great while it did.

Now that I had experienced what it was like bringing in and having the weed bag in prison, I was hooked. My mind immediately started plotting on how to get more in. If I could figure out a way to get more weed in, I could make enough money to help with my escape plans. There were many guys I knew inside who could and would send money to any address you asked them for some weed. That's called street money. Whenever a quantity of weed was available on the yard it didn't last long. Like sharks in a feeding frenzy, guys buy it up quick. At that time, a wholesale ounce of weed was $500 dollars street money. The guy selling the ounce would give the guy who was buying it an address to send the money to. The address would be to either a friend or family member on the street. Once the money arrived, the guy who paid would be given the weed. Not just anyone did these kinds of transactions in prison. You could get ripped off or killed if you dealt with the wrong person.

This is one of the reasons why your "name" or reputation is very important in prison. Kinda like a credit report or resume. Word gets around if you don't pay your bills on time. Your reputation will follow you to other prisons as well. Nobody doing any significant amount of time will ever get away with screwing someone over in prison. It will catch up with you. My reputation was very good. Many guys respected and looked up to me because of the way I carried myself. By this time, everyone knew I was doing a 30-year non-prollable sentence, and I had come from a USP. Before even doing time in the feds I had done time in the state of Texas twice. Just that alone earned me respect. I was already what guys considered a convict. Not just an inmate passing through but a seasoned veteran of the prison system. Not to mention being on the Federal Marshals fifteen most wanted list and captured in Colombia. It wasn't just my background or my story that gained me respect, it was the way I carried myself. I didn't disrespect or bully anyone, and at the same time no one was going to disrespect or bully me. The first time that happened was in the state joint working out in the fields as I mentioned earlier and that guy left in an ambulance. That reputation always follows you even in the feds. I learned early on that you can't let things slide in prison or people will constantly try and get over on you. I felt like I would do real good dealing weed in prison. After my first taste of it I was addicted. Now all I could think of was how to get more weed in.

One night, we had a little get together in the unit I lived in, with a bunch of us guys from Texas. One of the guys was going home the next day so we made a big spread of food to eat that consisted of a little of everything. Chili beans, refried beans, spam, ramen soup, and whatever else we had from the commissary were all thrown together and eaten with crackers or tortillas. We drank homemade wine and smoked a little weed. There were about 6-8 of us from Texas and a few guys from Oklahoma, all having a good time. The guy going home had done over 15 years in the federal system, and in the course of conversation, he started talking about all the different prisons he was in over the years. That's when I first heard in detail about FCI Three Rivers. Almost all the guys that were talking had been to Three Rivers before. They went on and on about how sweet it was there. Pool tables and snack machines in all the units, a concession stand on the yard where you could buy hamburgers, chopped beef sandwiches and ice cream with meal tickets you bought from the commissary. There was always a poker game going on in the rec. yard and everybody had cash money. They let you get $20 dollars in quarters every time you went to the commissary and you could also get $20 dollars in meal tickets which were redeemable at the concession stand on the yard. There was always weed available for purchase on the yard. The unit of measurement to buy weed was a chapstick cap. You could get the equivalent of a chapstick cap full of weed for $25 dollars. (referred to as quarters)

They told me the visiting room at Three Rivers was wide open, meaning it was very easy to bring in weed and everybody was doing it. What made it so easy was they would let you go in a separate room to take pictures, group pictures. Several guys and their visitors would all go into the room together to take pictures. The more people, the better. The people in the front blocked the view for someone in the back to allow their visitor to pass them a package. Some guys were even having sex with their girlfriends or wives in that room behind the group taking photos. My homeboys had my full attention as they explained how it was at Three Rivers. They kept on and on telling me about how sweet the place was. I could hardly believe what I was hearing. Although there were not as many weights as El Reno, the weights there were newer and better. All the units were air conditioned. What really got my interest was what they were telling me about the visiting room. How easy it was to get something passed to you. They said you gotta be careful though, because there were alot of snitches there. It's not the cops you have to worry about, it's the inmates. "So, where exactly is Three Rivers in Texas?" I asked. "It's a lot closer to Houston than El Reno, Oklahoma that's for sure." was the reply. Just so happens that our case manager was working late that night and was still in his office. After hearing all that was said, it was suggested that I should put in for a transfer to Three Rivers. Three

Rivers was closer to my family. I had not been in any trouble in El Reno so there's no reason why they should deny me a transfer. All this was new news to me. I didn't know I could request to be transferred. I stayed away from talking to any of the prison staff. The only time I had spoken to my case manager was when it was mandatory to do so.

We had program evaluations every six months where the case manager would go over your progress in any self-help programs, like education or drug classes. This stuff was for guys getting out in the next five years. My reviews were always depressing because they reminded me of how long it would be before I got out. I didn't like talking to any staff member and couldn't understand why anyone else would. Some guys seemed to really enjoy talking to staff, and these were the guys I stayed away from. My homeboys telling me about Three Rivers knew how I felt about talking to the prison staff, so they strongly encouraged me to just talk to my case manager. They said, "Go now!" "Go talk to the case manager." "He is in his office right now." "Go man, don't be stupid!" So I did.

I left the cell we were in and went straight over to the case manager's office. His door was open, and he was sitting at his desk shuffling papers around. I knocked on the door to get his attention. He looked up from his desk with a surprised look on his face when he saw it was me. "What can I do for you Andrus?" He said. "I want to transfer to Three Rivers," I replied, straight to the point. He said, "come in, sit down, and tell me what's happening." I entered and sat down reluctantly, feeling uncomfortable in his office and talking so cordially like I had seen many guys do. Whenever I would see guys laughing and joking with staff, it made me angry. These are the ones keeping me in here. No matter what job title they held, whether it be a regular "turn key" guard, secretary, unit manager or case manager, their first priority was to make sure I didn't escape. They are not my friends. I sat down and told

151

my case manager I wanted to be closer to my family in Houston so it would be easier for them to come visit me. He pulled my file, looked over everything, and saw that I met all the criteria for a transfer. He asked me a few questions and attempted to engage me in small talk as he filled out my transfer papers. He then proceeded to give me a speech about the type of inmates at Three Rivers. He said there were alot of "snitches" and "hideouts" in that yard. "*What will you do if you find out someone in your unit testified on someone else?*" Then he said, "*You know if you assault anyone for any reason, you will be sent back to a USP. Probably one furthest away from Texas. You may not be able to ever return to an FCI.*" My response was there were lots of snitches here in El Reno too. After giving me stern warnings about how I should act if I were to make it to Three Rivers, he finished up the paperwork and said he would submit my transfer. Less than three weeks after that conversation, I was on a bus headed to Three Rivers, Texas.

THREE RIVERS

The bus ride from El Reno to Three Rivers was an all-day ride. I was woken up around 4 a.m. in the morning to start the long process of transferring out of one prison and into another. Like always, whenever you are transported in the federal prison system, you are shackled up with leg irons, belly chain, handcuffs, and a black box. The leg irons are ankle cuffs connected together with an 18-inch chain that limits your leg movement when you walk to a shuffle. The black box is a box that fits over the handcuffs preventing any access to the keyhole and the little chain that connects the two cuffs together. The belly chain is a chain wrapped around your waist. It is used to secure the black box containing your handcuffs to your waist. The cops who escort me often grab hold of the belly chain from the back when moving me from one vehicle to another. When the Federal Marshals first transported me, there would always be 2 Marshals holding my arms as I shuffled about with my chains. This was the first time since my capture in Colombia that they seemed to ease up on the intense security with me. It was still super high security but just not as ridiculous as before.

The bus first took us to the Oklahoma City airport. The Federal Marshals used a section of the runway for transporting prisoners. Armed guards were spread out around the runway where the planes would park, unload, and load prisoners. The buses would pull right up next to the planes on the runway. I remained on the bus and watched as names were called to get off the bus. Some were getting off our bus and getting onto an airplane, and others were getting into another bus. The same with the guys getting off the planes.

153

They were either getting on one of the buses or on a different plane. It was kinda interesting to watch. I had been in El Reno for two years so seeing anything new was exciting and entertaining. I was looking forward to this 10 Hour bus ride, down south, through Texas. Once our bus was loaded up with all who were going to Three Rivers we were ready to go. My eyes were watching everything outside the barred windows of the bus. I had not seen anything like this in 6 years. 2 years on the run in Colombia and then 4 years in prison. I was always transported by plane so seeing the "free world" after all this time was nice. Even though I was shackled up with chains like a wild animal, I enjoyed the sites. I remember smiling and feeling happy just to be able to look at the landscape passing by. Checking out the people moving around going about their daily hustle and bustle. I noticed that almost everyone I saw moving around had an angry or serious look on their face. They all looked unhappy. Nobody that I saw was smiling. I never noticed stuff like that before. I thought to myself "*why aren't you people smiling!?*" How ironic that I am smiling and you are not. I was in a great mood taking it all in. Going to a new prison that's supposed to be way better than where I was. I heard so much about how sweet this Three Rivers prison was in comparison to other prisons. From what everyone was telling me about how good this prison was I was very optimistic. If half of what I heard was true, I should be smoking marijuana real soon which made me happy just thinking about it. I was feeling pretty good about my chances of scoring some weed. Hopefully, if all goes according to plans, I will bring my weed in through the visiting room.

The bus finally arrived at Three Rivers and we were all processed in. By the time I finally got to a cell it was after 10pm, and the unit was locked down for the night. The cell doors would not open again until 6 a.m. They put me in your standard 6' by 9' two-man cell with bunk beds. The guy who was in the cell chose the top bunk over the bottom so I went straight to the bottom bunk. I liked this place already. My new cell partner was a guy in his early 50's from Texas named Terry. He was doing an 8-year sentence for felon in possession of a firearm. He had previously done time in Texas state prison. Terry had been in Three Rivers for about two years by the time I showed up. We talked for about an hour that first night before going to sleep. I told Terry my story, and he told me his. Terry was very familiar with the visiting room. He got visits nearly every weekend. He had a really pretty younger girl in her 30's that came to see him. He explained to me how they met through a mutual friend. Initially, they were "pen pals" writing back and forth to each other. Apparently, Terry wrote some really good letters because the girl eventually came to visit him. Now they are engaged to be married. When I first saw her, I was taken aback by how pretty she was. Naturally good-looking with an athletic body. Everyone who saw the two of them together asked, "How did that guy score such a beautiful woman?"

After I had told Terry a little bit about my story of living on the run in Colombia for two years, he asked if I had ever read the book "Papillon?" He explained to me that the main character in the book, "Papillon," had escaped from prison and was also on the run in Colombia. I vaguely remember hearing about a movie named "Papillon." I had heard the name thrown around when I was in La Guardia with Yayo but I didn't really know anything about the story behind the name. Terry kept telling me I've got to read the book. Terry had a nice book collection. He spent a lot of time reading. Just like most prisons there are alot of books floating around. He didn't have the book Papillon, but he knew who was currently reading it. He said he would get it for me when the guy finished reading it. I would be next in line for it if I wanted. We talked about all the different books we had read and then suggested our favorite books. He could ask his girlfriend anything he wanted to read, and she would have the bookstore send it to him. Books had to come directly from a bookstore or you couldn't get it in. After a few days living in the same cell and talking back and forth getting to somewhat know Terry I started asking him questions about the visiting room. Specifically about bringing stuff in. Terry liked to do heroin but he would never try to bring anything in. His girlfriend was super straight, and even the suggestion that she bring him any drugs would ruin their relationship. He explained the layout of the visiting room and how guys were bringing it in. They no longer let visitors go into the separate "picture room" to take group photos like the guys in El Reno told me. By this time, the prison staff knew all about drugs being passed in that room so it had been shut down for some time before I got there. I assumed guys smuggled stuff in only by swallowing balloons like I had done in El Reno. Terry told me that was not the way to do it. He said the best way to smuggle something in was to "keister" it.

"What do you mean 'Keister' it?" I had no idea what he was talking about. Then he explained what the term \meant. *"You stick it up your ass,"* he said bluntly. "Stick it up my ass!?" "I'm not sticking anything up my ass." I laughed. "Guys really do that?" "That sounds pretty gay to me." "Surely only fags would voluntarily stick something up their ass!" He laughed and explained that's how it's done. *"That's the best hiding place to smuggle anything in prison."* I honestly thought Terry was joking around with me. I've been in federal prison for over four years, and this was the first I've ever heard of it. I went back and forth with him, insisting only a queer would put something up their ass. He assured me that hardcore convicts have been doing this for a long time. He would ask random guys in front of me to explain what it means to "keister" something in prison. They all answered the same that this is where you hide anything you don't want the cops to find. I still wasn't going for it. I was convinced they were all joking with me.

It didn't take me very long to settle into a routine at my new prison home. Just like El Reno, and Leavenworth before, I took full advantage of the weights and worked out every day. Being new on the yard I was introduced to many guys from Texas. I wasn't looking for any friends and preferred to stay to myself most of the time. There were a few guys there that I recognized from Leavenworth. One of the guys I remember seeing in Leavenworth was in my unit. He was a loud-talking white guy named Sammy. He was the one Terry introduced me to when I asked where I could score some weed. Terry didn't smoke weed so he didn't really know who to get it from. Heroin was Terry's thing. He was a very rare case in that he never got strung out on Heroin. He did it once or twice a month and that was it. Sammy on the other hand would use just about anything if it got him high. Sammy was the wine guy in our unit. He had a hiding spot in the unit where he made his own wine and sold what he didn't drink. Wine making was Sammy's hustle. Homemade wine was $5 dollars a quart. It's made from fruit juice and sugar. Typically grapefruit juice, orange juice, or both are mixed in a plastic trash bag with sugar and water. You don't need yeast if you have what's called a "kicker." A kicker is fruit that has rotted and is fermenting. You just need a little of the live bacteria to start the process. Once you throw the kicker in the bag with the juice and sugar the bacteria starts to eat the sugar and produce alcohol. Usually, the process takes about 10-14 days, depending on how much sugar you used and how strong you want it to be. Many times, the guys making wine get impatient and take it down too early. You can tell immediately when you taste it if it's done. If it's too sweet it was pulled too early and whoever drinks it is going to be sick the next day.

Sammy didn't have any weed of his own but he knew where to get it. The deal was I had to give Sammy the stamps to go buy the weed. He would get it for me under the condition that I smoked a little with him. I was just happy to get some weed to smoke and didn't mind smoking a little with him if that's what it took to get it. We started hanging out and talking more and more as time went on. He told me he was doing a 15 year sentence for felon in possession of a firearm. Sammy was a prime example of someone institutionalized. He was the child of a single mother who never knew his father. Born in Kentucky, his mother put him up for adoption when he was a young boy because she was too poor to take care of him. He grew up in Texas raised in foster homes and juvenile detention centers. He was a petty thief, alcoholic, and drug addict who had been in trouble all his life.

He didn't have anyone on the outside sending him money or letters. Just like when you feed a stray cat, Sammy was super nice and wanted to hang around with me because he saw me as a means to get high for free. Eventually I found out where to get weed for myself and mainly smoked by myself in private but I would still go find Sammy now and then and get him high. He could be a very funny guy most of the time and was cool to talk to. He turned out to be someone I talked to and hung out with more than anyone else at Three Rivers. My cell partner Terry was still the only one I talked to about bringing in anything through the visiting room. The fewer people who knew that information the better.

My mother was the first to come visit me after I had been there less than two weeks. She was doing great with her new job and was starting to make a little money. We talked and talked about everything. I asked her about John. What was he up to and did she think he would come visit me and bring me some weed? She said she would talk to him about it. While we visited I was checking out everything. Where the cameras were, where the guards were, how the guards acted during visitation, everything. The visiting room at Three Rivers was much bigger than the one in El Reno. There was even an outside patio you and your visitors could sit and visit. Terry was out there with his gorgeous girlfriend. He introduced me to her, and I introduced both to my mother. Again you gotta scratch your head when you see the two of them together and ask, "what does she see in him?" After the visit, I felt confident I could bring something in. I was still stuck on thinking about bringing in balloons of weed instead of the suggested "keister" pack. I had the scenario worked out in my mind of how I would do it.

It wasn't until I started reading the book Papillon that I changed my mind about the keister pack idea. The book is a true story about a French guy who was incarcerated in France and French Guyana for many years. French Guyana is a small country in South America the French used to incarcerate their prisoners. Papillon was the book's main character and was always looking for a way to escape. In the book it explained how many of the prisoners would hide their money in their asses. Not so much to get it past the guards but more so to keep it safe from getting stolen. Papillon planned to use whatever cash he could acquire while in prison for his escape. For that reason he called the package of cash he kept keistered his "plan." Reading the book changed my point of view. When Terry first told me about keistering something to get it past the guards, I thought he was joking about it. I thought the idea of putting something in my ass was the most ridiculous thing you could suggest. I would never, ever even consider such a thing. Now I am starting to think differently. I realized it was something that real convicts did on many occasions to survive in prison.

You are constantly being stripped and searched in prison. Guards are trained to look in every possible spot on your body that could be used to hide something. During a strip search the guard stands directly in front of you while you are completely naked. The guard searches the clothes you just took off as he instructs you to first stretch forward your arms and show your hands palms up and then down, spreading apart and moving your fingers as you do so. Then you lift your arms up to show your armpits. Next you open up your mouth and lift up your tongue while the guard looks in your mouth. Then you move your head side to side bending both ears back as you do to show behind the ears. If you have hair you bend over and shake your hands through your hair. Next you lift up the family jewels showing underneath your ball sack. Then you are instructed to turn around and lift each foot up one at a time showing the guard the bottoms of your feet. Lastly, you are told to bend over, spread your butt cheeks, and cough so that the guards can see the crack of your ass. The coughing part is supposed to release the grip your butt cheeks might have on any contraband. A strip search is very thorough and almost impossible to get away with carrying anything on your person. Every prisoner is stripped and searched in this manner after visitation. If you try to carry anything back with you either on your person or hidden in your clothes, you will get caught. The only way to bring something in is either swallow it or keister it. If I wanted to be serious about bringing some weed in through the visiting room, I would have to get over my phobia of keistering it and just do it.

I talked to John on the phone before he came to see me. He already knew I wanted him to bring me some weed again because my mother told him. Now that I had learned the real and best way to do it I wanted to talk to John in person first. We talked in code when I let him know not to bring me any balloons when he came to visit. I just wanted to talk about it first. He understood and said he would come to visit me next weekend.

I had been in Three Rivers for over a month before John came to visit me. I was pretty much settled in by then. The prison was just as sweet as the fellas in El Reno had told me. All the housing units had a pool table and vending machines inside the unit. The vending machines took quarters or you could use your commissary card. On the recreation yard was

160

a concession stand run by prisoners that sold chopped beef sandwiches, baby back ribs, and they even had an ice cream machine with your choice of cup or cone. The currency used to make purchases from the concession stand were tickets you could buy from the commissary. You were allowed to buy $20 dollars in quarters, $40 dollars in tickets and put $25 dollars on your card each time you went to the commissary, which was once a week. There was always a cash poker game going on out on the recreation yard. There was an outdoor weight pile with lots of new equipment as well as an indoor gym with cardio equipment and nautilus-style machine weights.

One part of the outside recreation center had boxing training equipment, including heavy punching, speed, and timing bags. You would think this equipment would be in high demand in prison but strangely, hardly anyone ever used it. I was very much into working out and staying in shape. Mainly, I just lifted weights. Occasionally I would work out with the boxing training equipment. Punching the heavy bag and speed bag was not only a great workout but also helped release a bunch of pent-up anger I was holding inside. Playing poker was another one of my favorite pastimes. I have been playing since I was a young kid and always loved the game. Typically, playing poker in prison is not a good idea. The "house" cuts a percentage of the pot each hand so if you play long enough, eventually the house gets all the money. Getting yourself in debt was inevitable in a credit poker game. This poker game was a cash game with no cut. There was no "house." It was just a bunch of sharks with money playing poker, trying to take each other's money but having a good time in the process. Whatever you won or lost was right now, cash money. The first month I was there I was very tempted to sit down and play but could not afford to, so I stood by and watched. All the guys at the table wanted me to play, of course, because they all wanted to take my money on the poker table.

After just being there for a month, I was beginning to get a feel for the place. It doesn't take long to see who's who and what's what. Because I love to smoke weed, I found out all about the weed market on the yard. The price of weed depended on how much you bought. A "dime" was $10 dollars. That was about enough weed to barely go across a rolling paper. When rolled up, a dime was just a really small "pin joint." A "quarter" was $25 dollars and was typically measured using a chapstick cap. A quarter was packaged in the corner of an envelope. Guys also called quarters "caps" or "corners." If you bought just one quarter you had to pay $25 dollars cash. The more you bought at one time the better the price would be. If you had the ability to have someone you knew on the streets, send money to an address you were given, you would get the best deal. That's called "street to street" money, and it is the most valuable. Some guys would want you to have the money put on their books. *"Just have your people send me $100 bucks and I'll give you 8 caps"* was a common deal. Again, that depends on how much weed is on the yard at the time. Sometimes $100 bucks would only get you 6 caps. An ounce of weed was $500 dollars street to street. One ounce was 60-80 caps, depending on who you got it from.

The guys who were bringing in weed knew the guys who could send the money and most of the time it was the same guys who always got to buy the ounces when they were available. These were the guys whose reputation was solid and never had any issues with sending money. There were more guys wanting to send $500 for an ounce than there were ounces available. This was a great investment that most guys wanted to take advantage of. Depending on how you sold it, you could make between $1,500 to $5,000 selling one ounce of weed. My mind was taking in all this information. The more I learned, the more questions I asked. I was strategic with my questions, asking something like "how much does an ounce of weed go for here?" while in a group of several guys, would get them all talking. Everyone contributed to the conversation trying to outdo each other about how much they knew. Before long, I knew everything I needed to know about the marijuana market at FCI Three Rivers. All I could think about was how great it could be if I had some weed on a regular basis. My main motivation was not so much about making money in prison as it was having my own supply of weed to smoke.

My friend John came by himself to visit me for the first time. He was dressed nice and could have easily been mistaken for a lawyer. He didn't look like a suspicious character at all. He was very professional looking. He asked if I wanted anything from the vending machines. I said sure I'll take a coke and some chips or something. He got us both some snacks and a drink. It seemed we sat and talked about everything for hours without taking a breath. John was a really cool guy with interesting conversation and a great sense of humor. In the beginning of the visitation the outside patio was closed. As the visiting room filled up, they unlocked the doors to the outside patio. They announced that it was now open and visitors were welcome to visit outside. John and I went outside to check it out. The patio was a nice area with lots of vegetation. A 10 foot cement wall enclosed the patio and separated it from the main prison yard. Visitors sat on a cement ledge that went around the base of the wall. Flower and hedge bushes were directly behind where you sat. It was a garden-style patio with raised cement planters. There were no cameras on the outside patio. All the cameras were inside. The door to the patio had a special glass that you could only see out into the patio from inside the visiting room. One of the guards would often hang out at that door, watching everyone on the patio. He could see you but you couldn't see him. John and I were amazed at how easy it was going to be for him to pass me something. We kept pretending as though he had a keister pack to pass me. He would pass me an imaginary package over and over like we were practicing.

I explained to him how to make the keister pack. I told him to wrap the weed as tightly as possible using black electrical tape. The package should be no bigger than a roll of quarters. Him handing me something would be no problem. I would wear tight underwear underneath my boxers so when John hands me the package, I will quickly drop it in my crotch area. The trick was going to be shoving it up my butt. While visiting, I had been to the restroom a few times and noticed the guards were not watching me at all as I used the toilet to pee. When you need to pee during visitation, you must ask the guard, who will escort you to the back room where the toilet is. The visitors have their own separate restroom in the visitation room where prisoners cannot go in. I asked to go pee a couple of times when my mother came and again this time while visiting John. I thought while I was standing there peeing, the guards were not watching me. They were always close by but not watching me. If I had something, I could keister it right here and now. I told John what I had noticed. My plan was once I had it on me, I would ask to go to the bathroom to pee, and while I was standing over the toilet pissing, I would push it up my ass. I felt confident everything would go according to plans. The patio was closed one hour before the rest of the visiting room. When visiting was over the guards announced that visitation was now over and instructed all the prisoners to go wait on the patio while they processed all the visitors out. The guards were now either escorting all the visitors out or strip-searching prisoners in the back. There were only 5 guards, so the strip-searching process took 30-45 minutes to complete depending on how many guys had a visit that day. That meant I was out on the patio with no cameras and no guards watching me for at least 15 minutes. I could easily make my move here. I was thinking I could just have John leave the package hidden in the bushes on the patio and I would get it after the visit ended. There were lots of options, which made me feel very confident.

John came back as promised the next weekend. All the confidence I had the week before was gone. I was nervous. John's demeanor was much different as well. He had that look on his face like he was up to something. All the anticipation of this moment made it much more intense. We started talking and tried to relax but we were both nervous and tense. A terribly uncomfortable feeling came over me and I just wanted to get it over with as soon as possible. I didn't want to wait for the end of visitation to get the package because my stomach couldn't take the nervous feeling for that long. It was impossible to relax. We both kinda just sat there wondering when and how to pass the package. We were not even talking to each other and laughing like the week before. It was bad. After about two hours, they opened the patio so we went out there to visit. We were sitting out on the patio trying to figure out how he was going to do it when I suggested he go to the vending machines inside and get us something. When you come back just hand me the package first before you hand me the snacks.

He came back with his hands full carrying chips and snacks. Right when he came through the door I got up and started grabbing stuff out of his hands like I was helping him. The first thing I grabbed was the package. I turned around and immediately dropped it in my crotch area. Sitting down now, I had it on me. I took a few sips of the cold coke John had brought me and looked around to see if anyone noticed what I just dId. My heart was beating really fast, but I felt much better now that I had it on me. I sat there for about two minutes before getting up and going to ask the guard to let me use the toilet. He escorted me to the back, pointed at the toilet and said to knock on the door when I finished. He exited the back room and left me there by myself. I couldn't believe my luck. I was left alone in the back room and had plenty of time to do what I needed to do. I started peeing right away and when I finished I started to shove the package up my ass. I had never done this before and wasn't sure what to expect.

It hurt really bad, taking my breath away and bringing tears to my eyes. Once it was in, I could feel it move its way up and stayed in place. I had the strong sensation like I had to shit. It was done. I had it now, and a feeling of relief came over me. I washed my hands and looked at myself in the mirror. I was grinning from ear to ear. Feeling really good I wanted to shout YES! You did it! The nervous pressure and stress I felt was replaced with euphoria. I knocked on the door and waited for the guard to come and let me back in the visiting room. I knocked a few times and waited a couple of minutes before the guard finally came. I walked back out to the patio where John and I were sitting. He looked very relieved once he saw me. He said he was worried and stressed out because I was gone for so long. He didn't know that I had already keistered the package, so I explained to him what had just happened. How the guard left me back there by myself to pee. I told him after I got done peeing I keistered it. Also I told him how bad it hurt. Now we were both laughing and joking. Both of us were relieved it was done, and we had gotten away with it. We had only visited a few hours and still had several hours before visiting hours were over. I was ready to go though. Anxious to get this package out and smoke a fat joint. John was ready to go too so we cut the visit short, said our goodbyes and I went back to my unit.

The unit was quiet when I got back. It was the weekend, and most of the guys were out in the recreation yard playing softball, basketball, lifting weights, or whatever activities they had going on. My cell partner, Terry, was still out on visitation so I had the cell to myself. I put the shitter sign up in the cell door window for privacy before sitting on the toilet. Then I put a couple of sheets of writing paper in the toilet to catch the package when it came out and prevent it from sinking down the toilet drain pipe hole. It came right out but not without hurting once again. The package had torn tissue on my anal cavity either going in and or coming out and there was a little blood mixed with my shit on it. After cleaning myself, I retrieved the package from the toilet and put it in the sink to wash it off. Using my bare hands to clean my own shit off this quarter-roll-size package was disgusting. The site and smell of what I was doing had me retching and wanting to throw up. My ass was sore, and it felt like it was on fire. Once I had it cleaned off real good with soap and water I started unraveling the black electrical tape. I kept unraveling until finally reaching a plastic sandwich bag containing the weed. I separated the tape and plastic sandwich bag from the weed and was very disappointed at what I was seeing. There wasn't very much weed at all. What little weed there was full of stems and seeds. I'm looking at the contents of what I just smuggled in; most of it was the tape and the bag. John didn't even clean the weed. After removing the stems and seeds from the weed what was left was about an 8th of an ounce of smokable marijuana. Damn John. I just wrecked my butt hole for this little bit of weed. I was very frustrated and disappointed. Now I have to figure out how to communicate this with John on the phone, knowing the guards are listening. It was a bittersweet moment. I told myself, I'm not selling any of this weed. I'm smoking all this myself.

It would be at least two weeks before I could see John again. He had come the last 2 weekends in a row and now it was my mother's turn to come. I thought it best not to try and explain anything to John over the phone but just wait until my mother came to visit and I would tell her what to tell John. Before my cell partner and all the rest of the guys in the unit came back I wanted to smoke. I made a little pipe using a pencil and the cardboard from a toilet paper roll. First, I removed the little metal piece that holds the eraser on the end of the pencil. Then I took the eraser out of the metal piece and crimped one end. I used this as the bowl to put the weed in. The crimped end was to prevent the weed from falling out but had enough space for the smoke to pass through. I used the cardboard roll from the middle of a roll of toilet paper to hold the bowl by cutting a small slit near the end of the cardboard roll. I stuck the crimped end of the bowl down into the cardboard slit. Placing my mouth on one end of the roll and hand on the other, I lit the weed in the bowl and inhaled. There was only enough weed in the bowl for one hit. This way, there was no excess smoke after inhaling as much as possible. All the smoke was inside my lungs. After holding the smoke in as long as I could, I would blow it out into a towel that I had soaked in soap and water. This would prevent any smell from getting out in the unit. I took about 4 or 5 hits, then threw the pipe away in one of the unit trash cans away from my cell. I got really high and just layed on my bunk. I layed there thinking for a little while until I went to sleep. I remember waking up to the sound of everyone coming back into the unit from the yard. Yard recall is at 3:30pm and stand up count is at 4:00pm. Everyone is locked in their assigned cell by 4:00.

It's the same in every Federal Prison in the United States regardless of the security level. Terry came back from visit just before lockdown. I told him all about what had happened. He was the only one I intended to tell, and I felt confident he wouldn't tell anyone. Even though I had faith he would not tell anyone I still told him "don't you dare tell a soul." I asked him if he wanted to smoke with me but he said no. He was too scared they would piss test him and he would come back dirty. Marijuana stays in your system longer than anything else. If he got a dirty UA (tested positive) he would lose his visits. Heroin only stays in your system for three days and he only did Heroin when he knew he would not get tested. I rolled up a fat joint and a couple of regular-sized joints. When the count clears, I'm going to go smoke with Sammy. Can't smoke the fat joint in the unit because it will smell for sure.

The best way to smoke a joint in prison so it won't smell is cut it into small one hit pieces. Lay the pieces out on the table and use a pen to smoke it. One of those click pens that come apart in the middle. Take it apart and use the half that the writing point sticks out of like a straw to suck the smoke out of the little pieces once you light the end. If you do it right, you will inhale the piece all at once, keeping all the smoke in your lungs and blowing it out in a towel. Since the joint is cut into little pieces it goes out instead of staying lit and smoking after you take your hit. This is how we got away with smoking in our cells without stinking up the Unit.

As soon as I invited Sammy to smoke he was like a kid in a candy store. He knew I had a visit earlier and was certain I had brought something in. He started asking me a bunch of questions all at once. "How much did you get?" "Are you going to sell any?" "Let me sell some for you!" "Who came to visit you?" "Are you going to have weed now on a regular basis?" "I know everyone who smokes." "I can get you whatever you want." "You want some commissary?" "Street money?" "Money on your books?" "Let me know, I can get all that for you." "I'll take care of everything for you." "You don't have to deal with anyone and no one will know it's you." Sammy was a cool guy at times but other times he was a real asshole. He talked way too loud and in situations like this he acted very immature. I told him to chill out. I just had a little bit to smoke, and I wasn't planning on selling any. He proceeded to tell me how much money I could make if I wanted to sell some. He said if someone brought him some weed, he would have a locker full of commissary and thousands of dollars on his books. He kept stating the obvious as though I had not thought about any of this. He was really getting on my nerves and ruining my high. I kept telling him to chill out and if I decided to sell any, I would let him know. I am a very private person and don't like anyone knowing my business. I told him, he and my cell partner were the only two that knew I had any weed and I don't want anyone else knowing.

169

When the unit opened up for chow we walked together to go eat. Sammy was all over me acting like a kid who's dad was taking him to the amusement park as we walked to the chow hall. He was excited, and his excitement showed. He was patting me on the back telling me how lucky I was to have someone come visit me and even more so to bring me something. He just didn't know how to shut up and be cool. The way he was acting towards me and the fact that I had a visit earlier made me feel vulnerable to others finding out. Guys pick up on little stuff like that quickly. Just put 2 and 2 together and it's not hard to figure out. Prison is a small community where everyone knows when anything of any significance is going on. Many guys in prison are like old, gossiping women. They always want to know their neighbors' business and thrive on telling each other any new news. I was too stoned from the weed I smoked to know how to tell him to act like his regular self and quit drawing attention to me. I didn't associate with too many people in prison. Sammy lived in my unit, he was from Texas, and we were in Leavenworth together. I knew his story, and he knew mine. He was one of the few guys I talked to, but now I regret that choice. He was just too much at times.

After we ate, we went out to the recreation yard. I told Sammy he needed to chill out, and quit showing so much excitement whenever I got a visit. It was drawing unnecessary heat. You could tell by the look on his face that he didn't like what I was telling him. As we talked I pulled out the fat joint I had rolled and handed it to Sammy to light. "Fire this up," I told him, as I passed him a monster joint. His demeanor completely changed when he had that joint in his hand. A joint that size would cost you about $25 dollars. No one ever rolled them this big because it was considered a waste and it smelled too strong. I had been imagining smoking a joint this size for a long time. We passed the joint back and forth until both of us got super stoned. We laughed and joked around for a while before going back to the unit. It was great being high on marijuana in prison. The stuff made me feel happy. When I'm high, it's easy to find humor in everything, forgetting all about the massive sentence I was serving and enjoying the moment. Back in the unit, still high, we played pool and ate snacks from the snack machine. During those days, Three Rivers was not a bad prison to do time.

The next weekend, my mother came to visit. We visited all day and talked about everything. She updated me on how everyone was. Mom was doing good with her new job and making a good income and I was very happy for her. During the visit, I was paying attention to everything in the visiting room, taking it all in and seeing many vulnerable spots to get the package again when John returned. While we talked, I explained everything to my mother to tell John. We also talked in depth about a code to use when referring to weed over the phone. It would sound like we were talking about something totally different to someone listening. We could communicate our messages without the guards, who were listening to our conversation, understanding what we were talking about. I told my mother to tell John to get the best quality weed he could find. My mother actually knew who to talk to about getting better weed, more so than John. Mom didn't smoke, but she had friends who did. We talked about how to package the weed better. First he must clean the weed thoroughly, taking all the stems and seeds out. Then use something similar to a pill bottle to put the weed in and pack it down really tight so that the weed will form into a quarter roll shape and make it hard. Once it's all packed together, push the weed out of whatever you used to pack it and wrap it in plastic wrap. Use as little plastic wrap as possible, wrapping it tightly, no bigger than a quarter roll. Then wrap that tightly with electrical tape. Don't use so much tape this time. I thought I communicated this message very clearly to my mother about how to wrap the next one. She said she would pass the message to John.

Another week went by, and John came back to see me. I knew he had gotten the message from my mother and was bringing me another package. This time it should be much more weed and much less packaging. The last batch of weed he brought me 2 weeks ago was long gone. I smoked it all and didn't sell any. I would need to sell some this time in order to send John some money for bringing it. He wasn't asking me for money and when I suggested it he would always say I don't have to send him any money. He was just trying to help me out because he knows it must suck being in prison with a 30-year sentence. John was cool like that. Regardless of what John was telling me, I knew I must make it worth his while or he will lose interest. This time we were both much more relaxed than the first time.

We talked about alot of different things and laughed like the first time he came without bringing anything. I kept my mind off thinking about how I would get the package from him and just tried to relax and wait. Once the patio was open, we went out and visited outside. The plan was about the same as last time. John would go to the snack machines and buy us something to eat. They had sandwiches, chips, chocolate candy and sodas. John got us a large assortment of everything and brought it back to where we were sitting on the patio. He set everything down in between us with the package under a chip bag. As soon as I saw it, I grabbed it, stood up with my back to the door and dropped it in the front of my pants. I did it smoothly without drawing any attention. We were both laughing and joking as we ate our sandwiches. When I grabbed this package, I noticed it felt bigger than the last one. I was telling John he was trying to kill me. After we ate, I went to the front and told the guard I needed to pee. He escorted me to the back and stood off to the side while I peed. He wasn't watching me but he was standing 3 feet away. Once I finished peeing there was no time to try and keister this package without drawing attention to myself from the guard. I zipped up, washed my hands, and returned to where John was on the patio. I told John I couldn't do it because the guard was beside me. "I'll ask to go again later, hopefully, it will be a different guard."

We went back inside to the air-conditioned room and continued our visit. After a couple of hours went by, I asked again to go pee. This time, the guard was in the other room while I peed. He was still in the back but not standing so close. He could hear clearly when I was peeing and when I stopped. As soon as I stopped I tried to push it up in me but it would not go. It was too big. I was cursing John under my breath for making it so big. I flushed the toilet, washed my hands, and returned to the visiting room. Sitting down next to John I told him I couldn't get it in because it was too big. He thought it was funny and joked with me about it. Until then, I had not asked him how he packaged it. As I started questioning him, he told me, "I did it like you said to do it. I cleaned it real good, taking the seeds and stems out and then put it in a prescription pill bottle. I had to add some cotton to the end of the prescription pill bottle so it would not be flat at the end." I couldn't believe what he was telling me. He left the weed in the pill bottle and wrapped that up in electrical tape. No wonder it was so big! This was not what I hoped to hear at all. I had to be cool with John, because after all, he was bringing me weed. Man, I was pissed though. How could he NOT understand!? The pill bottle was just to use to pack the weed in a roll shape. Then once it is packed down hard and tight you pop it out of the container and wrap it in thin plastic cling wrap used to wrap up food. "Why would I want to smuggle in a pill bottle?" I asked. "The whole idea was to reduce the packaging and maximize the amount of weed I could bring in. I'm not sure if I can even get this." I told him. John kept telling me it was the same size as the last one, only slightly bigger on one end. We spent most of the visit talking about how he should package the next one. When finally the visiting hours were over the guards announced, as they always do, "*Visitation is now over. We need all visitors to*

come to the front and all inmates to wait out on the patio."
Once all of us were out on the patio the guards locked the
door separating the patio from the visiting room. The guards
then started the process of escorting visitors out of the prison.
On the patio, I walked around with my shirt untucked and
found a spot to push the package up in me. I had to push very
hard, and It was terrible pain, but I managed to get it in. Once
it was in, I was very relieved. Even though it hurt like hell, I
was happy knowing I would be smoking big joints once
again.

When I returned to the unit, it was getting close to
lockdown/count time. I had to hurry to get the package out. It
was very painful and caused me to bleed. Once I got it out, I
cleaned it off with soap and water but didn't open it. The
guards were yelling, "count time!" "Everyone in your cells,
it's count time!" I showed Terry the package before opening
it. "Can you believe my friend packaged the weed in a pill
bottle?" I asked. *"Why did he do that?"* Terry asked. I
explained the miscommunication and joked that he was
trying to kill me. Terry told me about a guy who used to bring
in 2 keister packs every time he visited. One ounce in each
one. If you do it right you can pack an ounce of weed down
to about the size of a quarter roll. "One is plenty for me," I
joked. "This damn thing made my butt bleed. I can just
imagine two!" The guards yelled for everyone to stand up,
they were coming by to count. After they finished counting
we remained locked in our cells until the count cleared. Terry
kept a look out while I opened up the package. Instead of
unraveling the tape, I cut it off this time with some mustache
scissors. A big wad of cotton was on the end of the pill bottle,
just like John said. The pill bottle was full of somewhat
cleaned weed. It was not packed down and still had a few
seeds but it was much more than last time. I would make 15
corners to sell and smoke the rest. I wanted $200 bucks for
the 15 corners sent to John. I made them up by using a
chapstick cap for measurement. After filling up the chapstick

cap with weed, I dumped it out in the corner of an envelope. The corner is cut away from the rest of the envelope and then folded with the ends taped shut. I also made two corners for Sammy. After the count cleared our cell doors were opened. I left my cell and waited in the middle of the unit for mail call with everyone else. I acted normal like nothing new or special had happened. You couldn't tell by looking at me that I just scored nearly an ounce of weed. I didn't let my excitement show, but I was jumping up and down inside with excitement. After the mail call, and everybody went about their business, I went to Sammy's cell. This is what I told him: "I have 15 corners for you to sell." "I want $200 dollars sent to an address in Houston that I will give you." " I'll give you two corners for doing the deal." I could tell by the look on his face he thought I was going to give him more. Instead of being happy about the deal I offered him, he looked disappointed. "No sweat if you don't want to do it." I told him. "I think I know who will send me the $200 dollars for 15 corners. I just thought you wanted to make a quick two corners." In Sammy's greedy mind, he thought he should get more.

In the past someone hustling weed would get one as payment for every five they sold. Sell five get one was the deal. He thought he should get three since he was selling 15. He was too greedy to understand the difference in the deal I was offering him. I wasn't asking him to go out and sling corners for $25 dollars a piece to multiple people. If that were the case, selling five and getting one would mean he would bring me $250 dollars for selling ten and then get his two free. That's 12 corners for $250 dollars. I wanted him to sell 15 corners to one person who would send me $200 dollars street to street. For that one transaction, I would give him two corners. Easy Money but Sammy thought he was getting shorted somehow. I went back and forth with him trying to explain the difference, but he was too stubborn to listen. We parted ways with no deal and Sammy stormed off in a huff.

175

I really didn't need Sammy at all. I was just cutting him in because we were homeboys, and I liked that he had hustle. I was helping him out, not the other way around. It didn't take long before he realized how stupid he was acting and came back wanting to do the deal. He apologized and said he didn't understand the difference at first and he was convinced I was getting over on him somehow. Then the light bulb must have turned on in his head and he realized he was only selling to one guy and that guy was getting a really good deal. I knew several guys eager to send $200 dollars for 15 corners. All Sammy had to do was bring them the weed and the address and make a quick two corners for himself. The whole idea was for him to be a go-between and keep any suspicion off me. We talked and talked about it again and I had to explain to him the importance of being low key. I told him the names of a couple of guys who I knew would send the money for the 15 corners. All he had to do was go talk to them. After contemplating all of his options he finally did just that and the deal was done. I liked Sammy most of the time but when it came to doing any business deals he was turning out to be the wrong person to deal with. He was loud and loved attention. Whenever he made his wine he let everyone on the yard know he had wine for sale, loudly. He thrived on wanting to be perceived as "the guy to see" to get whatever you wanted. Low key he was not. It was time to reevaluate my decision to cut him in on any dealings with weed that I brought in.

I talked with John on the phone and he confirmed that he received the $200. He was happy about it. We talked in the code we had established and were able to communicate about him bringing me more weed. He let me know that he found a great weed connection with quality weed. He also said he has a much better system now in packaging the weed and I would be happy with the next package. I was very excited. It sounded like John was taking this much more seriously and starting to actually enjoy smuggling in weed.

The next time John came everything went really well. We talked and laughed and enjoyed each other's company while visiting. Neither one of us was overly nervous or feeling the pressure like at first. The pass off went smoothly, and I waited until the end of visitation to keister the package. It was still very uncomfortable going in but much easier than the last one. When I got back to the unit I went through the same routine of getting it out then cleaning it off. John did a great job this time, the package was done right. When I opened it up the smell of weed filled the cell. The weed looked beautiful! It was lime green with red hairs, and much more of it than before. Looking at this made me extremely happy. I had not seen weed this good in a long time. Not only was the weed much better quality but there was way more of it this time. Way to go John! I made up what I planned on selling and kept the rest to smoke. This was by far the best weed on the yard and guys were very eager to buy it. I smoked some with Sammy and gave him a few quarters to sling for some commissary. I didn't let him know how much I had or that I was handling the street money transactions myself. I was happy and things were going well. After talking to Terry, and hearing how guys used to bring in two ounces at a time, I thought about trying that myself. I told John over the phone to bring two next time. Same weed, same packaging, just two instead of one. The next time he came to see me he brought two ounces. He passed them both to me out on the patio with no problems. I waited until the end of the visit to keister them both. I did the first one, then walked around a little and let it work its way up, then did the second one. I got them both. The only difference was the overwhelming feeling of having to shit. I could not wait to get back to the unit and sit on the toilet. I walked really fast and went straight to the toilet like I was about to shit myself.

Once I had both packages out I felt really good. Now I had two ounces of high quality marijuana inside prison. It was almost like making parole. The feeling was awesome! I

177

immediately sold one of the ounces for $500 dollars and had the money sent to John. The other ounce I kept for myself to mainly smoke. I did sell the standard 6 corners for $100 dollars and had the money sent to my books. After that I started bringing in two ounces at a time almost every weekend for about three months straight. I didn't need to go to the commissary because I had guys going for me every day it was open. Most guys who bought weed wanted to pay with commissary. I would fill out a list of things I wanted from the store and they would get it for me on the agreed upon date. That included multiple new shoes, sweat pants and sweat bottoms, a new watch, bags of coffee and too much food to put in my locker. I had to "rent" other guys' lockers to store much of my excess stuff in. In addition to having large amounts of food, I also had stamps, quarters and meal tickets. I had it going on like Donkey Kong but that was just the start.

I was sending John at least $500 dollars every time he came. I noticed the quality of clothes he was wearing to come visit me had improved. John had a new girlfriend and asked me if it was ok if she came to visit me with him. I said of course she can and got her on my approved visiting list. She was a very pretty girl with an athletic body and pretty smile. John asked me if I had a friend who didn't get visits and would like to put her on his visiting list so we could all visit at the same time. We could bring him a package too, he suggested. I thought about Sammy. I told John I think I know the perfect guy. I will talk to him and let you know.

I returned from my visit with John and his girlfriend with two ounces of weed like I had done several times before. Sammy's cell partner was getting transferred soon and he wanted me to move in the cell with him. He had been asking me since the moment he found out his cell partner would be transferring. Terry was cool, and he gave me the bottom bunk but he did his time a lot different than I did. He was a good guy, but he was always scared about the weed I had. He didn't want me smoking in the cell while he was around because he was always paranoid about losing his visits with his gorgeous girlfriend. I was still reluctant about moving in the cell with Sammy, but after John asked about putting his girlfriend on someone's visiting list, I thought Sammy would be good and it would be best if we were cell partners. This way we could talk business all we wanted in private and not draw any attention.

After the count had cleared and the mail call was finished I told Sammy we needed to talk. When the unit opened up for chow we both stayed behind to smoke a joint and talk. First, I told him I had decided to take him up on his offer and move in his cell when his current cell partner left. He had already offered me the bottom bunk. Then I started telling him the business proposition I had in mind. "My partner in Houston, who comes to visit me, has a girlfriend who will come visit you when he visits me. This way we will both be out there visiting at the same time. John will bring us two ounces a piece each time they come. You get to keep one of yours and give me the other one. The one ounce you keep is yours to do whatever you want with." I pulled out one of the unopened keister packs that John had brought me earlier that day and showed it to Sammy. "This is what they will look like," I said, "It's the same lime green, red hair weed we have been smoking. All you gotta do is put the girl on your visiting list and the next thing you know ole Sammy will have the weed sack."

He couldn't believe what I was proposing. He actually thought I was setting him up to get busted. That was a much easier scenario for him to believe. He couldn't believe what I was saying was true and on the up and up. I could tell what he was thinking by his body language. "What?" You think I'm bullshitting you? You think I'm that low that I would lie to your face to try and get you busted? What would I stand to gain by setting you up? You think I've been bringing in weed

179

all this time and all of a sudden I decided to quit that and set you up instead? No more ounces of weed or visits for me. I would rather get you busted and go sit in the hole and hope they give me a gold star for cooperation. That's funny. Think about how stupid that sounds. I didn't tell on the guys moving tons of marijuana into this country. I didn't tell on my Colombian connections who were moving hundreds of kilos of cocaine into this country. Many of whom I still know today. But now that I met the notorious winemaker of FCI Three Rivers, Sammy Floyd, gosh dang! The temptation to turn in such a big fish like you is just too much." I laughed and kept on joking with him in this manner as we smoked a joint. Finally he realized I was not trying to set him up to get busted but was offering him this opportunity for him to come up. I was getting half of what he brought in as well.

Sammy filled out the necessary paperwork to get John's girlfriend on his visiting list. His cell partner got transferred just a few days after our conversation so I moved right in the cell with Sammy. It was a few weeks before John and his girlfriend came to visit Sammy and I. My mother and other family members came to see me before John came. After we got confirmation that John's girlfriend was approved on Sammy's visiting list, I called John to let him know. John told me they would be there the following weekend and planned on getting a hotel room and seeing us both Saturday and Sunday. He planned on bringing us both two ounces a piece on Saturday and again two ounces a piece on Sunday. Eight ounces total in one weekend. That was a half pound of weed! Six of those eight ounces were for me!

I got off the phone with John and went back to the cell to tell Sammy the good news. When I told him what we would be doing this weekend his eyes got real big and for once he was quiet. He looked stunned. He just stared at me wide-eyed, saying nothing, his mind was processing what I had just said. For that brief moment he was lost for words. Really funny if you knew him. He was never lost for words. He had a comeback for everything. He talked loudly just to hear himself talk most of the time. "What's the matter, cat got your tongue?" I teased him. "Did you shit your pants?" I kept teasing him as I sniffed the air around him. "Dang, I think you did shit your pants. Do you need medical attention? You're looking a little pale. Aren't you the guy who told me a few months back how you wished you had someone to come visit you and bring you some weed? Now look at you. Just shit all over yourself and look like you're about to faint. I thought you were a real convict." I laughed and joked at his expense. He deserved every bit of it because he was a real asshole much of the time.

John and his girlfriend came to see us that weekend just as planned. I wasn't nervous at all about bringing the weed in because I had done it many times before. I was actually very happy and having a good time. Instead of having John or his girlfriend pass us anything John hid the four packages out on the patio in the flower bushes. They close the patio one hour before visiting was over and then opened it up again when visiting was over to send all the inmates out there to wait while they process the visitors out. I knew the routine well. John's girlfriend was just there to visit Sammy. She didn't have anything to do with anything else. Everything went well just like we planned. The only ones we had to be careful about were the other inmates out on the patio with us. Always somebody watching. We made it back to the unit with the four ounces. Sammy kept one, and I kept three. We went back the next day and did it again. It all went smoothly with no problems. I immediately sold 2 of the 6 ounces I had for $500 dollars a piece and had the money sent to John. The other four ounces were mine to do with whatever I wanted. I had a pretty good hiding spot out in the factory. I didn't work out there but paid a guy to hide it for me. I kept one ounce for my personal use on me most of the time. I kept it wrapped up in the black electrical tape and carried it in my crotch area. If I needed to,

I could keister it. When I went out to visit I kept my personal stash in a plastic chewing tobacco container. I dipped Copenhagen and always had 10-20 cans in my locker. I used an empty jalapeno can stuffed full of toilet paper as a spit can. I kept the plastic Copenhagen container in the spit can underneath the toilet paper. I spit tobacco on the top of the toilet paper. It looked very disgusting. During a cell search the guards would never attempt to look underneath the tobacco spit covered toilet paper in the can. At the very worst they would throw it away. This never happened though.

Three Rivers changed significantly while I was there. Someone from a different, lower security FCI called in to a popular, nationally syndicated radio talk show and exaggerated about how good prison life was in the feds. The talk show host was outraged to discover how nice some federal prisons were and made it the topic of conversation for weeks. He coined the phrase "club fed" and had everyone believing that the federal prison system was like a country club. His listeners were also outraged and called their elected officials in protest. This quickly led to sweeping changes throughout the federal prison system. Many of the privileges we once had were slowly taken away. The concession stand out on the recreation yard was the first to go. No more baby back ribs, chopped beef sandwiches or ice cream. That also meant no more meal tickets, which was a convenient form of currency. They also did away with the change used for the vending machines.

I was spending more and more time at the cash poker game out on the recreation yard but all the cash eventually dried up. The only form of currency used now were stamps. The poker game turned into a week to week credit game. They took away all the boxing training equipment. They stopped replacing damaged weight lifting equipment and were letting the weights go through attrition. When anything broke they took it away, never to be replaced. During this time, a big fight broke out on the recreation yard between a bunch of Mexicans. The fight spilled into the weight pile area where the Mexicans started grabbing anything they could to use as a weapon. One guy got killed with a weight bar. All the Mexicans involved in the fight were illegals straight out of Mexico. (Paisas) Most of them were doing a light sentence under five years. None of them cared about lifting weights. This murder on the weight pile caused that part of the recreation yard to be closed for several months. When it reopened, much of the equipment was gone. All the dumbbells were gone, and the remaining equipment was welded in its spot. All of the weight bars had cables welded to them so they couldn't be carried off. The Mexicans who caused everyone else to lose the weights had all been transferred.

This is how it always went in prison. Whenever something major happens, everyone is punished for it. Lifting weights had become one of my favorite things to do. Working out in general makes anyone who does it feel great. Slowly but surely they took away most of all the perks that made Three Rivers such a good place to do time. I was there for two years, and most of that time, I had lots of weed. I lost my visiting privileges two times while I was there. Once my cell got searched, and they found some marijuana seeds and residue on the floor. That cost me 60 days in the hole, loss of good time and 3 months loss of visitation.

The second time I got a dirty U.A. (Urine Analyses), which cost me another 60 days in the hole, more good time loss, and 6 months loss of visitation. I was also placed in the hole two times under investigation. The first time I was under investigation for assault. A loud mouth guy in my unit named Vincent, or "Vinny," who I didn't like, kept disrespectfully saying my name. I told him to stop, but he kept on and on. I called him to come in the T.V. room and hit him four times in his fat stomach very hard. Left, Right, Left, Right. Hard punches, like I was hitting the heavy bag. Vinny crumbled down in the fetal position gasping for air. I bent down close to his face and told him "If you tell the cops on me for this, the next time, I'll bash your head in." Then I walked out of the T.V. room, back up to my cell, and stood by the rail watching. Only a few guys witnessed it, but word got around fast. The next day we were both in the hole under investigation. Vinny didn't tell, and we both acted like there was no problem between us, so they eventually let us out of the hole. The next time I was under investigation for "possible assault." I did nothing to earn this one but apparently the lieutenant can have you locked up under investigation for any reason at any time and it doesn't matter if there is any merit to the allegations. Each time the captain kept me there for 30+ days before letting me out without taking any privileges. I had a really good reputation while I was at Three Rivers. I was a man of my word. I did many financial transactions and never screwed anyone around. I treated everyone with respect and everyone respected me. I was a "convict." Not to be confused with an "inmate." The difference between the two was how you do your time. An inmate is just someone who is incarcerated. Could be a rat or a cho-mo or a rape-o. Inmates mostly abide by whatever the rules are. If disrespected, they will let it slide because they don't want to get in trouble.

Most of the time, an inmate is just passing through prison, whereas, with a convict, prison is his home. Inmates laugh and joke around with the guards. Inmates play grab ass games. Inmates are generally less serious about how they carry themselves. Inmates are not respected. A convict lives by a different code. Convicts don't joke around with the guards or play grab ass. Convicts don't talk to the guards or help them in any way. To a convict, your word and reputation means everything. If disrespected, a convict will handle his business. There is a big difference between the two. Anyone who says there is no difference between convicts and inmates has no idea what they are talking about. I earned the title convict and wore it as a badge of honor. My identity and self-worth was caught up in living by the convict code. I was doing a non parolable 30 year sentence for cocaine possession. I could have cooperated and received a much lighter sentence but I didn't. Before I had even started my sentence, I had proven that I lived by the rules of the convict code. My reputation was solid. I was considered a standup dude. I stayed to myself and worked out every day. My word and reputation meant everything to me. Looking back now I can see how my ego was inflated. I saw myself as more of a convict than anyone else in Three Rivers at that time. After only two years I was getting bored with it and ready for a change.

USP Beaumont

I left three rivers for USP Beaumont in 1997. The BOP had just built a huge Federal Prison complex in Beaumont, TX that included multiple prisons that varied in security levels from lowest to highest. I wanted to go to Beaumont to be closer to my family and friends who lived in Houston. Unfortunately, the same security FCI, like the one I was in, was not open yet. The United States Penitentiary (USP) in Beaumont was my only option at the time because it opened before the medium security FCI. The Medium was scheduled to open one year after the higher security USP. My case manager at Three Rivers was looking for volunteers to transfer to USP Beaumont as it was just opening. At first it seemed like a stupid thing to do. Why would you volunteer to transfer to a USP from an FCI? Only a crazy fool would choose to do something like that. The difference between a USP and a FCI is like college football vs. professional. The boy scouts vs. Marine corps. It's like swimming in shark-infested waters while bleeding vs. swimming in a backyard swimming pool. The difference between the two security levels can't be understated. You have to be on your toes anywhere in prison, especially in a USP. The USP's are the highest security level prisons in the federal system. In a USP, you will find the worst, most violent prisoners in all the United States. I could have waited another year at Three Rivers for the FCI to open but going now meant being closer to family and friends. It also meant I could get visits every week! My case manager at Three Rivers was making it sound like a good idea to go there, which added to my distrust. At first I said I will pass on volunteering to go but then we started to get word back from some guys who went there a month earlier on the first bus.

They said they had the whole prison to themselves. It had been open for only three months, and less than 100 inmates were in the yard. The plan was only to bring in one bus, about 40 guys, every three months. All of the first guys to arrive had at least one year clear conduct without any write-ups. These were hand-picked guys who they felt would not cause any trouble. Most came from other USP'S but they were the super low key inmates that stayed to themselves. We were told the food was great and everything was new. No lines for anything because there were so few people there. We were informed everyone there was super relaxed with no drama. They said as soon as the FCI opened next door, they were going to transfer all the guys who came from the lower security FCIs. This would happen before filling up the USP with the crazies. After hearing how it was at Beaumont, many of us were now changing our minds about transferring there. My celly at Three Rivers, Sammy, was wanting to go too. The more we talked about it the better the idea of going there sounded. Most importantly, visits! That was my main motivation. Visits. I had become really good at smuggling packages through the visiting room. When it came to smuggling in dope through the visiting room, nobody was better than me. I knew instinctively when, where and how to do it. I had multiple people who were willing to bring me packages of weed. I had done it too many times to count and no doubt I will be bringing it in at USP Beaumont too. Being closer to home made visiting friends and family much easier. I'll get visits all the time in Beaumont. Our case manager went around like a salesman trying to sell guys on transferring to USP Beaumont. Both me and my celly, Sammy signed up at the same time for transfer and two weeks later we were on a bus leaving Three Rivers. I was carrying about ½ ounce of weed, papers, matches and a striker.

When we got to the OKC Transit unit, Sammy and I were separated. He went to one floor, and I went to another. That meant he would not be smoking with me in the transit unit. The disappointment showed on his face as we parted ways. It was very late at night by the time I got to a cell with a bed and a toilet. I had been holding this package of weed all day traveling and couldn't wait to get it out. Everyone in the unit was locked in their cells asleep when I came in. The cell they locked me in was empty so as soon as the guard left the unit I put some paper in the toilet and pushed the package out. After retrieving it from the toilet I started washing it off in the sink and flushed the toilet. The toilet flushed with a loud high pressure flushing sound that echoed throughout the unit. It would not stop running and the water was coming so fast it was overflowing out of the toilet. Soon the cell was flooded, and the water was rushing out into the unit. I cleaned the package and hid it on myself. I had to beat on the door waking everyone up to get the cops attention. Finally he came and turned the water off and gave me a mop to clean all the water out of the unit. I kept a really good attitude with the CO because I had all this weed on me. When I finished, about 45 minutes later, the CO put me in the handicap cell. That is the best cell in the unit. Twice the size of a regular cell with adjustable bed and its own shower with a hand held shower wand. Not only did I have that cell to myself but I had weed with me as well. Sometimes it pays to keep a good attitude. The days there were spent reading, playing cards, chess, or watching TV. Just waiting for them to call my name to be transferred to the next place. My time there went by very well because I stayed stoned every day and had a great cell. After spending a couple of weeks there, my name was called to leave. From there, I was herded into that final holding tank before getting on the bus that would take us to USP Beaumont. There were around 40 of us in that cell and all of us were going to USP Beaumont. Kinda hard to explain, but when you are on the same bus with someone going to the same prison for the first time there is an unspoken bond between you. I knew many of the guys on the bus from either Three Rivers, El Reno or Leavenworth. Mostly guys from Texas, and the majority of us were white. Being in the majority group for the first time in my prison sentence felt good. Looking around at each other, the apprehension had gone, and the feeling was replaced with confidence. We all talked and got to know each other better. How long have you been down? What prison are you coming from? What are you doing time for? How much time do you have? Who do you know? What's going on in other prisons? Race wars, gang wars etc... We talked all day, and the general consensus was we were going to stick together at USP Beaumont. As we rode the bus from OKC to Beaumont, we were handcuffed, black boxed with belly and leg chains.

Pulling up to USP Beaumont and seeing it from the outside, you could tell right away that nobody was going to escape from this place. A 30 foot wall surrounds the prison that no prisoner will ever be on the other side of. If you were to find yourself on the other side of the wall, there is a double fence around the perimeter stacked to the top with razor wire and motion detectors. Armed guards patrol the outside perimeter in trucks. There are seven gun towers positioned around the yard and one in the Middle of the yard.

Processing into the prison was quick. They were fully staffed with guards and very few inmates. I was the #257th inmate to arrive. We finished getting processed, fingerprinted and photographed, then we were all issued a brand new prison mattress, sheets, pillow, and blanket. Everyone who came in together on that bus was escorted across the yard for the first time to our unit. When you come out of R & D you are literally on the yard. When you come out of anywhere to go anywhere else in that prison you are on the yard. The significance of this arrangement was mind-blowing to us. As we looked around shaking our heads in disbelief, it was obvious to us that this place would be a bloodbath. The entire prison population had immediate access to one another. Normally, the movement is much more restricted in a lower security prison. Units are typically separated and off-limits. If it is not your assigned unit you are not allowed to be near it. Here when you come out of your unit, you are on the yard. Someone on the yard can communicate with anyone in any unit. Each cell has a window that you can look out of and many face the yard. There are (4) four story buildings that contain four separate housing units in each building. The gun tower, (tower 8), sits in the middle and looks like an air traffic control tower. Obviously their plan was to let everybody out together and control them by threat of being shot.

We were shaking our heads looking at this crazy set up as we walked to the unit. When we got to the unit we were the first inmates to walk in that unit. They told us we could all pick whatever cell we wanted. All of us white guys from Texas took the most strategic cells on the 2nd tier furthest away from the stairs. We had a row of cells next to each other with a TV room on the corner. Everyone had their own single-man cell. There were four TV rooms in the unit, and we all agreed on what TV rooms would be White, Black and Mexican. Remember, out of the 40 of us on that bus who were now in the unit about 30 of us were white. This was a very unique and highly unusual situation. They would not be bringing another bus of inmates for three months and the next bus to come was not going into our unit. The whole prison population was only around 300 for the first 3-6 months I was there. We had first dibs on all the good hiding spots to make wine and hide weapons. A couple of guys in our crew got the building maintenance jobs and had access to tools. They would come into our unit as much as possible to "fix" things like broken sinks, toilets, etc.

During this time we had access to hundreds of knives. This was because the prison was brand new, and a lot of new construction had just taken place and we were the first to arrive. Steel was everywhere. We had bags of thick steel blank pieces that were plumbing straps. Once you bang them out straight and file down the edges they are lethal weapons. One of the homeboys from Texas brought a power grinder in the unit, supposedly to repair a pipe. He was the "plumber" and did all the pipe repair around the prison. The plumber was grinding out knives for us while it looked like he was doing his job. Otherwise, it would take hours to sharpen by rubbing the edges on the concrete. We had bags full of thick welding rods that easily sharpened into a point. All the groundwork tools like rakes and wheelbarrows were often left unattended so we disassembled those and used the steel pieces for knives. We had knives stashed everywhere. Buried out on the yard in multiple spots. In the ceilings of the TV rooms. Built into sinks and toilets in multiple cells. USP Beaumont was wide open in the beginning. We knew it was just a matter of time before this place filled up with many of the most violent and dangerous criminals in the Federal Prison system. Racial and gang wars were actively happening all over the prison system. DC Blacks and the Aryan Brotherhood were at war. The Texas Syndicate was at war with the California Mexican Mafia. California crips were at war with DC blacks. The prison staff would often tell us about the plan to fill the prison with the most violent and dangerous guys in the system. We were some of the first to get there and were preparing for the others to come like we were preparing for war.

Beaumont is only about 90 miles from Houston, making it easier for friends and family to visit me. My friend John was one of the first to come to visit me with his girlfriend. John's girlfriend was removed from Sammy's visiting list because she was not allowed to be on two different prisoners visiting list at Beaumont. The only reason she was on Sammy's list at Three Rivers was just to get Sammy out in the visiting room at the same time I was. Beaumont would not approve of her. I had not seen John in awhile because I had lost my visiting privileges at Three Rivers. I noticed his demeanor had changed. He had started using Heroin and was messed up when he came to visit me. Slurring his words and stumbling around the visiting room it appeared as though he was drunk. He was really out of it. One of the guards noticed his behavior and asked me if John had been drinking. I told him no, that John had been working long hours and had not slept much. The guard was convinced John was drunk and made him take a breathalyzer test. They would terminate my visit if he had been drinking and possibly not allow John to come back.

John passed the breathalyzer test but not without bringing major attention to both of us. The first two times I went out to the visiting room, I paid attention to everything and looked for vulnerabilities in the security. There were five cameras all positioned on the ceiling. The cameras were inside a tinted bulb to hide the direction it was pointing. There was an outside patio with nothing on it. No chairs, no tables, not anything. It was just a cement floor surrounded by walls. Big clear windows separated the patio from the visiting room. When the sunlight came in through the windows from the patio, I could see the little slit in the tinted bulb covering the camera lens. This allowed me to see where the cameras were pointed. Towards the back wall, in the center of the visiting room, was the guards desk. It was a large, counter-like podium that stood about four feet tall and was shaped in a half circle. Two of the seats were elevated giving the guards a better view of the visiting room. Below the counter were the camera monitor screens and controls. They could rotate the cameras and zoom in on whatever they wanted. The cameras were state-of-the-art hi-definition cameras that could zoom in and see the pores of your skin with clarity. If the cameras were on you and you tried to do something, you would get busted. They also recorded, so just because the guard was not behind the counter watching the monitors, they could always go back and rewind the recording to see what you did while they were gone. Knowing where the guards are and what they're doing is good, but the trick to beating them was knowing where the cameras are pointing. I got really good at recognizing where that little lens on each camera was pointing. I could tell when the camera moved. If I couldn't tell 100% where it was pointing, I would assume it was pointing at me. The cameras could also be monitored and controlled remotely. The lieutenant could be watching and moving the cameras from his office. I paid close attention to everything. When I was out there, I knew how many guards were working visitation and where they were at all times.

Even when they were not in the visiting room, I knew where they were. Whenever I walked up to their desk to ask a question, I observed their moves. They liked to hide behind the counter when watching the camera monitors. When I walked up they would try and conceal the monitors so I wouldn't see what they were looking at. They had to let prisoners and visitors in and out of the visiting room as needed and I knew when there was no guard monitoring the cameras. This only meant the cameras would be stationary while the guard was gone. It was still recording, so I would never do anything while the camera pointed at me. There were several moves I would make depending on the circumstances. One move was right when I first walked into the visiting room. I would greet my visitor directly in front of the guards podium. I already knew where the package would be concealed on my visitor. As soon as I hugged them I would grab the package. Directly in front of the guards podium. The podium itself was my cover. The guards don't have the cameras on me yet because I have not yet sat down. They would never have a camera pointed at themselves. I've done that move a few times. Grab it and drop it down my pants in one fluid motion. Once I have it on me I just wait for the right time to keister it. That would either be when I go to the toilet or wait until the end of the visit.

My most common move was grabbing the package while we were taking pictures. You are allowed to purchase photo tickets from the commissary to take pictures either on the yard with other prisoners or in the visiting room with your visitors. The guy with the camera taking the pictures is a prisoner. We would stand with our backs against the wall and hug while the picture was taken. My visitor would have the package in a back or side pocket behind them. I placed my arm behind them and grabbed it. Many times I would keister it right then and there. The more people in the photo who would stand in front of me, the better. Another one was to wait until the visit was over and pick the package up where my visitor left it. Sometimes it would be on a chair in a chip bag, under the chip bag, or in the trash itself. When visiting is over they always separate the prisoners from the visitors. Prisoners are to be seated on the far side of the visiting room while the visitors are being escorted out in small groups. We are asked to discard any remaining chips, sodas, or sandwiches. Much trash is left over after the visit so a couple of guys walk around with the trash bag from the trash can, picking up trash around the visiting room. The guards are no longer looking at the cameras at this time. Still I would go where the cameras are not pointing to make my move. I've done this countless times in Three Rivers and Beaumont. I've often had the package in my crotch area and waited until the end of the visit to keister it.

One such time was while I was at Three Rivers. I had the package in my crotch area, waiting for the guards to go in the other room and start strip searching so I could keister it. One of the guards called my name first to be stripped and searched. I still had the package in my crotch area. Normally, guys line up by the door to be searched and you go in order. This particular guard had previously worked my unit and thought he was doing me a favor by calling my name first so I wouldn't have to wait in line. My heart was beating fast, and I was really nervous that I was about to get busted. In the back the guards were searching us 3-5 at a time. I was in a small room undressing with the guard three feet in front me. As I got undressed I handed each piece of clothing to the guard to search as is the routine. First I handed him my shirt. My pants were loose and belt undone as he turned sideways to shake out my shirt. I reached in my pants as though to take them off and grabbed the package from the front crotch area and moved my hand to the back and pushed the package in. I was moving fast, getting undressed so he did not notice what I had done. I had just keistered an ounce right in front of the guard while he was strip-searching me. This boosted my confidence to another level. I knew what I could get away with and exploited it every chance I had. I got better every time I did it. It only took 1- 3 seconds to get the package from my visitor and drop it down my pants. Once I had it on me, it was as good as having it in the unit. I've smuggled packages into multiple prisons hundreds of times and never got caught.

Another time worth noting, and also the one I am most proud of is when I smuggled a package of bugler tobacco from visitation to the hole. I consider it one of the best smuggling moves I've ever done in prison. Afterwards the guards started calling me "Harry Houdini." I was in the hole at Beaumont. The "hole," as we call it, is officially referred to as the "SHU" or Special Housing Unit. This is the jail inside the prison, where they put you for disciplinary reasons. It is the most secure part of the prison. Prisoners are locked up in a tiny cell for 23 hours daily. I was lucky enough to receive a visit while in the hole. I was handcuffed and shackled with leg irons, then escorted by two guards to a locked visiting booth. A glass partition separated me from my visitor. A telephone is on each side for us to use to talk. After visiting for a while I needed to pee so I asked my visitor to go and let the guard know I needed to pee. The guard came and unlocked the visiting booth, and led me to the toilet. I was still in handcuffs and ankle cuffs so I shuffled over to the toilet, unbuttoned my orange jumpsuit and started to pee as I stood over the toilet. As I stood there peeing, I noticed someone had left a package of bugler tobacco sitting on the counter near the toilet. I immediately grabbed it and dropped it down into my jumpsuit while the guard was looking the other way. The ankle cuffs I was wearing prevented it from falling out. After I finished peeing, I flushed the toilet, washed my hands, and shuffled back to the visiting booth while being escorted by the guard. After the guard locked me in the booth I reached down and pulled out the package of bugler to show my visitor what I had found during my trip to the toilet. We both laughed. I was wearing socks and the orange slide-on shoes they issued me in the hole. I took off one shoe, slid the sock down, and placed the bugler pack underneath my barefoot. Then I put the sock back on and then the shoe. All the while having ankle cuffs on. I stood up to stand on the package and squash it down as best as possible trying to mold it to fit underneath my foot better. "How does this look?" I asked my visitor as I stood up. "Aren't they going to strip-search you?" She asked. "No, they just bring me straight back to my cell." "They never strip search me going back because I don't come into contact with anyone."

Less than 20 minutes went by and three of the guards came and took me out of the visiting booth looking for the bugler package. They patted me down and searched the visiting booth I was in. They kept asking me where the bugler was and what had I done with it. I found the whole scenario extremely entertaining. The more they insisted they knew I took it the more I laughed and told them they were crazy. I didn't even smoke tobacco at the time. They explained to me that the guy who's bugler it was is the only one in the visitation room. It had to be me because no one else went back there. I continued to deny it, and they searched every possible hiding spot back there. I wasn't worried because even if they find it on me, all they will do is take it. It's just tobacco, not dope. My visiting time ended, and it was time to go back to the hole. The guards were convinced I had taken the bugler package and told me they were going to strip search me when we got back to the hole. I told them they were queers and wanted to see my big balls. I don't even smoke, I told them. They radioed ahead to the guards working in the hole and told them they were bringing me back and needed to strip search me before putting me back in my cell because they thought I had tobacco on me. I heard the guard reply "ok," "if he's got anything on him, we will get it." As soon as I entered the SHU, the guard working the front asked me "Do you have anything on you?" to which I replied, "just these big ole nuts that these two queers seem to want to take a look at."

I was laughing at them and thoroughly enjoying the moment. They took my handcuffs and ankle cuffs off and told me to strip. I was standing in a small room facing the three of them. I started unbuttoning my jumpsuit and simultaneously kicked off my shoes in the direction of the guards. One of the guards picked up my shoes and bent them back and forth, examining them thoroughly. I let my jumpsuit fall around my ankles and at the same time, took my right foot and stepped on the sock holding the bugler package underneath my left foot. I pinned it down with my right big toe as I slid my left foot out of the sock, leaving the bugler package inside my sock underneath the jumpsuit. I slid off the other sock and then quickly stepped out of my boxers, leaving them next to the jumpsuit, and took one step back, completely naked. I continued verbally antagonizing the guards the whole time I was undressing, and now I stood before them completely naked, joking and smiling. They all stood there in stunned disbelief that I did not have the bugler tobacco package on me. I continued to laugh and make jokes that they just wanted to see my big balls. One of the guards picked up my jumpsuit and felt through it satisfied there was nothing hidden. They shook their heads in disbelief and told me to get dressed. Now I had to put the sock back on that had the package of bugler in it. I got lucky that my foot slid in the sock correctly with the package remaining on the bottom side. I got dressed quickly. After I dressed they put the handcuffs back on me and escorted me back to my cell. They knew I had beaten them; instead of being mad, they were genuinely impressed. This is how I got the nickname "Harry Houdini." I took pride in getting over on the "CO's." It was their job to catch me, and it was my job to get away with as much as I could. The next week I got another visit, and the same guards escorted me to and from the visiting room booth. They were pleading with me to tell them how I did it. "Can't tell you that," I said. "It's your job to catch me and my job to beat you. You guys are amateurs, not even in my league." They wanted to bust me after that but never could catch me.

It all started with my friend John bringing me those balloons of weed in El Reno, Oklahoma. Sadly, my friend John died of an overdose just a few months after I arrived at Beaumont. I was told he overdosed on methadone, trying to come off of the heroin. He was a good guy and a very good friend.

A year went by and I spent my time working out, playing poker, making and selling wine and occasionally bringing in weed through visitation. I got along with everyone and knew who most guys on the yard were. As new white guys would come in it was customary to brief them on the lay of the prison, find out where they are from, and try and get them shower shoes and hygiene items etc... until they made commissary or their property arrived. If a guy was from Boston, NY, California, etc., you would introduce him to one of his "home boys" from that state. It took about a year and half to fill the prison to capacity. Once the place was full, things started to change. My reputation and status in the prison was very good. I was known and respected by all the real shot callers on the yard. The poker game I had started in the unit eventually moved out to the yard. I was "the house" so I provided the cards, kept the books, and collected the money. I cut the pot 5% a hand so at the end of the month or week or however long we played, everyone would end up paying me. Sometimes one or two other guys would get lucky and win, but the house always wins.

The first murder at USP Beaumont happened right outside my unit. Jeff Moore killed Scot Miller. Scot was a 40 or so year old white guy from Louisiana who lived in my unit. He liked to drink wine and play poker and do a little heroin whenever he could afford to do so. Scot Was a likable guy. He played in my unit poker game and got wine from me so I knew Scot well and knew his financial situation. His mother would send him $100 dollars a month when she could. She loved Scot and apparently she was all he had. Scot always paid me what he owed. It may take him two months sometimes but he always pays. Scot had gotten himself in debt with another white guy in a different unit named Jeff Moore. Jeff was selling papers of heroin for an Egyptian guy that lived in his unit. Scot owed Jeff $100 dollars in commissary for the heroin he got on credit from Jeff. He was supposed to pay Jeff the week before but no money had shown up yet in his account. When they let our unit out for commissary, Jeff was outside waiting with a commissary bag to collect his stuff. Scot came out of commissary with an empty bag and yet another excuse as to why he couldn't pay. He felt ashamed and embarrassed that he couldn't pay and was under a lot of pressure when he approached Jeff to tell him it would be another week.

Scot did not respond well to Jeff's outrage, and they ended up getting into a shouting match, with Scot telling Jeff "fuck you! I'll kick your ass." I was standing about 5 ft from them when this took place. Jeff walks off back to his unit and says, "we will see." I tried to talk to Scot right then, but he was too mad to listen so we both walked back to our unit. As I was putting my commissary away in my cell, a couple of guys who saw the commotion came in and asked me what had happened. I told them what Scot said and that somebody should talk to them both and try to defuse the situation. After putting my stuff away, I went to Scot's cell to talk to him. Some other guys had already been talking to him, and he was still pissed. He said he had every intention of paying but just did not have the money yet. I told him he was wrong for talking to Jeff like that. Now he feels obligated to do something to you. He kept saying he was not scared of Jeff, "Fuck him, I'll kick his ass if he wants to go." he said, "I told him I would pay him, and he will get it when I get it." Scot was being hard headed and refused to apologize to Jeff. Later I heard back from guys who talked to Jeff that Jeff was going to wait until he collected what was owed to him before moving on Scot. Jeff wanted to pay the Egyptian guy what he owed him first. I knew the more time that went by without him doing something to Scot, the more he would be under pressure to do so for his reputation's sake.

Nothing happened that day or the next. I spoke with Scot a couple of more times about apologizing to Jeff but he remained hard headed. So after Jeff had finished collecting what he was owed he came for Scot. Jeff was with a self proclaimed "tough guy" named "country" from his unit when they came to my unit and called for me and another guy to come out. We four walked the yard, and I listened as Jeff and "country" told us he was going to get Scot when he came back from eating. They were letting us know as a matter of respect so we would not be around the unit when it happened. Jeff showed us the knife he was carrying around in a waist trimmer under his sweats. It was not a small knife but a knife that was considered a "bone crusher." It was a serious weapon. Looking at it my heart sank for Scot. He was in serious trouble. Jeff could have kicked Scot's ass one-on-one but didn't want to go that route. He had been convinced by those "tough guys" in his unit that this was the most honorable way to handle it. I thought Jeff would just ambush him and kick his ass, but instead he was given one of the most lethal knives you will ever see in a USP. The realization of what was about to happen had me questioning everything I thought about right and wrong and this BS prison convict code.

When the yard closed for count, they went back to their unit and we went back to ours. I wanted to tell Scot but couldn't. If I did at this point, I would be a target for betraying Jeff. Me and Jimbo talked in the unit and I was angry that Jeff had that knife. The guy who's knife it belonged to was in the hole and tough guy "country" gave it to Jeff to hit Scot. Couple of our homeboys saw me and Jimbo talking and asked us what's up? We told them Jeff was about to move on Scot, and Scot was in trouble. We locked down for count then after count they started calling units to go eat. Our unit was first out to go eat. I saw Scot in the chow hall as I was leaving and felt terrible that I could not warn him. I just hoped at this point that he would get away and survive. Jimbo and I didn't go back to our unit after chow but instead went to the handball courts on the other side of the yard and sat at a table. We only sat there for about ten minutes before the deuces went off. There was a C.O. near us with a radio so we could hear the panicked C.O. on the other end calling for backup. He was shouting over the radio that an inmate was stabbing another inmate. We stayed where we were as the C.O. ran towards our unit. Some cops ran across the yard with a stretcher to get Scot and then ran back to medical carrying him in a stretcher. As we were watching from across the yard, they started yelling lockdown over the loudspeaker. We walked back to our unit, crossing paths with guys who just saw what happened, going back to theirs. You could see the high adrenaline and panic on a lot of guys' faces. A couple of guys we passed told us "Scot is dead. No way he made it. Jeff butchered the shit out of him." Scot wore loose-fitting pants that slid down as he was trying to get away and it tripped him up. Jeff was all over him as the CO's just stood back and yelled at Jeff to drop the knife. I didn't see it but talked to just about every single person that did. It traumatized more than a few guys in our unit pretty bad. They walked around stunned with blank stares on their faces for weeks. These were guys who knew Scot. Lived in the same unit and spoke with him daily. They had watched him get killed. Some of the CO's quit because they were traumatized by witnessing the murder. Many were not psychologically prepared for what they witnessed. The entire prison was on lockdown while they did an investigation.

On the second day of lockdown, after Scot was killed, each of us was pulled out and interviewed one at a time and asked the standard BOP incident investigation questions. "Do you know anything?" "Would you tell us if you did?" Etc... This was the standard procedure with the same questions they ask everyone after any major assault or murder occurs. Everyone knows what you are supposed to say in such interviews. *"I don't know anything and I would not tell you if I did."* Period. Nothing else. That was the convict code, and that is exactly what I told them. A few days later, the FBI came and interviewed everyone one at a time with more questions. I gave them the same answers. "Don't know anything and wouldn't tell you if I did." About a week later the FBI had some additional questions for me concerning Scot owing me money in the poker game. Apparently he got on the phone and told his mother to send money to my account several months back. I only answered questions that pertained to myself and my interactions with Scot. I would not answer any other questions.

A few months after Scot got killed, Jeff was still over in the SHU unit, or hole, as we called it. Jeff's lawyer, who was defending him for murdering Scot, was able to get copies of all the statements taken during the private interviews with the prison staff. He gave those copies to Jeff, who sent them out to the yard with someone getting out of the SHU. The copies were delivered to the unofficial shot caller on the yard at that time, who was also my cell partner. He and I met with three

DWB (dirty white boys) gang members on the yard and read the copies. Very incriminating documents that exposed many who were still on the yard who cooperated and gave information during the interviews. It was surprising to see a few names on the list, who were generally thought of as convicts, who would never say anything to the cops. It was a 5-page list of names with their statements. Some were really bad, and others were just guys saying more than they should have, but not anything incriminating. We had the paperwork that proved these guys snitched, so now we were obligated to do something to them. There were blacks, whites and Mexicans from almost all the units who gave statements. We marked out all the white guys who told, it would be our responsibility to take care of them. The list of blacks went to a black shot caller and the list of Mexicans went to a Mexican shot caller. The plan was to move on all these guys who told at the same time in every unit. That night at 7pm, we did just that. Around 15-20 guys were assaulted simultaneously in multiple units. Four guys got beat up in my unit but no weapons were used. My unit was the first to start the planned, simultaneous assaults.

We were also the first unit for the "dueces," or the emergency signal, to go off for all available staff to respond to our unit. They entered our unit and broke up the visible altercation going on in the middle of the unit. Another victim was found coming out of the TV room, bloodied with torn clothing. They had not yet realized that 2 others lay unconscious in their cells. They yelled for everyone to lockdown in their cells. As they were locking everyone in their cells, the emergency "deuces" went off again. This time, the call came over the guards' radios to respond to another assault taking place in a different unit. Now that everyone was locked in their cells, we could see the guards running from one unit to another trying to stop the multiple assaults that were taking place. The other units got ugly as some drunk maniacs went wild and took things too far. Nobody got killed, but a few got worse than they deserved. They didn't find the two others who got beat up in our unit until the next day when they were pulling each of us out one by one to check our hands and bodies for any marks or signs of injury. We stayed locked down in our cells for a month over that. The CO's found copies of the list within a week after conducting cell searches and everyone on the list was transferred.

Most of the guys with lower security levels, who came in the beginning, had long since been transferred. I couldn't go three months without getting a write up so I could not get transferred. The prison became increasingly more violent as time went on. Just as promised, they had turned USP Beaumont into a disciplinary destination, sending many of the most problematic troublemakers from other prisons to Beaumont. By the 3rd year, USP Beaumont had become the most violent prison in the United States. There were more assaults and murders there between 97-2000 than any other prison in the United States. I know of three murders that were ruled as a drug overdose, and no one was even investigated. That's three times someone was murdered that I personally know about and nothing happened to the guys who committed the murders. The victims were each given a "hotshot" of heroin to purposefully take them out. A "hotshot" is a shot of heroin that was made to be too strong. The victim who shoots it up doesn't realize how much he is doing. Once he goes out, they will shoot him up again with more heroin just to make sure he never wakes up. When the guards find him dead, they have an autopsy performed and rule the cause of death as an overdose. Many guys were leaving the yard in stretchers and body bags. It got super intense and life was cheap. Mentally ill, seriously dangerous killers, who do not reason or show empathy, were all over the place like time bombs walking around you.

Walking back to my unit from the chow hall one day I passed three black dudes all wearing winter coats. I thought it strange that all three were wearing coats because it was warm outside. Two of the guys were confronting the one. As I walked past them, I could hear the one telling the other two, "I ain't no punk and you ain't going to talk to me like some kind of bitch ass MFR!" He was raising his voice loudly to the other two. All three of these guys lived in a different unit than mine. I kept walking past them and entered my unit. When I got inside, I noticed that we had a brand new, really nice microwave. It was a big Panasonic and was way better than any microwave we've had in the past. I stopped at the center desk to check it out. "Damn, this is nice!" I said to myself. A couple of others in the unit were calling out to me in agreement, "yeh we scored!" "Nice microwave!" As I walked away from the microwave and continued walking to my cell the three black guys I had just walked past outside the unit came running in. Two were chasing the one. The guy being chased grabbed the microwave and threw it at the two guys chasing him. It didn't even come close to hitting them but just smashed all over the floor. The guy that threw the microwave continued to run frantically around the unit, trying to get away from the other two. As the two closed in on the guy running, he ran inside a random cell. The two guys ran in the cell after him and started stabbing him. I couldn't see what was going on but I could hear it.

The guards came running in the unit, yelling "Lock Down!" "Lock Down!" as the two assailants exited the cell and walked toward the door of the unit. The CO's were continuing to run in and the guy who had just been stabbed by the other two, came out of the cell with a knife in his hand, wearing a blood-soaked t-shirt. The guards immediately focused on him and yelled for him to drop the knife. As all the focus was now on the bloodied guy with the knife, the two guys who stabbed him walked right out of the unit. The guy stood there dripping blood, refusing to drop the knife, while the guards yelled at him to drop it and lay down for about two minutes. Finally he laid face down on the concrete and dropped the knife. The guards handcuffed him and let him lay there for close to 10 minutes. Looking out of our cell windows we watched him die. A pool of blood formed around him as he lay there face down, handcuffed behind his back. Everyone in the unit could see the guy was dying. We were yelling at the cops through the doors to get him to medical. Don't just leave him there on the floor to die like a dog. Everyone was cursing the guards for not trying to help the guy. I doubt he would have made it but the guards showed no effort in trying to help him. Finally they put the guy's lifeless body in a stretcher and carried him out of the unit. The two guys who killed him were later caught and one was given the death penalty for the murder. I later found out it was over a gambling debt. The guy who got killed owed money to one of the guys who killed him.

I had been in and out of the hole for various infractions like dirty UA, possession of a knife, possession of weed and under investigation numerous times. Out of the four years I was in USP Beaumont, almost a year of that was spent in the hole. Each time I got out of the hole there were lots of new faces on the yard. People were coming and going at a fast pace and it was hard to keep up with all of the new guys. Many mentally ill guys were being put in Beaumont.

My unit was full of guys that should have been in a mental institution. One such guy was a white guy named "Shithead Bob." Bob wasn't around very long. He was a big, likable, funny guy in his mid 50s that seemed harmless. He was obviously crazy as crazy can be though. Everyone thought it was funny to joke and play around with Bob. Some guys took advantage of him for their own entertainment. Once, a couple of guys in my unit were playing around with Bob when they laid out a line of cleaning powder and told Bob it was cocaine. "You want to do some cocaine?" They asked Bob. "Hell yeah," he said. It was laid out on top of the guy's locker in his cell and Bob snorted it all. He was shouting "woohoo!" "That stuff is strong!" "Damn that's good shit!" Guys were laughing and thinking it was funny to play those kinds of tricks on Bob but I thought it was messed up. There was a reason everyone called him "Shithead Bob." When Bob first arrived at Beaumont he was in the hole before going out into the general population. I was in the same range as Bob in the hole. He was very funny and kept everyone entertained with the crazy things he would say. He had a very loud voice so everyone on the range could hear him whenever he talked. While he was in the hole, he decided to pack his own shit down on his head. He would shit in his hand, smear it on the walls and pack it down on his head. The guards would come by shaking their heads and tell us what he was doing, hoping someone would talk some sense into him. "BOB!" Someone shouted out through their cell door. "Did you put shit on your head?" Bob answered back, "Yeh!" "Fuck these mother fuckers!" Everyone was dying laughing.

The guards were hoping we would tell Bob to clean up and stop with the nonsense, but instead everyone yelled back, encouraging Bob. "That's right Bob!" "Fuck these Mother fuckers!" "You show'em Bob!" "That'll teach them!" "You get'em Bob!" "Stay strong Bob!" "You go hard Bob, fuck these mother fuckers!" It was so funny. Bob loved the attention he was getting and ended up covering himself in shit. What was even funnier, he was in the cell with another guy who had checked in. "Checking in" meant you voluntarily went to the hole for your own protection. The guy was quiet as a mouse while Bob smeared shit everywhere. Eventually they let Bob out into the general population. There were guys like Bob all over Beaumont. Bob only lasted a few months before they transferred him out of there. He should have never been sent to USP Beaumont.

My mother was coming to visit me often while I was at Beaumont. In one of our visits she told me that the daughter of her long time friend Betty had seen me on America's Most

Wanted and was asking how I was doing. She wanted to write to me if it was okay with me. I remembered Betty's daughter, Keli, from years past. She was a few years younger than me. I remember giving her a ride on my Harley-Davidson when she was around 16 or 17 years old. I told my mother of course it would be fine if she wrote to me. Having a female pen pal would be a good thing. Keli was living in Seattle, Washington working as a stripper at the time when we started writing to each other. She had a three-year-old son. The father of her son apparently was physically abusing her and beat her up a few times very badly. Her father was not going to tolerate anyone beating his daughter. He invited her husband on a fishing trip and killed him. Keli was now raising the young boy on her own up in Seattle. We started writing letters to each other back and forth for a couple of months, and I would call her on the phone now and then. She sent me pictures of herself that were impressive. Keli was very attractive with a gorgeous body. I had not been with a woman in years, so the pictures she sent me easily excited me.

After about two months of correspondence through letters and over the phone, she moved back to Texas and came to visit me. The rules in federal prison visitation are one kiss in the beginning and one kiss at the end. You were allowed to hold hands, but no other physical contact was allowed. We kissed very passionately that first day of visiting. I felt like a 15-year-old kid in love for the first time. Our relationship grew as time went by. She wrote me multiple letters everyday, and we spoke on the phone every day. Her young boy was also coming with her to visit me. After a while, he started calling me dad. He was the cutest little boy. Every time I walked into the visiting room to start our visit he would run up to me and shout daddy! It was a great feeling. The letters and telephone conversations we shared were very intense. I couldn't believe someone as good looking as Keli was showing this much interest in me. I'm sure when people saw us together in the visiting room they had to wonder why a beautiful woman like her was coming to see a convict like me. I felt like my old cell partner Terry from Three Rivers. Even though I had nearly 20 years left on my sentence, Keli insisted we get married. I knew it was a crazy thing to do but more for her than for me. I had nothing to lose. Our relationship consisted of letters, phone calls and visits. It was a temporary distraction from prison life. The relationship with Keli and my new son Jeremy had me thinking about the outside world more and more. It was nice getting letters and visits but also painful that I couldn't be out there with them. It was a trade off. It's not always a good idea for someone in prison with a lengthy sentence like mine to start a relationship with someone in the free world. You are constantly reminded of what you can't have and it's a big tease.

Many hours passed with me laying in my bunk, consumed with hate for Dale Henderson Walker, the guy who set me up to get busted by the DEA. It was him that stole my life away from me. He was the one responsible for this horrible mess I was in. He was the one responsible for keeping me from the chance of living a normal life. I lay in my bunk, remembering how I was home laying in my bed asleep when he called to set me up with selling cocaine to the DEA. What a piece of shit. I thought of different ways to torture him. I spent many hours thinking about hurting him badly. I've never hated someone so much as I hated him. I thought of all the methods of torture to use on him that I had read about in various books over the years. I didn't realize it at the time, but all of that hate I was carrying towards him was only damaging me. He felt nothing. I have since forgiven Dale and no longer hold on to hate towards him. Forgive that you may be forgiven.

Heroin was plentiful on the yard so guys were getting strung out and couldn't pay. The SHU or "Special housing unit" was packed with three, four and sometimes five guy's in a two man cell. Guys who couldn't pay their dope debts would check in the hole or do something stupid to go to the hole in order to get out of paying. Many would be attacked in the hole if they got in the wrong rec. cage with the wrong guys. That happened just about every day. We called those rec. cages the "Thunderdome" because it was like going into a fighting arena.

You never knew if you were going to be a spectator or a participant. Somebody could be put in the rec. cage with you that you have no problem with but someone in a different rec. cage does. So maybe someone I know who's out there in a different rec cage tells me "Hey, you see that guy? he checked in owing me money or he snitched on something. Do me a favor and kick his ass." Some guys don't even have to say all that verbally; they could just give the sign and you know what you're supposed to do. Now I am obligated to kick the guy's ass. If the guy is a tough guy, and many were, then multiple guys will kick his ass. The same is also true if I see a guy in a different rec. cage that checked in owing me money. This is what separates what we call real MFR's or "convicts" from fake MFR's or "inmates." Most of the guys who checked into the hole owing money never went out to the rec. cages. Some of them occasionally wandered out, thinking nothing would happen to them and they would get beat up. The SORT team, or "goon squad" as we liked to call them, remained suited up in the S.H.U. 24/7 "Suited up" meaning they were dressed in full riot gear. "Cell extractions" became an everyday occurrence.

I was in the hole when they forced four and five guys into a two man cell together. I was the third man in a two-man cell. The other two guys I was in the cell with were complete maniacs. They would not allow anyone in the cell with them until I showed up. The third man has to put his mattress on the floor. If someone needs to use the toilet, you have to roll your mattress up. It sucks. Other guys had four and five guys in one cell. About a month and a half into this living arrangement, the CO's came by our cell telling us we had to take a fourth guy in. Of course, we told them "f*** you!" "We are not taking a fourth guy in." They tried the same thing on us a couple of times before but we refused. This time the lieutenant came by and told us if we refused a fourth guy, they would extract us from the cell and put us in a "four point room." The four-point room is the jail inside of the jail inside of the prison. You are laid down and restrained with four different points of restraint on your outstretched arms and legs. Imagine a steel bunk bed with no mattress with steel loops on each corner of the bed. These steel loops were used to attach one end of the handcuffs; the other end of the cuffs were attached to each arm and each leg. "Fuck you!" the maniacs screamed back at the Lieutenant. After he left one of the COs came back and set up a camera in front of our cell. They also covered up all of the windows of the other cells on our range. That's so no one from the other cells could see what they were doing. We picked everything off the floor and put it on the top bunk. We put shampoo and water on the floor so it would be slippery when they came in. The plan was, if we could get them to fall down, we could crawl over them. We know they were coming in to kick our ass. That was inevitable. We just must go out fighting as hard as we can. It's the "convict code" and the only honorable thing to do. We could hear the goon squad as they shuffled up the hall near our cell. The captain was in front of our cell now confirming on camera that we refused to "Cuff up." "Cuff up" means voluntarily putting your arms behind your back and sticking your wrist out of the door slot so that they can put handcuffs on you. "F*** you!" "We ain't cuffing up!" Was the only response they got from us.

At this point the captain started reciting his spiel for the camera that "inmate number blah blah and inmate blah blah has refused to cuff up." "We will now extract the inmates from the cell." First they shot pepper spray in on us through the door slot. After about 10 minutes of coughing and eyes burning the door popped open and in they came. Shield first, they came one right behind the other, pushing their way in like a centipede. They pinned me down with their weight stomping me with their steel toe boots. My wrists and ankles were zipped tied as they carried me to the 4-point room. My eyes were swollen shut and burning like crazy. Tears streamed out of them and snot was running out of my nose. The 4-point room that I was brought to had two metal four-point restraining tables in the center of the room but both were empty. Eight other guys were already in the room handcuffed in the front with the belly chain, Black Box and wearing leg irons. Everyone was buck-naked and filthy. The room was full of shit and piss. The smell was so bad I fought back throwing up. It was very hard to breathe with no ventilation in the room. The nurse came and looked at me and wiped my face. Afterwards they took the zip ties off, stripped me naked then put handcuffs with a belly chain, black box and leg irons on me. Chained up buck naked like a wild animal, I could hardly breathe as I sat in piss. My eyes still burned and watered from the pepper spray and snot continued to run like a river out of my nose. Everyone was yelling as loud as they could and the sound was deafening. Most of the guys in the room were completely out of their mind. The other two maniacs that were extracted from the cell with me were placed in two different four point rooms and both were restrained on tables. At least they got to be in a room by themselves. I fought back the urge to vomit knowing that I would just have to sit in it if I did. Each minute that went by felt like an eternity. This was serious torture. Anything that I write to describe how bad it was doesn't come close to the actual experience. It was one of the lowest points in my life.

The lieutenant comes by once every 24 hours to ask if you still want to refuse a cell partner. He is only going to ask one time so if you do not answer correctly you stay there another 24 hours before you get the opportunity to reconsider. The longest anyone has ever lasted was 13 days. That was a mentally ill Cuban guy. He was famous for his stand. All the COs in the hole talked about him because he lasted 13 days. He told them f*** you for 13 days! He was out of his mind and near death before they finally got him out of there. I could not wait until the lieutenant showed up the next morning to ask me if I was ready to cell up. "Hell yes I'm ready!" "You don't have to ask me twice." "I had enough."

On a separate occasion, when I was in the hole, two guys I knew well were in the rec cage together when one killed the other. I would have been out in the rec. cages at the same time but was called out for a visit. At that time I was in a cell with two other guys. They had made all the bunks triples instead of double bunks so all of us had a bunk. Both of my cellies were out there when the murder happened. Even though the killing happened in the rec. cage in the hole, the entire prison went on lockdown. Visiting was closed and everyone who was in visitation had their visit cut short and sent back to their cells. One of the guards who came to escort me back to the hole was the CO who was working the rec. cages. He was the CO who decides who gets put in each cage together. He was visibly shaken after just witnessing Richard kill Tootie by stomping on his throat. Contrary to popular belief, the CO's did their best to NOT put enemies together in those cages. I've read stories where it was claimed the CO's at Beaumont put guys together who they knew would fight. That's BS. Not true at all. I was there from 97-01 and spent a lot of time in the hole. If I didn't have a visit I never missed going out to the rec. cages. I can say with all certainty the CO'S tried their best to NOT put enemies together.

The CO knew I was cool with both Tootie and Richard and assumed those guys were cool too. He told me what happened as he escorted me back to the hole from visiting. He was surprised over the murder like everyone else because everyone thought Richard and Tootie were cool. He asked me rhetorically what the hell was going on? I shook my head in surprised disbelief. "Who knows man." I said. "Could have been anything." "Prison is a fucked up place to be." That's how it was. One day you think you know your enemies and the next you were killed by someone who you thought was an ally.

Richard Wanksky killed Luther Plant basically because he didn't like the way he carried himself on the yard. Luther went by "Tootie" and was from Beaumont. His mom and dad came to see him regularly so I've met them and have said hi whenever I saw them in the visitation room which was often. Tootie did the tattoo that covers my back and a portrait of my son on my arm. We lived in separate units but I knew Tootie. He liked heroin and drinking wine. He got himself in debt and was running around high or drunk all the time causing drama. Richard had intervened for him and gotten him out of debt with the stipulation that he quit doing heroin, getting in debt and causing drama. That lasted only a few months. Richard ended up going to the hole for a knife that was found in his cell and Tootie got back in his old routine of doing more dope than he could pay for. Then Tootie wound up going to the hole owing money. Which is never a good thing. Richard was in a cell with Peter Gump in the Hole. Peter Gump is a gang member who killed a guy at USP Atlanta in the center hallway while AG Janet Reno was there touring the prison. I was cool with both Richard and Peter. It was my interactions with these two on the yard that made me totally change my way of thinking. The turning point for me came after a conversation with Richard and reinforced by a conversation with Peter .

I learned from these two individuals that the "Convict Code" that I lived by for so long didn't mean shit. There was nothing "honorable" about living by this code. It was all BS. The real code in prison is this: The one who will kill you for disagreeing gets to decide what is honorable. After Richard's older brother and crime partner had died in prison, Richard was able to purchase him an expensive gravestone. It was a large black headstone engraved with a picture of a Mustang and the words "Mustang Jim." Apparently this was his brother's nickname. He had the pictures of his brother's grave with the gravestone he had purchased in a folder out on the yard. It was just him and I talking privately. He explained to me how he had inherited a bunch of money from his mother and father who had died. I was surprised to learn that Richard came from a stable home that had plenty of money.

His parents owned a large farm. Richard grew up not wanting or needing anything. His brother was a few years older and Richard looked up to him. They basically robbed a bank for the thrill of it more than the need for money. As we sat out on the rec. yard talking, I started asking him questions about the bank robbery. He told me how he and his brother kidnapped and tortured the bank president. The guy was tied to a chair and after they had tortured him they threw him off a bridge into the water below, still tied to the chair alive. Richard was the one who told me this story. I didn't hear it from someone else. I asked Richard "why did you throw the guy in the water instead of just leaving him tied to the chair on the side of the road?" He said, "because I wanted to kill him." Then he looked me straight in the eyes, clearly agitated at my questions and said, "Do you have a problem with that?" I did, but I didn't say so. I can understand a man robbing a bank but what Richard and his brother did was just pure evil plain and simple. Richard is a highly revered, respected, dangerous prisoner in prison. Even though he had unnecessarily and cold-bloodedly killed the president of the bank he and his brother robbed. The general consensus in prison was that Richard was considered a "good dude." That's how prison politics work.

I don't think most guys even knew the details of Richard's case. Not that he was hiding it. He would tell you to your face what he did. Now that he had told me the details of his case my attitude towards him had changed. He didn't come from a broken home or raised in poverty. There was no sense or need to do what he did. He was a spoiled rich kid who wanted to be a killer for the sake of killing. I was never the same after that conversation with Richard.

Peter Gump was revered at Beaumont because of his reputation. He was in federal prison for dealing cocaine like I was. His notoriety came from killing a guy in USP Atlanta while the Attorney General of the United States (Janet Reno) was touring the prison. Supposedly he was paid by someone on the streets to kill the guy. After the murder, Peter was sent to Florence Colorado supermax for a 5 year program. While at Florence, he joined a notorious prison gang. After his 5 year program at Florence they sent him to Beaumont. I got along really well with Peter. We ate at the same table in the chow hall. He seemed to be an ok guy. I told him all about my case and he told me about his. There was a guy in Peter's unit who claimed to know the law really well who said he might be able to help me with my case. I let him have my paperwork to look over. It was no secret that I told the DEA that I would co-operate if they let me out. However, I never cooperated.

Instead, I fled the country and subsequently was put on the Federal Marshals 15 most wanted list. I told the guy who had my paperwork the whole story just like I had told everyone else. The guy went to Peter with my paperwork and acted like I did something wrong by scamming the DEA. Peter then got my paperwork and came out on the yard questioning me about it in a very accusing kind of way. Holding my paperwork in hand he asked me, "What about this?" This is something I had already told him. I told them I would cooperate in order to get out and run. The Colombians I was working with hired the lawyer. I shouldn't have to explain myself like this. I got a 30 year non parolable sentence because I didn't cooperate. I didn't have any co-defendants. It was just me. I was so pissed that he was questioning me of all people. He was insinuating that I co-operated. I didn't deserve that. Not at all. Peter was a killer, and a gang member, however, at the time he had really bad back problems. He was not in very good physical condition at all. The only reason I didn't beat the shit out of him was because he was in a prison gang. You can't touch those guys without getting marked for death. It was BS. In my mind I was a stand up guy in every sense of the word. Guys like Richard and Peter were not "honorable dudes." They were both killers who were never getting out; somehow, that's what made guys look up to them. I was now disgusted with this "convict code" and wanted no part of it.

Killing someone in Prison gives you a very high status. The more bodies you have in prison the higher you are revered. Richard had already killed a bank president on the streets when he was only 17. He was doing life without parole and was the kind of guy who would love to have multiple bodies on his resume. A few days after Richard killed Tootie he was moved into a cell across from mine in the SHU unit. I was in a cell with two other guys because of overcrowding and Richard was by himself. We talked through the doors and he sent me over his shot for killing Tootie. *100 killing. He said "I never got one of these before." We all get shots for different infractions but he got one for killing. Richard was showing me the shot as a matter of pride. He didn't show any anger or remorse or offer any conversation at all about what happened. His attitude was just very matter of fact. In his mind he did the right thing by killing Toottie. Yep, he is a bad dude. Lots of guys like Richard are revered, feared and respected in prison. Richard got the death penalty for killing Tootie. As of this writing he is still on death row in Terre Haute Indiana awaiting his date with the Executioner. May God have mercy on his soul.

This was not the trajectory I wanted for my life. Even though I had a lot of time to do and having respect and a good name in prison was very important, I didn't want to be THAT guy. I was NOT that guy. Not like Richard, Peter or Toottie. The prison culture there had become where one week a guy was a "good dude" and the next, he was getting killed because he was really a piece of shit. I decided then, when I was in the hole, that when I came out this time, I was going to change my routine, stay out of trouble and try to get transferred out of USP Beaumont. My case manager told me my points were low enough to send me to an FCI, but I had to have at least three more months of clear conduct. My unit manager told me he would transfer me to any FCI I wanted if I stayed clean and participated in some of the self help programs they had. I got a job in the factory and stayed out of trouble for three months. I enrolled in all the self help programs and classes that were available at the time, and true to his word, my unit manager put me in for a transfer. Finally in 2001, after spending four years in USP Beaumont, I was getting out of there. As the bus left the prison, I was looking back at it with relief. The further the bus took us away from the prison the more relieved I felt. I thought of all the guys who left out of there in body bags or on a stretcher because they were beaten severely, and was thankful to God that I made it out of there. Even though I was still in custody, headed to another prison, it felt like an enormous weight had been lifted off of me. I was being transferred to one of the best FCI's in the system, Sheridan, OR.

FCI Sheridan

The bus took us to Houston where we flew to the OKC federal transfer facility. I was there a couple of weeks then flew to Seattle federal transfer unit where I stayed for over a month. I almost did not get to go to Sheridan because I beat up a child molester who they put in the cell with me at the transfer facility in Seattle. I wasn't looking for trouble or trying to play the role of a tough guy at all. The guy literally told me he had kidnapped and raped a 14 year old boy. The first cell partner I had, when I first got there, transferred out after about two weeks. I remained in that cell by myself for another two weeks before they put the cho-mo in with me. I couldn't believe it. He came in straight off a bus. He was older than me and in reasonably good shape, covered in prison tattoos. I was laying on the bottom bunk reading a book when he entered the cell carrying his sheets and blanket. He set them on the top bunk as we started talking. I asked him the standard questions: where are you coming from? How much time are you doing? How long have you been down? What other prisons have you been in? What are you in here for? I gathered from what he was saying that he was doing a 40 year sentence in Washington state but the feds were charging him with terroristic threats to the president. He was doing a lot of talking but avoiding the question about what he was doing state time for. I let him ramble on and on about what a bad ass he was by talking back to the guards who transported him. He had already gotten a write up for insubordination and was proudly showing it to me. When he stopped talking, I asked him again point blank what he did to get that 40 year sentence in Washington state.

Then he looked at me with an angry look on his face and said "Does it really matter?" "You're damn right it matters," I told him. "If you're going to be in the same cell as me I want to know." What he said next was totally unexpected. He said, "Alright I'll tell you. I'm a homosexual. I didn't know that boy was 14 years old." I was laying on my bunk, covered up with a blanket and had a book in my hands when he started telling me what he was in for. As he continued to talk, I set my book down, sat up on my bunk and put my shoes on. When he saw me putting my shoes on he knew what was about to happen. He started beating on the door, yelling for the CO, before I even landed the first punch. In Seattle my cell was the closest one to the CO's office. His desk was literally 5 ft from my cell door. Although he wasn't at his desk, he was nearby and heard the commotion going on inside my cell. I only got off a few solid punches but they were good ones. The CO opened the cell door in time for the child molester to scoot his way out before getting beaten to a pulp. I was in a rage, very mad and my adrenaline was running high. The CO quickly shut the cell door and locked me in. I started cussing out the CO who put that guy in with me. I felt disrespected that they would put him with me. The lieutenant in charge came and spoke with me through the door. He was not sympathetic to my argument. In his mind we were all the same. A prisoner is a prisoner no matter what you are in for. He regarded me no different than the kidnapper/child molester. I disagreed with him vehemently and now wanted to punch the LT in his face. I was yelling at him through the door for all to hear. He threatened to send me back to Beaumont to which I responded "Send me back to Beaumont." Of course I did not really want to go back, but it sounded good.

Thankfully, that situation worked itself out, and I ended up finally making it to Sheridan. I was transported there by bus and the ride was amazing. The Mountains and hills, trees, rivers, lakes and farms were all things I had not seen in a long time. Just looking at everything, drinking in the beauty of it all, gave me a great feeling of joy that I had not felt in awhile. Again, I thought it ironic watching everyone go about their lives while looking out of the bus window. Most had frowns and grumpy attitudes while I was smiling ear to ear, happy and full of optimism, while chained on that bus going to yet another prison.

FCI Sheridan had a reputation of being one of the best FCI's in the BOP. The food was good, there was hardly any drama, lots of productive activities, and the compound looked like a college campus. Before I left Beaumont, a few guys there gave me names of a couple of guys they knew in Sheridan to look up when I got there. One of the guys lived in the unit next to mine and I ended up meeting him right away. His cell happened to be very close to the unit offices where I was getting signed in. We talked for a while before I ever went into my unit. He was about 10-15 years older than me and had been locked up longer than I had. He had a scar across his neck where a guy slit his throat in USP Atlanta. He took the knife from the guy, threw it down and beat the guy senseless. He was a big guy, in good shape that was not someone to mess with. He had done a lot of time in USP's that had similar circumstances as Beaumont, where I had just come from. Now he was nearing the end of his sentence with about three years left to do. He was a very smart guy that was functioning well in society when he was out. He was a broker for Chicago mercantile exchange on the streets.

He had a stand up reputation in prison as well. He introduced me to his cell partner who also was an older convict who had done a lot of time in USP's and had about 3-4 years left on his sentence. They gave me the rundown on the prison when I first came in. They told me the atmosphere was completely different here. There were a lot of "hide outs" here. Meaning there were more rats than convicts. Best to do your time and stay to yourself because the majority of the inmates here have some kind of dirt on them where they could not make it on another yard. It's best to NOT try and expose or beat them up because it's YOU who they will transfer back to a USP. I had to get to my cell for the count, but afterwards, we would meet up again to walk to chow together and they were going to show me around.

Coming out of the unit, we started walking down the sidewalk towards the chow hall. The air was super fresh. Noticeably super fresh. I can't ever remember breathing cleaner, fresher air. It was really nice because the air from the jet stream, traveling over thousands of miles of nothing but the Pacific ocean, hits those fertile Oregon mountains. In contrast, where I had just come from in Beaumont, the air was polluted from the countless nearby oil refineries. As I was breathing in the air with deep breaths through my nose, it amazed me at how clean and fresh it was. Then the wind blew through the leaves of a huge poplar tree above me. That sound stopped me in my tracks on the sidewalk. It was like electric chills went up and down my spine when I heard it. It was amazing. I stopped walking for a brief moment and just stood there in awe. The realization that I had not heard that sound in a long time hit me. Just the sound that leaves on a tree make when the wind blows through them gave me goosebumps. The guy walking with me asked "What's the matter?" I told him "I haven't heard that sound in so long and the air is so fresh, I'm just in awe." He smiled and said he was like that too when he first got here.

The landscape was very nice to look at. Flowers, bushes and very tall beautiful trees on the yard. Very different from Beaumont. The recreation center had an indoor track and a very nice weight pile inside and out. There were several credited classes you could enroll in. I was determined to do my time differently here. How could I utilize this time to better myself? At first, I was only concerned about getting in the best physical shape possible. One program that caught my interest was a class where you could become a certified personal trainer. Many guys with less than five years left on their sentence were interested in this program for a possible career in PT when they got out. I still had 17 years left on my sentence and wanted to take the class just to learn the information for myself. It was a nine month class, four hours a day, five days a week. I was able to get in the next class starting despite the one year waiting list. My routine, the first year, was working out and studying. I only hung out with about four or five guys. All were older convicts who had been around the craziness in other prisons but who were now doing their time differently and preparing to get out. I had never done my time like I was preparing to get out because my out date was so far off. I still had 17 years to go so why bother? The guys I met were telling me they wish they would have started preparing to get out earlier in their sentence. I was enjoying the class and putting a lot of effort into studying the material. I was also working out hard everyday and feeling really good physically. The majority of guys around me had less than five years left on their sentence and the smart ones were all making preparations to get out.

My name was on a waiting list to go work in the furniture factory and finally came up soon after graduating from the personal trainer class. Working in the furniture factory, I got a job on the same crew with two of the old convict guys I hung out with. One day, when we were on break, I saw my friend sitting on a box reading the Investors Business Daily financial newspaper. This guy was a big intimidating looking character. Old convict full of tattoos catching up on the stock market. The scene looked funny and out of place to me. I laughed and asked him why he was reading the financial news and not the comics. He laughed back and understood my amusement with him. He told me his celly was a stock broker on the streets and got him interested in the stock market. I sat down and listened as he explained.

He had his brother on the streets open an online trading account for him. He would deposit some of the money he made each month, from working in the factory, in his online account and buy stocks. He was trying to save as much as he could to have when he got out. I was very interested in what he was telling me and wanted to learn more. He introduced me to his celly who was always happy to teach and answer any questions I had. He gave me several books to read about trading. Once I had a decent understanding of how and why stocks go up and down I was hooked. I read and studied all I could and got my own subscription to IBD. Months went by with this new routine of working in the factory, exercising and studying stocks every day. This new idea of saving and investing money for when I get out was great once I understood the potential growth over the years with compound interest. Those guys were right, the sooner the better. I wanted to open an online trading account like my friend had ASAP. I sent $300, that I saved, to my sister to open an account for me. It was exciting to have money invested and watch it grow. Now I started to feel like I was doing something worthwhile. I was working my butt off in the furniture factory to earn about 100 a month and would also receive money from home most months. Many guys around me, who were close to getting out, were very stressed about it because they were going out to nothing.

For the first time in my sentence, I started taking steps in preparation for life after prison. I actually had a plan and was working on that plan. My stock investments were making me money, and I continued to add money to the account. In a year's time my investments were worth $2,000. I was staying out of trouble and doing all the right things. As a result, my security level dropped again. I was now eligible to go to a low-security prison. With 16 years left on my sentence, I never stopped thinking about escaping. I had heard the low security prison in Fort Worth, Texas was a place you could escape from. When I found out my points had dropped and I was eligible to go to a low, I requested a transfer to Fort Worth Texas. They did transfer me to a low, but it was not Fort Worth. I ended up in Stafford, Arizona. I hated that place from day one. Before I left Sheridan, a friend came to visit me and brought me some weed. I sold half of it before I left and took the other half with me. I was smoking fat joints by myself out on the yard in Stafford. That only lasted about two weeks before someone told on me. They ended up giving me a urinalysis in which I tested positive for marijuana. Immediately after, I was put in for a disciplinary transfer and sent back to a High security prison in Phoenix Arizona.

Phoenix

FCI Phoenix was very similar to Sheridan Oregon. Both facilities are set up the same way. The housing units are separate from the rest of the prison. The recreation yard is actually pretty big with a huge running track. When I arrived in Phoenix, I remained in the hole for about a month before finally getting assigned to a housing unit with the main population. Several guys that I knew from other prisons were there. A guy that I knew from Leavenworth worked in the prison factory. The waiting list to get a job out in the factory was at least 6 months, if you had prior experience. My friend from Leavenworth told me if I wanted a job in the factory he could help me get out there quickly. He worked in the parts room where they were making radio mounts for the military. He only had about three months left on his sentence and was looking for someone to train to take over his job when he left. I was all for the idea. This was how I now prefer to do my time. Working out in the factory not only earned you money, but it kept you out of trouble. I was determined to continue saving money and investing in the stock market. My routine at Phoenix was very similar to the one I had in Oregon. I would work in the factory as many hours as I could, save money, work out and stay out of trouble. I started to really enjoy working out at the factory. We were assembling circuit boards that went inside the radios for the military. I started out in the parts room but soon became the lead guy on the line. The lead guy is the prisoner who is in charge of the flow of production for that particular line. The cops that work in the factory are just there for security reasons. The prisoners operated the factory and made it run. The position I had also paid more than any other position on the line. The sense of accomplishment I had working out there was something that I really needed. I put a lot of effort into the job. I was determined once again to do something each day to better myself, spirit, mind and body. I felt like work ethic was a big part of improving myself. Kind of like making my bed in the morning and keeping my cell clean. It gave me a sense of accomplishment. A sense of pride. I felt like I was doing all the right things and it made me feel good about myself. A lot of guys could not understand why I was taking my job so seriously. It was just a prison job. I wasn't taking it seriously for anyone else but myself. I wasn't trying to suck up to the man for any special favors. I was trying to do a good job for myself. You can't really explain that to somebody in there.

After a while, I got a subscription to Investors Business Daily newspaper and started following the stock market again. Apple was one of the stocks I bought when it was around $80 a share with only 266 million shares being offered for trading. Later, I sold it for $200 a share before it ever split. As of this writing, Apple shares are at $365 a share with 4.33 billion shares being offered for trading. I kept saving as much money as possible and investing it in the stock market. Also, working out at the factory as many hours as they would let me. Whenever overtime was offered, I would work. When I was not working at the factory I was either working out on the weight pile, reading or studying something about the stock market or playing in the unit poker game. Time keeps marching on and as the months went by I was adding more and more money to my stock market account and watching it grow. No longer was I focusing my energy on how to get away with whatever I could. I didn't want to run a poker game or make wine, bring in weed through the visiting room or plan an escape. I didn't involve myself with any of the prison politics, gangs or social groups. My focus was entirely on bettering myself each day Spirit, Mind and Body. I made it a point to do something to improve myself in these three areas everyday.

227

One Friday afternoon, I was walking back to my unit from the chow hall when my unit manager was walking the opposite way down the same sidewalk. She saw me as we passed and she said "Andrus, the US attorney from Texas called and he would like to talk with you. If you give permission to talk with him, we will set up a time for the call. Do you authorize the call?" she asked. Of course my obvious question was "what does he want?" She said she doesn't know nor was that any of her business. She just needs my permission in order for me to agree to speak with him on the phone. I persisted with my questioning. This was totally out of the blue. I didn't have any pending charges and I've been doing my sentence for over 14 years now.

All of my appeals are exhausted. The only thing that I have pending is a petition for a presidential pardon. I kept thinking it had to be something to do with the pardon that I had filed. What else could it be? She told me it was the US attorney from the eastern district of Texas. My case was out of the southern district of Texas. This added even more questions in my mind. I said "Okay, sure." Only way to find out what he wants is to agree to talk with him on the phone. Being that It was Friday evening, my unit manager was leaving for the weekend. She said she would call his office back Monday and let me know when the call would be arranged. I went back into the unit, wondering with excitement, what it could possibly be. I kept telling myself it had to be something to do with the pardon that I had filed. It was all I could think about over the weekend. This little sliver of hope gave me such an adrenaline rush. It had to be something good. Why else would he be wanting to talk with me? I was clearly sentenced illegally and finally someone has agreed with my argument.

Monday came and the unit manager told me that a phone call appointment had been made for later in the week. After much anticipation the eagerly-awaited phone call finally arrived. The US attorney on the other line introduced himself as John Malcolm Bales. He was the US attorney for the eastern district of Texas. He asked me if I had any idea why he was contacting me. I told him that I was hoping it had something to do with the presidential pardon that I had just filed. He explained to me that it was not. And he was very sorry to disappoint me. He then went on to explain that he read over my case briefly before contacting me and he agreed that I was serving a much larger sentence than I should have. He seemed very friendly and very sympathetic. He was actually very kind and easy to talk to. He then explained that he was prosecuting the murder of Scot Miller. The original prosecutor on the case, eight years ago, had committed suicide. The case lay dormant for a long while and now is being picked up again. He said he read my name on a FBI report that Scot lived in my unit and we played poker together. I told him "Yes, I knew Scot."

"I was in the commissary line with him the night he and Jeff got in an argument over the money Scot owed Jeff for the heroin." I assumed he knew more than he did. The murder happened eight years ago. It happened in front of half the yard including ten or fifteen CO's. No question Jeff did it. The only thing really in question was why did Jeff kill Scot? The US attorney on the other line told me I had substantial information on this case that could help. If I was willing to help him by telling him what I know he would recommend a sentence reduction in my case. He said because of the amount of time that I've already done for cocaine possession meant, more than likely, I would be immediately released after his recommendation. He said he would like to come to Phoenix and talk to me in person if that was okay.

I sat there dazed in a fog. This was it. This was my chance to get out. My only chance. Go or stay. What are you going to do? All the physiological programming I've had over the years concerning the "convict code" told me I can't do this. What has that code done for me so far? How has abiding by this unwritten law served me or anyone else all these years? Was it worth my freedom? Was it worth missing every holiday and birthday of every family member? Was it worth literally giving up my life for? What are you going to do? Stay or go? I'm going. How could I not? I've been given the chance to walk out the door. Can you believe it? The original prosecutor in Jeff's case commits suicide? This new prosecutor calls me out of the blue eight years later? What are the odds? It seemed like all the stars had aligned perfectly in my favor.

I was in Phoenix now and my mindset and routine was totally different from how it was back in Beaumont. I was 14 years into a 30-year non-parolable sentence for possession of cocaine because I would not cooperate. No co-defendants, just me and some cocaine. 30 years. I was very heavily connected, and I never told. If I had cooperated, I would have gotten three or four years in a low-security camp. Did this mean anything to anyone in prison that added any value to my life? Hell no. It didn't earn me a metal, a trophy or a badge of honor. All it got me was a 30-year sentence and a trip to USP Leavenworth. Even though I never told and carried myself like a convict in and out of prison the respect I thought I deserved didn't follow me around. Nobody really cared. My honor still came into question by some dope fiend losers while in Beaumont. The heroin addicts who will kill a man for a shot of dope are the ones who get all the respect in prison. Gang members who will kill their own brothers for saying the wrong words are the ones who get respect in prison. If you disagree or disrespect what they do you can get killed too. It was all a bullshit game. Once the realization of how stupid that life-changing decision was to not cooperate it was too late to go back and change it. So here I am, by the grace and mercy of God, being offered a chance at Freedom. I told Mr. Malcolm Bales yes, yes I would talk with him in person and yes I would cooperate.

Soon after our phone call I met with an FBI agent and two US Attorneys in the visitation room at Phoenix. It was there that I told them the truth about what had happened in Beaumont eight years prior. It felt good telling them the truth about what happened. It was the right thing to do. Scot was a likable guy. I liked Scot and regretted badly that I did not do something to stop it. I thought about it over and over again. Seeing the knife, knowing that it was going to happen and not being able to warn Scot. Had I told Scot what was coming, I would have put my own life in jeopardy. Prison politics. At least now, I would be speaking up for Scot and telling his side of the story. The US Attorney told me that ultimately it was up to my sentencing judge to reduce my sentence. He could only make the recommendation. He told me he would make the recommendation after the trial was over and he believed that I would be released from prison. He said he could not promise me anything.

My immediate concern was my safety now that I had agreed to testify. I know very well how quickly word can travel through the prison system. Jeff would find out way before the trial. All the evidence the prosecutors had against him would be his right to see. He is going to see my name on the list of government witnesses. Once he does, that information will be spread throughout the system and I will be a target. The prosecutor assured me they would keep me safe. That ment entering in the federal witness protection program. I remained at FCI Phoenix for the next few months until it got close to Jeff's trial date. About two months before the trial began, I was transferred to the county jail in downtown Beaumont. Once I arrived at the county jail in Beaumont, I was separated to an isolated part of the jail. I would never be placed back in the general population again after this.

The US attorney informed me who the guys were that Jeff called as his witnesses. All of them were doing life sentences and most of them had been convicted of murder. All of his witnesses had a reputation in prison for being cold blooded killers. All of them had murdered someone in prison before. Richard was one of the witnesses Jeff called. Richard was on death row in Terre Haute Indiana for killing Tootie. Mr. Bales asked me, "Do you have any idea why Jeff had chosen these guys for his witnesses? They were not exactly the model inmates you would want to put in front of a jury to speak on your behalf." It was clear to me that Jeff had called these particular guys hoping that while being transported one of them would run into one of the government witnesses testifying against him such as myself. It was a very common mistake that happens often while being transported. They put guys together that aren't supposed to be together. Thank God the government made sure that this was not the case during this trial. All of Jeff's witnesses were housed in the hole at USP Beaumont. All of the government witnesses, including myself, were housed at the county jail in downtown Beaumont.

The federal prosecutors coordinated it in such a way that we would not be at the courthouse at the same time. All of Jeff's witnesses testified at a separate time than the government witnesses. Many of Jeff's witnesses, including Richard, were not even at Beaumont during the time of the murder. Jeff had called them as character witnesses. The trial finally started, and I was called to testify on the second day. I had been to court many times in my life but never called on to testify. Security was very heavy for this trial. The Federal Marshals came to transport me from the jail to the court house. They used three black SUV's to transport me. I rode in the middle vehicle. Two Marshals were in the front seat and me in the back. I was handcuffed and leg cuffed with a belly chain and black box over the handcuffs. Looking out of the tinted windows as we sped through downtown to the courthouse it reminded me of how the security was when they transported me to the prison in Colombia. Only then, I wasn't handcuffed at all. The prosecutor assured me that no other prisoners would be present at the courthouse when I got there. This was extremely important to me because I was putting myself in mortal danger by testifying for the government. Once we arrived at the courthouse, the Marshals escorted me to a court holding cell. While I was in the cell waiting, the US attorney and FBI agent came to talk with me.

They went over what was about to happen. He told me he was going to ask me a series of questions and just answer them truthfully. He said after he was finished asking me questions, Jeff's attorney was going to ask me questions as well. Just be truthful with my answers. He said to relax and take my time when answering the questions. I felt calm, confident and totally at ease. I was ready to get it over with. Finally, I was called to the witness stand and sworn in. Jeff was just a few feet away from where I was sitting. It was very hard to look at him and I felt really bad. This was going against everything that was programmed in my mind over the years. I had to keep reminding myself that this guy had unnecessarily killed Scot. That fact was never in question because he did it right in front of dozens of people, including prison staff. He didn't care if anyone saw him do it. The big question was why? Why did Jeff kill Scott?

All I had to do was tell the truth. For that it would forever change my status as a criminal. I didn't care. I'm trading that in for my chance at freedom. A chance to live a real life outside of prison walls. It would be worth it in the end. I hoped. The hardest part for me was when they asked me if I recognized him in the courtroom. Then they asked me to point him out. I had to physically point my finger at him and say "That's him sitting right there." It was a very hard thing for me to do. It was a defining moment when I knew that everything in my life had just changed. No going back. Only going forward. The US attorney proceeded to ask me a series of questions in which I answered truthfully. After a few questions he just let me tell the story which I found to be much easier than just answering questions back and forth. I told the truth. Like the U.S. Attorney later told me "The truth always rings true." It never changes. The courtroom was full of people, and everyone stared at me wide-eyed hanging on every word that I said. Everyone looked at me in complete silence with interest on their faces. I don't know what they had been told before my testimony but it seemed like what I was saying was all making sense to them. It should because it was what happened. The whole story. The truth. I was there from beginning to end during the whole ordeal. When it came time for Jeff's lawyers to cross-examine me his questions were weak. He had no defense for my testimony. He asked if I was promised anything in return for my testimony. Again, I told them the truth. "My understanding is, in return for my testimony, the US attorney would request a reduction in my sentence. I was not promised a time reduction. That would be completely up to my sentencing judge." After I was finished testifying I was escorted back to the holding cell. A little later the FBI agents and then the US attorney came back to talk to me. They were very happy with my testimony and smiling ear-to-ear. The US attorney said my testimony was one of the best testimonies that he had ever heard in his many years as a US Attorney. It was very clear, articulate and concise. This is when he said "The truth always rings true." A saying that I often repeat to this day.

After the trial was over and I had done my part in testifying, I was eager to find out what the government was now going to do for me. My life was literally in their hands and I felt very vulnerable. Was the U.S. Attorney really going to request a time reduction for me? Even if he does file the request, how effective will it be? After the U.S. Attorney requests it the judge could still say no or just reduce my time by a little bit. If they placed me back in the general population, I would be killed. All of these thoughts came to my mind, creating a rollercoaster ride of emotions. The next step for me was to enter the federal witness protection program and wait.

Soon after the trial, I was transferred to a special prison that houses government witnesses who are in the protection program. It was a small unit with less than 100 prisoners. The U.S. Attorney was true to his word and filed for a sentence reduction in my case. After speaking with some of the guys there, many were telling me I would more than likely be released after the judge ruled on the motion. I walked around very optimistic and grateful at the possibility of getting out. I waited and waited for the decision to come back. I called the U. S Attorney twice a week to find out if he heard anything concerning my motion before the judge. I was in daily contact with my family on the phone. My mother came to visit me and everyone was so excited about the possibility of me coming home sooner. Finally, the judge's ruling came out. I was on the phone with the U.S. Attorney when he informed me of the Judges decision. My sentence was reduced by 10 years! Instead of a 30 year sentence, I now had a 20 year sentence. By this time I had done over 15 years. When counting the little good time I had acquired over the years, I would still have to do about 2 ½ more years before being released. It was a bittersweet moment. I was so happy that it was done and grateful for the reduction, but at the same time expected it to be more. The U.S. Attorney and everyone I talked to told me they thought the judge would rule "time served" and I would be released immediately. Still, I was very happy to get the reduction. Now there would be no more speculation. The wait to find out what would happen was finally over. It was done. I no longer had a 30 year sentence but a new sentence of 20 years. A new out date and it was one I could actually see. 2 ½ years was just around the corner. After serving time for the last 15 ½ years and all that I had been through, I could do 2 ½ more standing on my head so to speak.

Preparing to get out

The thought of finally getting out of prison after doing so much time was exciting and scary at the same time. So much has changed over the years—the internet for one. I didn't even know what that was. The use of cell phones and computers, all the new technology that had come out had changed everything. The whole world had changed, and I was unfamiliar with all of it. How was I going to fit in? What would I do for work? I was very apprehensive to say the least. I knew I needed to prepare myself for getting out but wasn't really sure how. I was determined to do whatever it took to be a productive part of society. Breaking the law was out of the question. I tried to use my time to be as productive as possible each day doing something to improve myself, mind, body and spirit. With no mentor and no one to help give me directions, I had to figure things out for myself the best I could. The strong desire to change for the better was there but knowing what I should do to be a better person was not.

The physical part, improving my body was easy. I knew how to do that. I exercised like crazy every day. First thing in the morning, before breakfast, I worked on my abs. There were a couple of machines for doing cardio in our unit that I took full advantage of. Outside was a track for running and I ran 3-5 miles almost everyday. While keeping a log of my running times, I tried to push myself to better my previous time each time I ran. There were no free weights, but they did have a bar for pull ups and dips. Sticking with the routine for bettering my body everyday was working. I was in excellent physical shape and felt really good. Now I needed to know how I was to improve my mind? What exercise do I need to do to be smarter? I knew that I needed to do something, but what? There was a "computer class" available but only to those who had 18 months or less left to do on their sentence. I was signed up and on the waiting list. While waiting for the class, I wanted to learn new things but wasn't sure what. I wanted to do something each day to also better my mind and searched for a routine that would produce results for my mind like the one I was doing for my body.

I started reading self help books. Many, many self help books. Napoleon Hill, Dale Carnegie, Stephen Covey, Tony Robbins and John Maxwell to name a few. The prison library was full of self help books and I consumed them one after another. Very inspiring and I learned a lot. They all seemed to teach the same underlying message of universal laws. These same principles I remember learning from reading the bible. The prison unit I was now housed in had a small chapel that was very rarely used. I first went there to pray and explore ideas of how to improve myself spiritually. Inside the chapel were many books from various religious teachers. The chapel also had a library of DVDS you could sit and watch. In the inventory of different DVD's I came across one from Joel Osteen. There were four sermons on the one DVD. It was the only DVD by Joel Osteen in the chapel. I heard that Joel Osteen was now the pastor of Lakewood church after his Father John Osteen had passed away. I have a history with Lakewood Church. I had gone to that church off and on with my mother since the age of 14.

It was much smaller back then. As I stated earlier, I went to Bible School at Lakewood in 1984. It was the first year they had it. I was 18 years old then and had just been kicked out of high school for setting it on fire. I remember Joel from going to Lakewood over the years. He was just a couple of years older than me. I remember when he came back from college, he was working with the TV production in one of the trailers behind the church. He drove a Porsche 928 that I thought was so cool. Every Time I saw his car I admired it like most guys my age did. All the single young girls at church were after Joel. Joel was a very shy kind of guy. He was very polite and courteous to everyone. Everybody wanted to hang out and be friends with him but he was super shy. Always smiling and always in a hurry to get somewhere. The TV production kept him busy, and he seemed to love it. I saw Joel a few times a week while going to Bible School. He worked a stone's throw away from where the bible school classes were so we crossed paths with him often. Now he was pastor of Lakewood church. I couldn't believe it the first time someone told me. "Joel?" "Joel is Pastor?" Very hard to believe. Not that he wasn't a good Christian guy, he very much was.

Joel was just too shy to talk to three people for any amount of time before running off. He seemed like an unlikely candidate to speak in front of thousands of people each week. I was told that not only was he Pastor, but he was doing a very good job. Now this was my first opportunity to finally hear Joel Preach, and I was very excited about it. I put in the DVD and sat alone in the prison chapel watching Joel Osteen preach for the first time. All the old memories of Lakewood church, bible school and the Osteen's came back to mind as I sat and listened. It seemed like the message he was teaching was just for me. It was just what I needed to hear at that moment in my life, it felt so encouraging. Tears filled my eyes as my emotions overtook me. To add to my excited emotions, he made reference to my old bible school friend and roommate, Jerry, in his message. Jerry and his wife Jana were now missionaries living in Africa and had been there for years. Old friends of mine being mentioned on the one and only Joel Osteen DVD in the chapel. What are the odds? I'm sure Joel had preached hundreds if not thousands of sermons that were available on DVD. This was the first and only message I'd ever heard from Joel Osteen and he makes reference to my friends Jerry and Jana? It was a powerful message and an emotional moment for me.

I felt God was talking to me, not audibly but impressing on my spirit. Calling me back to live an obedient life to his word like I once did while going to bible school. Immediately after hearing the first message on the DVD, I got on my knees and prayed. I cried and prayed. Thanking God for not turning away from me even though I had turned away from him. Overwhelmed and thankful, the tears ran down my face. Tears of gratitude. Grateful to be alive and have a second chance at freedom. I had to call my sister and tell her what had happened. We went to Lakewood church at the same time. My sister was a counselor there in the early 80's. She knows I've never heard Joel before and I'm sure she will appreciate the significance of him making reference to Jerry and Jana on the one and only Joel Osteen DVD in the chapel. I was feeling really excited when I called to tell her about it. She seemed to be impressed by what I told her as well. What are the odds? She reminded me that God sometimes speaks to our spirit like that. She told me that it was not by random chance or accident that my sentence had been reduced either. The changes that I made within myself while in prison allowed for that miracle to happen. I started taking steps towards planning on getting out even though my out date was 15 years away. I acted like I was getting out by saving money and investing in the stock market. My energy and focus shifted into preparing myself for release. Whatever it was or however it happened I was so grateful that it did. I thanked God for his mercy and forgiveness. I feel like I don't deserve God's forgiveness but so thankful that He gave it to me anyway. I prayed that God would help me be a better person. That He would lead me on the right path. Guide me through life. Now more than ever, I worked on preparing myself for release. I made an effort to do something each day to better myself, spirit, mind and body. After that day, I started going to the chapel on a daily basis as part of my routine. If for nothing else, I just wanted to pray and give thanks to God.

My attitude inside prison had completely changed for the better. After my sentence reduction, the remaining time I had to serve was as productive as I could make it. Once I got down to my last year I couldn't help but count down the days until I got. With each passing day my excitement grew as I got closer and closer to finally getting out. Someone told me I could go to a halfway house and get out up to six months earlier than my out date. I heard mixed reviews about going to a halfway house. Some said they were very strict and would send you back to prison for the smallest infraction. However, if you had a job you could be at work instead of stuck inside the halfway house. In a halfway house you are allowed to leave for work each day unsupervised. You still must live there and abide by their rules but if you have a job you can leave to go to work. It sounded like a good deal to me so I requested to go to a halfway house. My case manager applied for me and surprisingly, I was approved for four months. That meant the last four months of my sentence would be served in a halfway house.

I was on the phone daily with my family and Keli, the woman I had married while in USP Beaumont and later divorced. Keli and I had started talking again. When she found out my sentence had been reduced and I was getting out, she insisted on being the one to come pick me up from prison. We started talking more and more on the phone as my release drew near. Both of us were excited about the prospect of finally being alone together. Something we had both talked about in anticipation for years. Even though I knew by this time she was not the right person for me, I had an uncontrollable physical desire to be with her. My mind and spirit were telling me "NO, don't do it, she's trouble!" My body screamed "DO IT, DO IT!" Strange that I could be so disciplined over my body while working out but when it came to this physical, sexual urge, I seemed to always give in and make the wrong decisions.

Getting out

The day had finally come for my release. I had been in prison for the last 18 years almost to the day. If you count the 2 years I was on the run in Colombia it had been 20 years since I walked free in the United States. It was difficult to believe it was really happening. Even as I was being processed out I kept thinking something was going to happen and they were going to change their mind and keep me. They gave me sweat pants and a sweatshirt to wear out. I had a little over $200 dollars on my prison account that they gave me in the form of a check. The BOP also gave me a check for $150 as my "release money." I was given some paperwork with the address to the halfway house in Houston. They told me I had 48 hours to report there or a warrant would be issued for my arrest. I was still technically in the custody of the BOP. I also had 5 years "Supervised Release" to complete after the four months of halfway house was finished.

They escorted me to the front door of the prison where I stood waiting. I was carrying a large manila envelope that contained some legal papers, personal pictures and a couple of self help study books. 18 years inside and this was all that was coming out with me. Wearing no handcuffs, no chains and only facing one more locked door before being out. I just knew at any second they were going to change their mind and keep me. I had an overwhelming feeling that something from my past that they missed would come up and I would be charged with it. Finally, the door was opened, and I was allowed to leave. The guard who escorted me to the door said "Good luck Andrus. Stay out of trouble and don't come back." I started rushing towards the visitors parking lot where I knew

Keli was in her Jeep waiting to pick me up. As I got closer, I heard her shout my name and come running towards me. We hugged, and both said we couldn't believe that I was out. "Let's go before they change their mind" I said. I just wanted to get as far away from the prison as possible. I still had a strong feeling they were going to find some last minute hold or charge to keep me. As we drove out of the parking lot and away from the prison I started to feel more at ease. The further we drove away from the prison the better I felt. Finally, after about 10 minutes of driving, I started to feel relieved and the realization that I was out of prison began to hit me. I started shouting "YES! WOOHOO! I'M FREE! THANK YOU, GOD!" I stuck my arm out of the jeep window as we went down the highway. It was so nice to not be in handcuffs. I was enjoying the view and smells of the Florida countryside as we cruised along. My senses were bombarded with all new sensations. Keli began asking me questions nonstop one after the other that was taking me out of enjoying the moment and started to aggravate me. Finally, I had to tell her to please stop with all the questions. Let's enjoy the moment and I'll answer all your questions later. It was going to be a long ride back to Houston from Florida.

Soon we stopped to get gas. She asked if I wanted anything from inside. A beer maybe? she suggested. "No beer, thanks. I don't want to damage my liver with alcohol." I debated for a moment if I should get some Copenhagen chewing tobacco. I used it for years until they took all the tobacco out of prison. It had been a few years since I enjoyed a dip of Copenhagen. "Celebrate," she says, "you just got out. I'll get you some if you want." That was all the encouragement I needed. "Yes, get me a can of Copenhagen," I said. Later I wished I would have never decided to get that first can. That one can was all it took to get me hooked back on dipping tobacco for the next several years. Hindsight is always much clearer and looking back I know now I would have been much better off not getting involved with Keli at

242

all. She was not the strong positive influence I needed at this vulnerable point in my life. She was very good looking with a body that would turn heads wherever she went. I hadn't been with a woman for 18 years so my sexual desire for her clouded any good sense I may have had. Even after all the self-help books I had just read, all the praying I had been doing, together with my strong, sincere desire to change and rehabilitate, It was still going to be a daily struggle to make the right decisions.

Keli asked if I wanted to call anyone using her cell phone while she went inside to pay. I had never used one of these little wireless phones before. I wanted to call my son Joseph. Standing outside the jeep while getting gas she handed me her little phone after calling Joseph's number for me. Joseph answered, and we talked for about 10 minutes as I stood outside the jeep. I wasn't used to talking on a wireless phone and was stuck to that one spot near the jeep while we talked. Keli motioned for me to get back in the jeep so we could go but it never occurred to me that I could keep talking on the phone and get in the jeep and go. I remember telling Joseph I had to go and would call him again later. I didn't realize until after I hung up that I could have kept talking while riding in the jeep. This new technology was going to take some time getting used to.

We continued to drive towards Houston for a couple of hours when Keli suggested we stop at a Walmart to buy a few things, including a change of clothes for myself. I heard about Walmart and saw the commercials on TV but had never been inside a Walmart before. My mind was not prepared for the experience. "Sensory overload" would be the best term to describe the experience. In prison, your choices are very limited as to what you could have. You basicly don't have a choice at all. They take away that decision making process from you. You are told what you can have, when you can have it, and how much of it you can have. Years of prison life without making simple, independent decisions, had my brain disconnected from knowing how to make selections of merchandise. I didn't know what I wanted because there were way too many choices for my brain to handle. I stared in awe at all of the stuff they had. As I walked down the aisles, seeing all the merchandise, I got dizzy. Stopping every few feet and looking in amazement at all the different items for sale. Keli told me to pick out whatever snacks I wanted, to munch on for the ride. There were so many different things to choose from I was stuck staring at everything, unable to decide what to get. My head was hurting, I was dizzy and became physically ill. It was too much for my brain to take in. All of this new information at once was just too much for me. I felt overwhelmed and disoriented. I was completely out of my element, almost like I was walking on a new planet. It was difficult being in there and I had to force myself to look forward and concentrate on finding my way out of the store. If I looked at any display of merchandise, I would get stuck staring at it like a moth to a light bulb. When we got back in the jeep she asked me what I thought of Walmart? It was too much, I said. It made me dizzy looking at all the stuff to the point where I felt like I would throw up.

We continued our journey westward in the jeep. As we drove I eventually spoke with all my family on the phone who were very happy about my release. They were all eager to congratulate me and everyone wanted to know how it felt being out after 18 years of prison. The one person I really missed talking to that day to share in the celebration of my release was my father. Cancer took him out about ten years prior while I was in USP Beaumont. He came to see me a couple of times while he was battling cancer with chemotherapy. Now he was gone and I miss him very much. He was buried in his hometown of Lafayette, Louisiana. We would be driving through there on our way to Houston and I wanted to stop to visit his grave. My cousin Susan, who lived in Lafayette, agreed to meet me at the graveyard and show me where my father was buried. By the time we arrived, the sun had already set and it was dark outside. It had been raining earlier in the day and everything was still wet. Susan was in her car waiting at the entrance to the graveyard when we pulled up and motioned us to follow her. We followed her through the winding maze of driving paths that went into the graveyard until finally she parked and we all got out to greet each other. We stood by her car talking for a few minutes, excited to see each other, when Susan said "You ready to go see your daddy's grave?" she asked, "He's buried right over there." Her and I walked alone to the gravesite while Keli waited in the Jeep. It was very dark and wet outside as we stood in front of my father's grave. Susan was very close to my father and was with him in his final days. She started telling me all about his last months and days alive, his death and the funeral. I just stared at his name on the gravestone and cried as I listened. I felt heartbroken and guilty. My stupid life decisions had not only put me in prison but had also essentially robbed my father and myself of a precious father/son relationship we could have had. I missed my chance. It was over. Susan and I hugged and cried together. It was very emotional. We were both still crying as we said our goodbyes and promises to stay in touch.

The visit to my father's grave affected me more than I thought it would. He had been dead for ten years so I thought visiting his grave would not be so hard emotionally. I was wrong. It was very hard emotionally. As we continued to drive towards Houston, I was quietly lost in my own thoughts. Looking back on how stupid I was to choose to live a life of crime. The heavy price I paid for the bad decisions I made. Being incarcerated for all those years was tough but the hardest part for me was not where I was but where I wasn't. I wasn't with my father or any other family member enjoying moments together. Celebrating birthdays, holidays, marriages, laughing and enjoying each other's company over a good meal. Many other special moments that could have been shared together. Now he's gone and I'll never have that opportunity to share any moments with him. I can't go back and change anything. The only thing I can change is how I will act going forward. You grow to appreciate these things while in prison that you took for granted while you were out. Holidays like Christmas and Thanksgiving, birthdays, weddings and special occasions where family is grouped together. You give all that up when you go to prison. Life keeps going on the outside and you miss it.

Nobody in their right mind who gets out of prison plans on going back. Almost everyone who gets out says they are never going back. Unfortunately, 85% of people who get out end up going back. For people like myself, who have done more than 15 years in prison, and are on 5 years supervised release, 90% don't make it. The odds of me staying out are not good. I was fully aware of the statistics and they were not very encouraging. Regardless, I was determined to make it. I can't forget this moment. I must be strong. Obviously it's not going to be easy but I must do whatever it takes.

It was still 3 ½ more hours of driving before we made it to Houston. My sister wanted me to come to her house where all the family was waiting to see me. Everyone was very excited and even though it was late into the evening they were all up waiting for me. The last couple of hours driving in that jeep was miserable. I had gotten car sick and was feeling terrible. When we finally arrived at my sister's house my head was pounding, I was dizzy and sick to my stomach. It was very nice to see everyone and my sister's house but I was too sick to celebrate like I should have. My head was pounding, and I felt nauseous. I just wanted to shower and lay down in bed. We didn't stay very long at my sister's house. Soon we got back on the road and drove to Kelis' house. It was a very long day of traveling. My youngest son Jeremy was there waiting when we arrived. I would stay that first night and the next with Keli in her house before having to report to the halfway house.

Halfway House

The halfway house was located in downtown Houston. It was right next to Minute Maid park where the Houston Astros played. I was processed in and assigned to a bunk in a dormitory. My first week there I was not allowed to leave. I would attend several classes over the next couple of weeks, including drug treatment, finding a job, writing a resume, opening a bank account and getting ID. My first major obstacle was getting a Texas ID. Before I could get a job or anything else I needed a driver's license. I studied the drivers manual, scheduled an appointment to take the test and got it done. I was allowed to leave for my appointment once I could show proof one was made. Walking alone on the streets of downtown Houston that first time was an amazing feeling. I was so grateful to be free. The new sights, sounds and smells were exciting. Once I had my driver's license, I felt a huge barrier had been crossed. It wasn't until then that I felt somewhat like an official citizen. Like I belonged out of prison.

Now what I needed was a job. Not too many people are willing to hire someone fresh out of prison. A friend of a friend of Keli's referred me to a guy who sold wood flooring and was willing to hire me working in his warehouse. It was hard work for minimum wage but it was a job. That's all that mattered at that point. I needed a job, any job. If you can't find a job within a certain time frame the halfway house would send you back to prison. People were getting sent back every day for various reasons. The halfway house charges you to stay there and the charge depends on how much you make. The good thing about having a job meant I would be able to leave the halfway house each day to go to work. The job was hard work for little pay but I was happy to be working. I used the money I had saved to buy myself a car and parked it right outside the halfway house. Each morning at the designated time I would get up, get myself ready and go to work in my own car. I was beginning to go through the regular routine of a normal, everyday citizen.

My mother regularly came to visit me at the halfway house. They were allowed to bring food in so we would sit in the eating area and eat something different every time they came. My mother was in a wheelchair because of multiple health issues. It was sad to see her in that condition, but I was thankful to see her alive. She never let it get her down and remained her upbeat jovial self every time we visited.

I stayed in the halfway house for the first three months after being released. I remained working at the same job in the warehouse for minimum wage the entire time I was in the halfway house. The 4th and last month was spent living with Keli on home confinement. I went to work every day and still paid the halfway house a portion of my pay. I wasn't making very much money. I had not even officially finished my sentence of incarceration when Keli started pressuring me about not paying my share of the bills. She would get drunk and say awful things to me. When she sobered up she would always apologize and act better but once those hateful words were spoken they could never be brought back. Finally, I finished my sentence of incarceration. The last month of it was home confinement. Now I would start 5 years "supervised release." This meant I had to report to a probation officer once a month and submit to random urine tests. I was allowed to come and go as I pleased but if I left the county I needed permission from my probation officer. Living with Keli didn't last long. It was a bad relationship from the very beginning. My sister and her husband were kind enough to let me live with them until I got on my feet. I stayed in their guest bedroom and worked various low paying low-skill jobs until I found what I thought was a halfway decent job as a waiter in a Mexican restaurant. After some time waiting tables and not making very much money, my sister's husband referred me to an expensive restaurant that was nearby. He told me the waiters there made good money. He knew the owners and put in a good word for me. After interviewing with one of the owners, I was hired on as a waiter. By this time, I had been out of prison a little over a year.

Restaurant Manager

It was considered a "casual fine dining" restaurant, serving steaks, seafood, and chicken with unique sauces. There were also expensive wines and cocktails available. It was a pricey restaurant where a waiter could make decent tips. Typically, customers tip between 15-20% of their bill, so the more they spend, the more the waiter usually makes in tips. No one I worked with knew anything about my past, and I wouldn't dare tell anyone that I was in prison. I took the job seriously and tried to give each customer the best possible service. Many of the customers who came to eat there were people I considered rich. This was my first time ever interacting with so many highly educated and financially successful people, and it felt very awkward at times. My circle of friends and acquaintances have for the most part always been thugs, criminals and low IQ individuals. I had to adapt and learn to communicate very differently with this class of people. Many of the customers who came to this restaurant were people my age who were living the good life because they made better life choices than I did. The fact that I was serving people younger than me, who were way more financially successful than I was, got to me at times. I was continually comparing myself to the people who I was waiting on. It was a constant reminder of the success I could have had if I had made better choices with my life when I was younger. In my mind the fact that I was waiting tables at my age was evidence of my lack of education and poor life choices. It was embarrassing and degrading at times. I struggled with this, but I stuck it out because my options were limited, and I needed the money. Many times I would have to remind myself that although they were more financially successful than I was, they would have never made it in many of the places I did. I was successful in surviving extreme situations that most would have not survived. I came out of a life of crime and incarceration and changed. Keeping that in mind, I have to consider myself very successful. Just not so financially successful. Yet.

Eventually my contribution and great attitude that I brought to the restaurant was noticed by the owners and I was promoted to assistant manager. No longer waiting tables and depending on tips I was paid a salary. I moved out of my sisters' guest bedroom and into a brand new rental house in a very nice neighborhood with my son Joseph. It was a dream come true to live with my son. I had missed out on being a part of his life for all those years. After he had graduated from high school, he went straight into the army and was promptly sent to Iraq. Now that he was back, the opportunity presented itself for us to live together while he was going to school. I was working long hours at the restaurant and after six months as assistant manager, I was promoted again to manager. I was completely dedicated to the job.

My probation officer was very happy not to have any problems from me and congratulated me on the success that I was having at my work. Within two years of working with this very popular restaurant I was promoted to General Manager. I was in charge of nearly 100 employees. The restaurant was thriving, averaging over $100,000 in sales a week. While I was General Manager, we became the number one rated restaurant in Houston on TripAdvisor, beating out over 7,000 other restaurants. My hard work and dedication was paying off. The owners wanted to capitalize on the popularity of the restaurant and open a second location with the intention of starting a franchise. After months of considering multiple different locations it was finally decided that the second location would be in the Galleria Mall. It was exciting times but also very long hours and demanding work.

Working 50-60 hours a week, I was literally married to the job with hardly any personal life. My five years of supervised release was finally over and I was finished with my federal sentence.

I had beaten the odds. The first thing I did after completing my sentence was apply for a passport. I didn't have any particular plans or places in mind to travel but now that I was able to go anywhere I wanted to be ready. I wasn't sure if they would even issue me another passport because my last passport was confiscated from me in Colombia. I went through the steps of filling out the necessary paperwork and applying for the passport and waited to see if it would go through. After a couple of months of waiting the passport came in the mail. I could now travel just about anywhere in the world I wanted. It was a great feeling. I was getting restless and tired of the demands that the job was requiring of me. A few months after the second location in the Galleria was open, I had a falling-out with the owners and quit but quickly got another job managing a different restaurant. The new restaurant was almost as demanding as the last. Long hours on your feet all day is what you can expect when you manage a restaurant. It had been nearly five years of working straight through without a break from work. I had not taken any vacation time.

My longtime friend, Jerry, who I went to Bible School with, came to see me one day while I was working in the restaurant. I had seen Jerry two other times since I had been out but very briefly on both occasions. As I stated before, Jerry and his wife Jana had been Living in Africa as missionaries for the last 30 years. He would come back to the United States to visit now and then but Africa was now his home. It had been a very long time since going to Bible school and Jerry and I were roommates. I was only 18 years old then.

After completing Bible School, Jerry and Jana got married and they went to Africa to do missionary work. As for me, I eventually went back to my rebellious ways. Now I am embarrassed and guilt-ridden to talk to Jerry. Of course, I truly believe in the Bible and in God. I was so sincere while I was going to Bible School. I can't put my finger on what happened. I just fell away from the faith. Now sitting across from Jerry he reminded me of God's forgiveness. Even though I am not worthy of God's forgiveness, He forgives me anyway. I understand the principle and I understand the Bible's teachings. The hard part for me was forgiving myself. Jerry and I sat at one table in the restaurant while we ate lunch together and talked for a good while. He told me all about Africa and the work that he and Jana had done there over the years. He was pastoring a church and had founded a Christian School as well as an orphanage where he lived in Botswana, Africa. He had dedicated his life to serving and helping people. I was so proud of Jerry. So proud that I knew someone of this caliber and called him my friend.

In the course of conversation, Jerry asked me when I was going to come visit him in Africa? He had asked me that question before and my response was always "One of these days I will go." This time Jerry persisted and said, "If you really want to go you have to set a date. When you just say 'one of these days I will go,' you will never go. You have to make definite plans," he told me. "Set a date when you will come and work towards that date. Make plans and follow through." We finished eating and having our conversation and Jerry had to go. I told him I would work towards setting a definite date when I would come to Africa and then let him know. We parted ways, promising to stay in touch.

The more I thought about going to Africa the more I wanted to go. Since getting out of prison, I had not even traveled outside of Texas. How exciting would it be to travel to Africa? I had always been a big fan of National Geographic and could watch African wildlife shows all day. The plan that Jerry and I discussed was for me to actually live and work there for several months. My Visa would be for three months but Jerry felt confident that we could have it extended, If that was what I wanted to do. I was feeling very apprehensive about going there without any plan for any type of income if I was going to be there for that long. I had made a little money managing the restaurant but not enough to have saved a significant amount to hold me over for several months in Africa.

Jerry had offered me a place to stay as well as a job managing the small gym he had recently added to the community center he was in charge of. The community center was also where he held his church services every Sunday morning. I needed to be able to do some kind of work so I could have a little income. I knew Jerry's real plan for me was for me to get into the ministry. Teaching the bible and helping people. I was all for helping people but at the same time felt like a complete hypocrite to be preaching to people. If I was going to talk the talk I needed to also walk the walk. Even though I was a completely changed person at this point, I was still not walking the walk of a dedicated Christian. I felt ashamed for so many stupid things that I've done in my life even after I went to Bible School. Although I had paid a very heavy price with all the years I spent in prison, I still could not forgive myself. I missed out on life that I will never have the opportunity to get back. I can't go back and change the past. All I can do is go forward and not make the same stupid mistakes.

I am a completely changed person now. Although I'm not a saint. Far from it. And far from walking a life as a Model Christian. The evidence of the change I've made was in my successful completion of the five year supervised release. Even though I had changed for the better and was not out committing crimes, God was still missing from my life. I had a strong desire to get back to reading my Bible, praying and getting closer to God. After thinking and talking about it for several months, I finally set a date that was also good with Jerry when I would go. I bought my ticket three months in advance to get the best deal. Once I had bought the ticket there was no turning back. Part of the low price deal that I got was there were no refunds on the ticket. I continued working at the restaurant up until just a few days before my flight was scheduled to leave. I had sold most of all of my belongings and stored the few things that I kept with my brother.

Africa

The day had finally come to go. After saying my goodbyes to family and friends, my sister dropped me at the airport and off I went to start the long journey to Africa. It had been over 25 years since I'd traveled anywhere by myself. The farthest I had been since getting out of prison was an hour drive away to Galveston beach with some friends. This journey I would be taking alone would take me all the way to the other side of the world and down into the southern hemisphere. I was smiling ear-to-ear, full of excitement as I left. The first part of the flight took me from Houston to Doha, Qatar. After several hours there in the airport, I changed planes for the second part of the journey. The second plane took me to Johannesburg, South Africa. In Johannesburg, I had to get my bags and go through customs and then board another flight that would take me to Gaborone, Botswana. Gaborone is the capital of Botswana. The airport there was much smaller than the one in Johannesburg. It was very quiet with not a lot of activity. It would be several hours there waiting before connecting with the next flight so I walked all around, checking everything out, so excited to be in Africa. The main attraction was a statue of an elephant, made out of elephant tusks, located in the middle of the airport. The plaque explained that all of the ivory tusks that made up this beautiful statue were confiscated from poachers who kill the elephants just to cut off and sell their ivory tusks. Possession of these ivory tusks was against the law and the penalty if caught was prison time and a heavy fine. As I stood there admiring the statue and reading the plaque, I heard the quiet sound of someone walking nearby. When I looked up to see who it was, I was surprised and shocked to see what I later found out to be 300 young kids ages 5-9. Surprised because they were so quiet and well-mannered for being so young. They were all wearing their school uniforms and obviously were there touring the airport on a school trip. They were all smiling ear-to-ear, happy as could be, but none were making any noise. They were the most well behaved group of kids I had ever seen. Never in my life could I imagine 300 kids together that age all happy but none making any foolish gestures or noises. They all walked in a single-file line in a very orderly manner. Their faces were bright with excitement as they looked around at the airport smiling and happy. As they toured the airport, I stood there watching in awe. This was the first moment that I realized I was in the presence of a people and culture that did not fit my preconceived ideas. I was somewhere very unique.

From Gaborone, yet another plane took me to my final destination, which was the village of Maun, Botswana. After traveling for almost two days straight, I arrived in Maun. It was a small airport mainly used by tourists who were going on Safari. Jerry was there to pick me up. As we drove away from the airport and through the village of Maun, Jerry explained how things had changed over the last 30 years since he had first arrived here.

The main road we drove on was a two-lane highway in serious need of repair. Jerry told me it used to be a dirt road when he first arrived. On either side of the main road were houses thrown together with what looked like whatever kind of materials were available. Some were cinder block and cement structures, others were made from mud, tree branches and dried grass. Most of these dwellings were not equipped with indoor plumbing or electricity. Basically they were cement and cinder block square rooms with grass roofs. Most people here lived in extreme poverty. There was no green grass covering the ground but instead brown sand was everywhere. Surprisingly, there were many beautiful trees that bloomed with bright colors growing out of the sand.

People were walking around everywhere going about their day-to-day business. Many were outside of their houses, just hanging out socializing, and many were walking up and down the sides of the sandy dirt roads. Most of the vehicles on the road were small taxis. The majority of people either got around in taxis or they walked. Very few owned their own vehicles. Herds of cows roamed freely looking for grass to eat wherever they could find it. I asked Jerry about it and he told me you could own cattle here without owning any land. Most of the cattle owners didn't fence their cows in because there were no laws or regulations that said you had to. The donkeys also roamed around freely. They seem to just wander around wild on the sides of the road but Jerry told me that all those donkeys also belong to somebody. It was about a 30-minute drive from the airport out to where Jerry lived. As we drove out to his place, he explained how things were when he and Jana first arrived in Botswana and how he came about living where he's living now.

They struggled for many years when they first started ministering in Botswana. It was not easy. The only income that they had was a few churches back in the United States who donated to their ministry now and then. They had dedicated their lives to that of helping people and teaching the Bible under difficult circumstances. Both Jerry and Jana are smart, capable people who could have had successful careers in the United States if that's what they had chosen to do. They both left everything behind and answered what they believed was a calling from God to help the people of Africa. After living in Botswana for several years doing missionary work, Jana giving birth to, and now raising three sons, they lost everything they had in a house fire. It was a devastating blow. They almost gave up then and came back to the United States and called it quits in Africa. In spite of their hardships, they were still convinced that this was God's calling for their lives. They remained in Africa, rebuilt and pushed on, continuing to spread the word of God and give hope to people who needed hope.

Many months were spent living in a tent with no running water, no electricity and sleeping on the bare ground. They went through very tough times but they stuck it out. Jerry continued to preach and teach the word of God to all who would listen. Then out of nowhere, a miracle happened. An older German man and his wife were vacationing in Africa and stayed briefly in Botswana while on Safari. The man was a Christian, who had made hundreds of millions of dollars in the pharmaceutical business over the years. While staying in Botswana he felt a love and compassion for the people there. He and his wife were touched by the sweet spirit and kindness from the people of Botswana. Seeing the extreme poverty that most of them lived in, he wanted to do something to help. They searched the internet looking for a Christian Ministry doing work in Botswana so that they could get involved and possibly help financially. Their internet search led them to "Love Botswana," which is the ministry of Jerry and Jana Lackey. The wife called Jana, and they spoke over the telephone for a long time. Jana explained all the different projects and plans they had in the making that just lacked finances to go forward. Before long the German couple came and met with Jerry and Jana and got involved with the ministry in a very big way. They built a large community center where Jerry now holds his church services every Sunday.

The building also has offices for community outreach programs and rooms for children's church services. In addition to the community center, they built a private Christian school and an orphanage on a nearby separate property. As the ministry grew, Love Botswana was now employing several dozen full-time employees who must be paid. The Ministry required a steady flow of income in order to stay in operation. They were mainly dependent on churches and individual donors for income. In order to have a steady flow of income, and not worry about depending on donations from churches back in the United States to survive each month, the German man also bought and gifted to Jerry and Jana a private game reserve with 12 rentable rooms. Jerry and Jana now lived out on the property of the game reserve in a comfortable 2-bedroom house.

I would be staying in the guest house next to their house. Jana's brother was also there when I arrived. He had been there for the last couple of months and was heading back to the United States just a few days after I got there. Jerry surprised me with the news that he had plans for us all to go visit Victoria Falls the next day. They wanted to take Jana's brother there to see the falls before he went back to the United States. It was only about 350 miles away, but the drive would take us about 8 hours on the African roads. Jerry knew that I had an interest in seeing Victoria Falls because I had asked him about it before. I told him the story of the first time that I remember seeing or hearing about Victoria Falls. It was in a National Geographic magazine that was given to me by someone from the United States Embassy in Bogota, Colombia while I was in prison there. There was a large fold-out centerfold picture of the falls. I was so impressed with the beauty of the falls that I took the center fold out of the magazine and stuck it to the wall of my prison cell with toothpaste. To me it was one of the most beautiful places on Earth. Needless to say, I was super excited to have the opportunity to go see it in person.

When we arrived at the game reserve, we stopped to open the gate and I took a picture standing in front of the gate. Once inside the gate, it was another 15 minute drive on a winding, bumpy dirt road to get to his house. The place was huge! There was an abundance of wildlife on the land including giraffe, zebra, springbok, ostrich, eland, gemsbok, kudu, lots of monkeys and wildebeest. Jerry's house is situated not far from the banks of the Thamalakane River. It was a beautiful place. Walking around the game reserve I felt an amazing sensation of peace, excitement, freedom, wonder and happiness all at once. It was incredible being out there in the African bush surrounded by wild animals. There were no predators on the reserve and Jerry's house was fenced-in from the rest of the reserve so none of those wild animals could get in.

The first night there was incredible. Seeing the African sunset for the first time was an awesome sight to behold. As the sun was going down, the sky was displaying magnificent colors of yellow, gold, orange, violet and blue. Acacia trees silhouetted the sunset. Flocks of many different types of birds dotted the sky as they were headed back to where they would nest for the night. The sounds that the birds and other animals made as the day turned to night was like a symphony of beautiful music. The feeling that overwhelmed me was total awe of God's creation. Completely immersed in nature with every site, every sound and every smell being nothing but the creation of God. Once the sun had set, the clear, dark sky was filled with stars, twinkling like colored jewels. Looking up at the night sky and admiring the beauty, I prayed and thanked God for bringing me to this place and allowing me to experience this moment of wonder. After we had all eaten, we sat outside around a campfire and listened to Jana's brother play the guitar. That night, I went to bed very happy and slept like a baby.

Early the next morning, we left while it was still dark outside. The sun came up as we drove on the main Highway out of town. Traveling down a two-lane highway through the flat African landscape, the view was unobstructed for miles around in every direction so we could see clearly the untamed wilderness. The sunrise was just as beautiful as the sunset. So beautiful that we pulled over to the side of the road to take pictures. As the sun rose, we watched wild herds of zebras roam freely across the great expanse of land. We continued the drive north, taking our time and stopping often. Parts of the highway had huge holes right in the middle. There were long stretches of highway where you had to come to almost a complete stop and drive around these huge potholes.

The highway took us through Chobe National Park. The landscape through this area was breathtakingly beautiful. We saw several different groups of elephants near the road. As we got closer to the hotel, where we were to stay, elephants were actually blocking the road that we were traveling on. We just stopped and waited for them to pass. All the while everyone was taking pictures and recording videos. The road trip there was amazing; things kept getting better. The hotel we stayed in was located out in the bush on a game reserve on the banks of the zambezi river where many wild animals were. We watched herds of elephants bathe in the river, crocodiles sunning themselves on the river banks and hippopotamus snorting as they swam around in the same river.

The door to my hotel room opened up to a patio that faced the river. The patio had its own furniture and a hammock to lay in and enjoy the view. Monkeys, warthogs and meerkats were all over the beautifully manicured hotel property, roaming around. The weather was very nice and cool this time of year. When the sun goes down, it gets kinda cold. A cool breeze made it really pleasant to hang out outside. I left the doors and windows open to the hotel room to enjoy the fresh, cool air. Jerry warned me to lock everything up whenever I left my hotel room. He said if I left with it open for just a minute when I came back the monkeys would be wearing my boxers. It was funny when he said it but I understood his point just a few hours later when I watched a monkey go into a nearby hotel room and grab some bread. Those monkeys are super fast. They could be up in a tree or on the roof of the hotel and then in and out of your room and back up in the tree within seconds. Watching them was very entertaining. The entire setting was amazing.

No pressure, no stress and an overwhelming feeling of peace and freedom. The energy there felt completely different from that of the United States. Here, I was surrounded by nature and wildlife, beautiful scenery, sounds and smells that I had never experienced before. The people that I came into contact with were happy, friendly and smiling. There was no work schedule to deal with. No bad attitudes, no drama. It was heaven on earth for me. Smiling from ear-to-ear, the happiness I felt inside was hard to contain.

The next morning we left again before the sun came up. This time we got in a safari truck and went on a safari with a professional tour guide from the hotel. We drove deep into the bush as the sun was rising and all the animals started moving around. We saw two lions eating their kill as giraffes and elephants passed near them. We saw another set of lions that had lion cubs that we're playing in a tree. Elephants, water buffalo, zebras, giraffes, and countless monkeys were everywhere. It was incredible how close we got to them in their natural habitat. The tour guide explained they were used to the truck and that we would not be attacked as long as we stayed in the truck. It was still very intense to be that close to lions out in the wilderness. It was an experience of a lifetime. We stayed out in the safari truck cruising around, looking at all the animals for several hours. We finally came back to the hotel around lunchtime. After we ate, we took a short rest in our rooms and then met back up a little while later to head out to Victoria Falls.

It was about an hour's drive to the falls from the hotel where we were staying. The hotel was out in the bush, and there was nothing else around but animals. The entrance to Victoria Falls was situated in the center of what appeared to be multiple tourist attraction businesses. Restaurants and souvenir shops lined the main road as you approached the Falls. Jerry dropped us off at the entrance to the falls where there was a short line to buy tickets to get in. He didn't come in with us. He was going to use the time to do some errands around town. He had seen the falls many times before. You couldn't see anything from the road or even from the ticket booth. Once we bought the tickets we walked through a huge cave-like structure that brought us out to a walking trail. Once we started walking on the trail, we could hear the roar of the falls but we still couldn't see it. Dense, tropical vegetation was on either side of the walking trail. It was incredibly beautiful. Mist from the falls kept all the vegetation thoroughly watered. We rounded a corner on the trail and were led straight to the edge of the enormous falls. At this point we all split up and everyone went at their own pace and their own different direction. The Falls were breathtaking. There were no safety barriers so you could literally walk directly off the edge if you wanted to. Standing on a rock ledge, taking it all in, I was stunned and in awe. The mist from the falls was like standing in a light rain. The afternoon sun was shining through the mist and created a rainbow.

Walking alone along the edge of the falls, looking at it from all different vantage points, I stopped at one of the main areas along the edge where you could view almost all of the falls. It appeared to be the exact spot where the picture that I had seen from the National Geographic magazine was taken. Until then, I hardly thought of that picture or prison at all. It was vaguely in the back of my mind because it was my first reference to Victoria Falls, but I didn't really think about it until now. Just being in this place under any circumstances would give a normal person great excitement. The beauty and the energy here felt supernatural. "Look where you are," "Look where you are," those words kept ringing in my head. My heart was racing and my breathing was fast. Hard to believe where I was standing. I was soaking wet, overwhelmed with uncontrollable emotions that I had never experienced. Tears of joy had welled up in my eyes as I stood there taking it all in. It was a very intense moment that I didn't quite understand.

My mind drifted back to that first prison cell in Bogota, Colombia, "La Picota" where I had placed a picture of this place on my cell wall—remembering the empty feelings of hopelessness and despair that had eaten at my stomach while incarcerated. Remembering how I would stare at the picture of this place and imagine myself being here instead of inside the prison cell I was actually in. It was the first of many prison cells I would live in over the next 18 years. All the years of incarceration that followed came to mind. It seemed like everything that had happened to me from then until now came rushing back to my memory all at once. It was intense, and I was feeling extremely grateful. I raised my arms up to the sky as the mist from the falls was drenching my clothes, and I just thanked God for rescuing my life from destruction and bringing me to this place where I stood at this moment. *"Thank you God! Thank you for forgiving me for all the wrong that I have done. Thank you for never giving up on me even though I turned my back on you, you never turned your back on me. Thank you for your mercy and your forgiveness. Thank you for hearing the prayers of my mother, my sister and others who prayed for me while I was locked up. You answered those prayers and here I am. Even when my situation looked completely hopeless, You made a way where there was no way. You delivered me from the clutches of death more than once. You rescued my soul from destruction. Thank you God for giving me a second chance in life."*.

Made in United States
Orlando, FL
09 March 2023

30861116R00148